The Beholder's Eye

Also by Walt Harrington

*The Everlasting Stream*

*Intimate Journalism*

*Crossings*

*At the Heart of It*

*American Profiles*

# The Beholder's Eye

## A Collection of America's Finest Personal Journalism

Edited and with an
Introduction by
## Walt Harrington

Grove Press
*New York*

"Prisoners of War" © 1997, reprinted with permission of International Creative Management, Inc. First appeared in *Harper's*.

"To Seem Is Not to Be" © 1994, reprinted with permission of the author. First appeared in *Los Angeles Times Magazine*.

"A Day at the Dogfights" © 1979, reprinted with permission of the author. First appeared in *Esquire*.

"Missing Alice" © 1986, *The Washington Post*. Reprinted with permission.

"The Endless Hunt" © 2000, reprinted with permission of the author. First appeared in *National Geographic Adventure*.

"Journey to the Center of My Mind" © 1999, reprinted with permission of the author. First appeared in *The New York Times Magazine*.

"A Family Portrait in Black & White" © 1990, *The Washington Post*. Reprinted with permission.

"My Dinner with Ali" © 1989, reprinted with permission of the author. First appeared in *Sport*.

"Resurrecting the Champ" © 1997, *Los Angeles Times*. Reprinted with permission. First appeared in *Los Angeles Times Magazine*.

"Her Blue Haven" © 2001, *Los Angeles Times*. Reprinted with permission. First appeared in *Los Angeles Times*.

"The Passions of Mario Cuomo" © 1985, reprinted with permission of the author. First appeared in *Manhattan, Inc.*

"Last Tango in Tahiti" © 1987, reprinted with permission of the author. First appeared in *The Washington Post Magazine*.

Published simultaneously in Canada

Printed in the United States of America

FIRST EDITION

Library of Congress Cataloging-in-Publication Data

Grove Press
an imprint of Grove/Atlantic, Inc.
New York, NY 10003

05 06 07 08 09    10 9 8 7 6 5 4 3 2 1

To Ed Lambeth,
a wise and good man

# CONTENTS

# CONTRIBUTORS

**Scott Anderson** is a journalist and novelist who splits his time among New York City, the Catskill Mountains, and Third World war zones. His journalism articles, mostly focused on foreign conflicts, have appeared in *Harper's, The New York Times Magazine, Esquire, Men's Journal,* and *Vanity Fair.* His most recent nonfiction book, *The Man Who Tried to Save the World,* was an investigation into the life and mysterious disappearance in Chechnya of world-renowned relief worker Fred Cuny. His first novel, *Triage,* was translated into seven languages. He is at work on his second novel, *Moonlight Hotel.* He is the co-owner of the Half King bar in Manhattan, the result of a long-held ambition to find someplace where he and his friends could drink for free.

**Mary Kay Blakely** is a journalist, author, professor, and mother—the order of importance depending on the year, circumstances, and nearest emergencies. Her work has appeared in *Ms., Vogue, Lear's, The New York Times Book Review, The Washington Post, Mother Jones, The Nation, Life, Working Women,* and other publications. She was a "Hers" columnist for *The New York Times* and a contributing writer for the *Los Angeles Times Magazine.* Her books include *Wake Me When It's Over, American Mom,* and *Red, White and Oh So Blue.* She is a frequent speaker on women's issues and has contributed her share of sound bites on *Oprah, Larry King Live,*

*CBS This Morning, The Today Show,* and NPR's *Fresh Air.* She is an associate professor of journalism at the University of Missouri-Columbia, where she teaches nonfiction writing.

**Harry Crews** is best known for his many novels set in the hardscrabble South. The books build on his own poor childhood in Bacon County, Georgia, which he left for the Marines during the Korean conflict. Crews returned home with a consuming ambition to become a writer. He used the GI Bill to attend college and published his first novel, *The Gospel Singer,* in 1968. Numerous novels, including *A Feast of Snakes, Body,* and *Celebration,* have followed. Crews eventually became a professor at the University of Florida. His nonfiction articles have appeared in *Esquire, Playboy,* and *Fame.* He has written with unusual insight about American icons of various stature—Robert Blake, Charles Bronson, David Duke, Jerry Falwell, and Madonna. His column in *Esquire,* titled "Grits," ran for fourteen months in the 1970s, and explored topics such as cockfighting, alligator poaching, and the lives of carnival workers. His acclaimed memoir, *A Childhood: The Biography of a Place,* appeared in 1978. His nonfiction is still read by a cult following in the collections *Blood and Grits* and *Florida Frenzy.*

**Pete Earley** is the author of seven nonfiction books, including *Family of Spies,* a *New York Times* best seller that was made into a five-hour miniseries for CBS. His book *Circumstantial Evidence* helped free a black man wrongly accused of murdering a white woman from death row in Alabama. The book won the Robert F. Kennedy Book Award and an Edgar Award from the Mystery Writers of America. His book *The Hot House* was based on a year Earley spent inside Leavenworth maximum-security prison with hardened criminals. He is a former reporter for *The Tulsa Tribune* and *The Washington Post,* and the author of two novels, *The Big Secret* and *Lethal Secrets.* He is at work on a nonfiction book about the inadequate mental health treatment given the imprisoned.

**Gretel Ehrlich** was born on a horse ranch in California and was educated at Bennington College and UCLA film school. She is the author of thirteen books, among them *The Solace of Open Spaces, Heart Mountain, Islands,* and *The Future of Ice.* Her articles have appeared in *Harper's, The New York Times Magazine, The Atlantic, Life, National Geographic, Outside,* and many other publications. Her work has been anthologized in *Best Essays of the Century* and *Best Travel Essays.* She has won a Guggenheim Fellowship and an award from the American Academy of Arts and Letters. For more than a decade, Ehrlich has traveled extensively in Greenland and the Arctic. She otherwise divides her time between California and Wyoming. Her article in *The Beholder's Eye* appears in slightly different form in her book *This Cold Heaven.*

**Stephen S. Hall** has been called "our nation's best chronicler of biomedicine." He has served as the science editor and as a contributing writer for *The New York Times Magazine,* where he has written cover stories about the biology of fear and memory, teenage male body image, and the science of embryonic stem cells. His work also has appeared in *The Atlantic, Smithsonian, Science,* and *Discover* magazines. His most recent book is *Merchants of Immortality: Chasing the Dream of Human Life Extension.* His other books include *Invisible Frontiers, Mapping the Next Millennium,* and *A Commotion in the Blood,* which won the Coley Award from the Cancer Research Institute. All three books were selected "Notable Books of the Year" by *The New York Times Book Review.* Hall also has worked as a reporter at the *Chicago Tribune, The Washington Post,* and the *San Francisco Chronicle.* He lives with his wife and two children in Brooklyn.

**Walt Harrington** was a staff writer for *The Washington Post Magazine* for nearly fifteen years. His book *The Everlasting Stream* is the story of what he, while working as a city-slicker reporter for *The Washington Post,* learned during his many years of rabbit hunting outings with his Kentucky country father-in-law and his friends. He is also the author of *Crossings: A White Man's Journey Into Black America,* which won the Gustavus Myers Center Award for the Study of Human Rights in the U.S., *American Profiles, At the Heart of It,* and *Intimate Journalism.* His work has been anthologized in

*Literary Journalism* and *Literary Nonfiction*. He is head of the Department of Journalism at the University of Illinois at Urbana-Champaign, where he teaches literary journalism, and the editor of *The Beholder's Eye*. His e-mail address is: wharring@ uiuc.edu.

**Davis Miller** is the author of *The Tao of Muhammad Ali* and *The Tao of Bruce Lee*. His articles have appeared in *Esquire, Rolling Stone, GQ, Men's Journal, Sports Illustrated,* and *Sport,* where he served as both a contributing editor and an editor-at-large. His work also has appeared in *The Washington Post, The Boston Globe,* and the *Los Angeles Times*. He is now at work on a memoir of his adolescence, *So May It Secretly Begin*.

**J. R. Moehringer** attended Yale University and was a copyboy at *The New York Times*. He worked as a reporter at *The Rocky Mountain News* before joining the *Los Angeles Times* a decade ago. He has been a Nieman Fellow at Harvard University and is the winner of the PEN Literary Award, the Livingston Prize, and the Pulitzer Prize for Feature Writing. His memoir, the *Tender Bar,* will be published soon.

**Bill Plaschke,** a sports columnist for the *Los Angeles Times* since 1996, has been named National Sports Columnist of the Year by the Associated Press, Sigma Delta Chi, and the National Headliners. His work appears in several annual editions of *Best American Sports Writing,* and his columns are collected in *Plaschke: Good Sports, Spoil Sports, Foul Balls and Odd Balls*. He is the winner of a Pursuit of Justice award from the California Women's Law Center for his coverage of women's sports, and he is a regular panelist on the ESPN daily talk show, *Around the Horn*. Plaschke made his film debut with three lines in the movie, *Ali,* starring Will Smith. In what some of his more cynical colleagues considered a casting stretch, Plaschke played a sportswriter.

**Ron Rosenbaum** graduated from Yale University, where he studied English literature. He worked as a staff writer for the *The Village Voice* and as a contributing editor for *Esquire*. He cowrote the award-winning PBS/*Frontline* documentary *Faith and Doubt at Ground Zero*. His articles have appeared in *Harper's*, *The New York Times Magazine*, *The Atlantic*, and *The New Yorker*. He writes a biweekly column for *The New York Observer*. His most recent books include *Explaining Hitler: The Search for the Origins of His Evil* and *Those Who Forget the Past*, an anthology of essays on anti-Semitism that he edited. His article in *The Beholder's Eye* also appears in his book *The Secret Parts of Fortune*, one of four book collections of his essays and journalism articles.

**Mike Sager** quit law school after three weeks to work the graveyard shift as a copyboy at *The Washington Post*, where he soon became a reporter. He left the paper after six years to write for magazines, which have included *Rolling Stone*, *GQ*, *Vibe*, *Spy*, *Interview*, and *Playboy*. He is now a writer-at-large for *Esquire*. Known for his deep-immersion reporting, Sager has chronicled the lives of crack addicts in Los Angeles, expat Vietnam veterans in Thailand, teenage pit bull fighters in Philadelphia, Palestinians in the Gaza Strip, heroin addicts on New York's Lower East Side, Aryan Nation troopers in Idaho, and Tupperware saleswomen in suburban Maryland. His article on the life and death of Irish journalist Veronica Guerin was made into the movie *Veronica Guerin*, starring Cate Blanchett. His articles are collected in *Scary Monsters and Super Freaks: Stories of Sex, Drugs, Rock 'n' Roll and Murder*. He teaches literary journalism at the University of California-Irvine and lives with his wife and son in La Jolla, California.

# PREFACE

## When Writing About Yourself
## Is Still Journalism

*Walt Harrington*

This is a book of stories by journalists writing about themselves, so I will begin with myself. Twenty-five years ago, I was a young desk editor on the Metropolitan staff of *The Washington Post,* when I decided to take an evening class in short fiction writing. I spun a tale that was really about my mother and father. Naive beyond belief in those days, I submitted the story to Stephen Petranek, editor of the *Post* Sunday magazine then, for possible use in its summer fiction issue. A few days later, Mr. Petranek called me into his office and politely explained that only prominent fiction writers were considered for the annual issue. Naturally, I was embarrassed at my breach of etiquette.

As I turned to go, he asked, "Is your story true?"

"Pretty much," I said.

"Could you fix it so it's all true?"

"Sure."

"Do that," he said, "and I'll run it."

I did and he did.

The short article brought a tremendous response, from colleagues in the newsroom as well as from readers, who sent me a dozen or so thoughtful letters. I had been a journalist for five years by then and had never gotten so dramatic a reaction to a small story. And this story wasn't about a raging issue or a notable public figure. It was a personal story about my father, a milkman, and my mother, a housewife, about their triumphs and disappointments and their way of staying optimistic through it all.

The reaction violated everything I had been taught in my prestigious university journalism education and during my years in the field. People don't want to read about *you,* the logic went. *You* are never the story. A journalist writing about himself was at the least self-indulgent and, quite likely, narcissistic. Sure, a few columnists got to blow on about themselves, but a real journalist stayed out of his stories, maintained the cool authority of the distanced observer. Most journalists believed that; most still do.

Yet you didn't have to be a literature professor to realize that this iron logic had been violated brilliantly again and again. Way back, there was Ernie Pyle's World War II story about the death of Captain Henry T. Waskow. "I was at the foot of the mule trail the night they brought Captain Waskow down. . . ," Pyle wrote in a dispatch that appeared in newspapers all across America. "Dead men had been coming down the mountain all evening, lashed onto the backs of mules. . . . I don't know who that first one was. You feel small in the presence of dead men, and you don't ask silly questions." From the classics: George Orwell's *Down and Out in Paris and London* and *The Road to Wigan Pier,* James Agee's *Let Us Now Praise Famous Men,* and Edward Abbey's *Desert Solitaire.* From the New Journalism of the '60s and '70s: George Plimpton's *Paper Lion,* Hunter S. Thompson's *Hell's Angels,* and Michael Herr's *Dispatches.* From travel writing: John Steinbeck's *Travels with Charley,* Peter Matthiessen's *The Snow Leopard,* and William Least Heat Moon's *Blue Highways.*

In all these works, the writers were characters in their own stories, people with personalities that shaped what they saw and reported, people who were touched and changed by the experiences about which they wrote and who shared their personal impressions, emotions, and conclusions. We know today that Orwell fictionalized portions of his books and that they violated modern rules of journalistic accuracy. Yet I didn't know that when I was reading them as a young man, and he and these other writers opened me to all sorts of possibilities for journalists who were committed to following the rules of accuracy. These works weren't armchair memoirs or navel-gazing exercises. They weren't stories where the journalist was an emotionless tour-guide narrator without a personality. They were stories with action taking place around the journalists, action that created insight into a subject or place at the same time it created self-discovery in the journalists themselves and, by extension, in their readers. In short, the stories combined the personal essay and deep reporting into a distinct form.

I eventually moved from Metro to *The Washington Post Magazine*, where I wrote mostly traditional third-person stories about other people. Yet I never shared the journalistic disdain for personal journalism, and, over the years, I occasionally wrote a piece about myself. Always, the reaction was the same as it had been after that story on my parents—more mail, more phone calls, and more unsolicited remarks from neighbors.

One day, a magazine colleague, Pete Earley, came into the office complaining that he was exhausted. He hadn't slept well in days because he was having disturbing dreams about his sister, Alice, who had died nineteen years earlier in an accident while riding his motorbike. Pete couldn't even remember the last time he had thought about his sister. I suggested he write about her, and Pete, a straight-ahead journalist then, went ballistic: "I'm not gonna write some psychological thumb-sucker about my repressed memories of my long-dead sister," he fumed

No, not a thumb-sucker, I said, but a reported piece. Go out and investigate your own sister's life and death and its meaning to you. After some prodding, Pete bit on the idea and wrote "Missing Alice," a story included in this book and that is still compelling twenty years later. For his story, Pete returned to his Colorado hometown and walked the streets, sat in the pews of his old church, climbed down into the ditch where his sister's body had been thrown in the accident, interviewed the police and medical officials who had handled the case, his own parents, and, finally, the woman who had driven the car that killed his sister. When the story ran, Pete was stunned at the overwhelming response.

"I've never had that kind of reaction to a story," he said.

I took note and began keeping a file of personal journalism stories that had caught my eye, which is where this anthology really began: Pete Earley's quest to understand his sister's death, Harry Crews at a bloody pit bull fight, Ron Rosenbaum in philosophical conversation with then-New York governor Mario Cuomo, Davis Miller at the home of Muhammad Ali, Mike Sager stalking Marlon Brando in the Tahitian jungle.

These stories were personal but not self-indulgent or narcissistic. In fact, the journalists writing them were brave souls willing to reveal themselves—often in a strange or sorry light—in order to bring readers insights that were deeper than supposedly objective third-person stories. Sager's story on Brando, for instance, was really a exploration of how easy it is for a journalist to get sucked into the tawdry obsession with celebrity and the lengths a normally responsible reporter would go to satisfy that lust—and how Marlon Brando knew this well before Sager did. Yet the depth of journalistic animosity toward Sager's piece was staggering. The *Post* newsroom gossip was vicious: Sager had written 10,000 words about trying to meet Marlon Brando, the newsie logic went, and he never got to meet Marlon Brando! So why'd he write the story? What was the news here? Why'd the magazine's editor even publish it? The story was so vilified that it was the beginning of the end for the *Post* magazine's new editor, who later found a new job. To Mike, I could only quote Louis Armstrong: "Some people, if they don't know, you can't tell 'em." There did turn out to be justice in the universe, though. After the Brando story ran, editors at the glossy New York magazines began ringing Mike Sager's phone off the hook, and he went on to *Rolling Stone, GQ,* and *Esquire* to become one of the most distinctive journalistic voices of his generation.

I continued to do my traditional journalism at the magazine. On the side, I wrote two books of personal journalism—one is the tale of this white man's 25,000-mile journey through black America, the other the story of what I learned from years of rabbit hunting with my Kentucky country father-in-law and his friends. Besides generating intense reader response, these books and the personal pronoun "I" had their own weird power among my journalist friends, who sometimes asked if I had decided to leave journalism to become what they called "a writer." When I became a university professor, I noticed that my new scholarly colleagues often introduced me to their colleagues not as a "journalist" but as an "essayist," a considerable job promotion in their view.

Yet in my view, when writing about myself, I was doing exactly what I'd done when I was writing strictly about other people. I was going out into the world, reporting what was in front of me, writing down people's words, noting the colors of their eyes and the brands of shirts, while also asking probing questions. I used exactly the same standard of literal documentary accuracy that I used in all my other journalism, which is really the only criterion we need to decide if an approach is or isn't journalism. The only difference was that in my "essays" I also was trying to do the same kind of reporting on myself. Along with the characters in my stories, I, too, had become a character.

I'm not sure why the word "I" has always been so scary to journalists. I suspect it has had much to do with journalism's desire to be respected in the way that scientists are respected in society. If journalism could strip the appearance of all personal judgment from its stories, each would carry not only the authority of one person, one byline, but the power of the royal we—the voice from on high. By the 1960s, journalists had begun to abandon the idea that individuals could be "objective"—without bias—for the idea that journalists should instead strive to be fair and balanced despite their biases. All of this resulted in a dry journalism, indeed. When the New Journalism of Tom Wolfe and Gay Talese arrived in the '60s, it assaulted this emotionless journalism and demanded that journalists capture and evoke the sensations of human experience, the music of it.

The innovators borrowed the storytelling techniques of fiction—scene, action, description, dialogue, character, and plot. It wasn't the first time journalists had cribbed the devices of fiction. John Hersey's famous 1946 "Hiroshima" piece in *The New Yorker* was influenced by Thornton Wilder's *The Bridge of San Luis Rey,* and I don't think you can read Ernie Pyle's writing without

hearing the cadences of Hemingway. Yet, for whatever reasons
of history, the New Journalists wrought a revolution in journalism. Curiously, when the techniques of these rebels were adapted
by mainstream journalists, they borrowed heavily from fiction told
by a third-person omniscient narrator—fiction's version of the
voice from on high, the narrator who can, like God, go in and
out of every character's head and report action with undisputed
authority.

The voice of God was perfect for journalism. It allowed for the
power of narrative storytelling without undermining journalism's
commitment to its own authoritative voice, spoken as if from
on high. In the way that mainstream journalists rarely looked
at, say, *Let Us Now Praise Famous Men,* as a model for journalism,
they also ignored the parallel literary model in fiction. Ernest
Hemingway's Jake Barnes narrates his own story in *The Sun Also
Rises.* Jack Burden narrates his story in Robert Penn Warren's *All
the King's Men.* Ralph Ellison's nameless narrator tells his own story
in *Invisible Man.* In fact, you can probably name as many works of
fiction narrated in the first person as in the third, although that is
nothing more than a curious footnote.

Still today, newspapers from *The New York Times* on down the
line run first-person pieces as afterthoughts, usually in their Sunday magazines or feature sections. In a recent collection of newspaper articles that had won the Pulitzer Prize for Feature Writing,
only two of the nineteen stories were written in the first person.
Glossy magazines, on the other hand, have gone crazy in the other
direction, filling their issues with frothy reports about what their
writers thought and felt as they dined with, oh, Charlize Theron
or Brad Pitt. Many of the truly excellent magazine articles that
end up as finalists for the National Magazine Awards these days
also are written in the first person. Even *The New Yorker* person-
alizes its traditional articles with attributions such as "the secretary of state told me," instead of plain old "the secretary of state
said."

We live in the *People* Magazine Epoch. Our fascination with
personality, with pop psychology and talk-show therapy, has created some awful journalistic schlock. At the same time, the era

also has freed journalists from a straitjacket of tradition and created a window for them to do some very good work. As the truism goes, "Every discovery can be used for good or for evil." If *Us Weekly, Entertainment Tonight,* and *The Jerry Springer Show* are the evils of our obsession with personality, I hope the stories gathered here are the "good" of that obsession.

Before you dig into them, let me warn you that this is an idiosyncratic collection. I have made no attempt to cover the history of classic nonfiction written in the first person, the early works of Orwell or Agee, or those of the New Journalists. That work is out there to be read in books and anthologies. Instead, I've culled a handful of stories from hundreds of fine personal journalism articles that have appeared in the last couple of decades. The stories illustrate how a deeply reported personal journalism can inform and touch readers in ways that are unique to the approach. Some stories in *The Beholder's Eye* demanded to be told through a personal lens: Pete Earley's story about his sister's life and death, my own story about my wife's family, and Scott Anderson's story of his lifetime of covering war after war.

Other stories here did not so much demand to be told through a personal lens as they allowed for the opportunity. The stories could easily have been written in traditional third person without the presence of the journalist as a character. Harry Crews could have written only about the men and women who fight pit bulls and left himself out. Mary Kay Blakely simply could have profiled the autistic author Donna Williams without being present in the story. Gretel Ehrlich could have focused the narrator's lens only on her Inuit hunter friends. Stephen S. Hall could have taken pictures of the brain of a much more famous writer than himself. J. R. Moehringer could have discovered the identity of an aging prizefighter without making that search a personal quest. The same is true for Davis Miller in his profile of Muhammad Ali, Bill Plaschke in his story about a woman with cerebral palsy who runs a Los Angeles Dodgers Web site that nobody reads, Ron Rosenbaum on Mario Cuomo, and Mike Sager on Marlon Brando.

These writers didn't have to be in their stories. Yet the choice allowed them to add insights and touches and observations that only being personal could create. Their stories were not the *only* stories that could have been told from the material, but they were all made more vibrant by the journalist's presence.

At least *I* think so.

Finally, making personal journalism stories work requires a searing honesty on the part of journalists. Traditional journalism consciously pretends away the presence of the reporter-writer, while personal journalism exposes not only subject but also writer in order to reveal more of substance and texture to readers. It's not an undertaking for everybody. Down deep, any journalist who attempts the approach must have a touch of the hard-earned confidence of Harry Crews, who writes, "Once I realized that the way I saw the world and man's condition in it would always be exactly and inevitably shaped by everything which up to that moment had only shamed me, once I realized that, I was home free. Since that time I have found myself perpetually fascinating."

May you, too, find these journalists—and their stories—perpetually fascinating.

The Beholder's Eye

# PRISONERS OF WAR

*Scott Anderson*

I've never known precisely what to call it, but this is how it begins: heat, thick tropical heat, still air that smells of sweat and
paddy water, and Athuma being led into the hut, the afternoon
sun behind her so that she is only a silhouette against the hard light.
She moves toward me, emerges from shadow, and I see her, always as if for the first time, a slender woman with long black hair,
a floral-print sarong, and that is where I stop it—I've become quite
good at stopping it there. But if I am not vigilant, the scene continues. Athuma is in the wicker chair, just four feet away, and then
she leans toward me, looks into my eyes—hers are brown with
flecks of yellow—and is about to speak, and if I am not vigilant, I
hear her voice again.

What I can say is that this remembrance comes when it wants
to. I can be content or unhappy, on a crowded street or standing
alone, I can be anywhere at any time, and I will suddenly be returned to that hut, all the sounds and smells and tastes there waiting for me, the black silhouette of Athuma fixed in my eye like a
sunspot, and until I close off the vision there is the peculiar feeling that I am being asked to try again to save Athuma, that the
events of that day ten years ago have yet to be lived.

The sensation comes on this night, the second of November
1995. I am in Chechnya, standing in the courtyard of a house,
trying to count off the artillery against the sky. Normally, this is

not difficult—you see the flash and count off, five seconds to a mile, until you hear the blast—but on this night so many shells fall their flashes are like sheet lightning against the low clouds, the roar rolling over the land, a steady white noise of war.

But I am patient when it comes to such things, and I wait for my moment. I spot three quick, nearly overlapping, pulses of light streak out along the base of the clouds, and I begin to count. I count for a long time, so long I imagine I've missed the moment, but at fifty-five seconds I hear it: three soft knocks, little more than taps amid the avalanche of sound.

Fifty-five seconds. Eleven miles. They are shelling Bamut again. It is a small village up in the mountains, a place I think about so much I no longer even refer to it by name. They have shelled it every night I have been in Chechnya—just a few dozen rounds some nights, several hundred on others. The shelling has never been as heavy as tonight.

As I have done many times these past few days, I travel the path to the village in my mind. Not eleven miles by road, more like thirty-five. The paved road cuts across the broad plain until it climbs into the foothills. After a time, a narrow dirt track appears, and it leads across the river and into the mountains. At some unmarked spot on this track, perhaps an hour or so past the river, neutral ground is left and the war zone begins. One is then quite close to the village, maybe just another half hour, but there are mines some-times, and sometimes the helicopter gunships sneak in over the hills to destroy whatever they find.

The road ends at the village. It is built along the exposed flank of a mountain valley, and the Russians are on the surrounding heights with their tanks and artillery batteries. The way in is also the only way out, but any decision to leave is up to the rebels, and they do not trust outsiders. Since this war began eleven months ago, a number of people have vanished in the village, and there are stories of torture, that some of those missing were buried alive. I have been frightened of the place since I first heard of it. On this night, its name sounds like death to me.

I am both astonished and appalled by what is about to happen. I have come to Chechnya to look for a middle-aged American man who disappeared here seven months ago. He was last seen alive in the village. I did not know this man, and he is dead, of course, but there is a part of me that has not accepted this, that holds to the fantastic notion that he is still alive and I might save him, and in the morning I will go to the village in hopes of finding him.

But this is nothing; who cares if I choose to do something stupid? What is appalling is that I have maneuvered four others into sharing my journey, and on this night, I can no longer ignore the fact that I have done this simply because I need them, each of them, that in the very simple moral equation between my needs and the safety of others, I have chosen myself. Not that this changes much; even now, I feel incapable of stopping what I have engineered.

If I wanted to keep things simple, I would say that this is a story about war, about modern war and the way it is fought. Or I would say that this is a story about obsession, the dangerous lure of faith and hope. What would be harder for me to explain is that this is also a story about truth. Not the truth of the mind—rational, intellectual, able to make order out of chaos—but emotional truth, what is known before the mind takes over, what seeps in when the mind relaxes, the truth your heart believes.

Rationally, I know I did not kill Athuma. I was in a difficult situation, and I did what I could under the circumstances to save her. I remind myself of this often. The few people to whom I've told the story reassure me of this.

But there is something about that day I have never told anyone. Before Athuma was led into the hut, I believed I was the one they meant to kill. When the vision comes and I am sent back to that afternoon, my very first sensation upon seeing Athuma is relief, a profound relief, because it is only then I understand that I am to live, that it is she who is about to die. And in that moment, there is the blossoming of my own private truth. Emotional, irrational—to anyone else, perhaps absurd—but whenever I see Athuma's silhouette, I believe that she is coming forward to die in my place, that once again I am being called upon to play a part in her murder.

I don't wish to make too much of this. What happened to me is nothing compared with what happens to other people in war.

And, of course, what happened to me is nothing compared with what happened to Athuma.

Yet the events in that hut carved a neat division in my life. Before I was one way, and afterward I was another. And just as my life before made it inevitable that one day I would come face-to-face with Athuma—some Athuma—so after her it was inevitable that one day I would come to this night in Chechnya.

I first went to war because I thought it would be exciting—and I was right. It is the most exciting thing I have ever experienced, a level of excitement so overwhelming as to be impossible to prepare for, impossible to ever forget.

This attraction is not something to be discussed in polite company, of course. Yet I know I am hardly alone in my reaction. For a great number of people, and perhaps especially for those who traditionally have been called upon to wage it—young men—war has always been an object of intense fascination, viewed as life's ultimate test, its most awful thrill. Of all the easy, comfortable aphorisms that have ever been coined about war—that it is hell, that it tries men's souls—I suspect the odd utterance of General Robert E. Lee, made at the Battle of Fredericksburg in December 1862, may come closest to capturing the complicated emotions of those who have actually experienced it. "It is well that war is so terrible," Lee said, gazing over a valley where thousands of soldiers would soon die, "or we should grow too fond of it."

But if the guilty attraction endures, it now comes with a heavier price. This is because the modern war zone bears little resemblance to that of 130, or even 50, years ago. What were once the traditional inhabitants of a battlefield—soldiers, or journalists like myself—today represent only a tiny minority, their numbers overwhelmed by the purely innocent, the civilians who find themselves trapped in war's grip. On this modern battlefield, comparisons to the Fredericksburgs and Waterloos and Guadalcanals of history—ritualized slaughters between opposing armies—are largely useless. For a true comparison, one must reach back to man at his most primitive, to the time when barbarous hordes swept over the countryside laying waste to everything and everyone in their path, when a "battlefield" was defined simply by the presence of victims.

A few simple statistics illustrate this regression. In the American Civil War, civilian casualties were so low that no one even bothered to count them. From 1900 to 1950, civilians constituted roughly 50 percent of all war-related casualties. By the 1960s, civilians represented 63 percent of all casualties, and by the 1980s, the figure was 74 percent. For every "conventional war," such as Operation Desert Storm, that pushes the percentage down a fraction, there is a Bosnia or a Rwanda that sends it ever upward. The world has seen many of these wars. Since 1980, according to World Military and Social Expenditures, a periodic compendium, 73 wars have raged around the globe. "War," of course, is a relative term. According to human rights groups, last year alone there were 22 "high intensity conflicts" (defined as 1,000 or more deaths), 39 "low intensity conflicts," and 40 "serious disputes." The 250-odd wars of this century have taken a collective toll of 110 million lives. There are those who say that the truest mark of the last hundred years is not industrialism, or the rise of America, or the moon landing, or the computer, but the waging of war—that war is the greatest art form of our century. Human ingenuity, it appears, has perfected the technologies of death and, like a kid with a new slingshot, cannot help but find targets everywhere.

The result is that today's "hallowed ground" is not at all like the pastoral valley Robert E. Lee gazed upon at Fredericksburg, is barren of the trappings of heroic folly that can be immortalized by poets and painters. Instead, this hallowed ground is a ditch or a filthy alley or a cluster of burned homes, and it is inordinately populated by the elderly, by mothers and their children, by those not quick enough to escape.

To be sure, there are the lucky few who are able to traverse this landscape with a degree of physical immunity (journalists, most obviously, but also soldiers and guerrillas now that most "battle" means the risk-free killing of the defenseless rather than fighting other combatants), but even they cannot arrange an immunity for the soul. If for them war still holds an excitement, it is an excitement that the healthy conscience recognizes as obscene. And if war can still be viewed as life's greatest challenge, it is now less a test of any concept of courage or manhood than of simple human resiliency.

As a child, I always thought of war as something that would eventually find me. The youngest son of an American foreign-aid officer, I was raised in the East Asian nations of South Korea and Taiwan, briefly in Indonesia—"frontline states," as they were called in the 1960s, in the global military crusade against Communism. Although culturally very different, there was a certain continuity to these places: In each, the people lived in thrall of a venal American-allied dictatorship, soldiers ruled the streets under martial law or state-of-siege decrees, and the long-awaited Red invasion, we were constantly told, could come at any moment. In South Korea, soldiers rounded up and imprisoned student demonstrators, then labeled them Communist provocateurs. The entrance to my elementary school in Taiwan was guarded by an enormous antiaircraft gun, two soldiers constantly scanning the skies with binoculars for some sign of the marauding Red Chinese. Every October 10—Double-Ten Day—Chiang Kai-shek amassed tens of thousands of his troops in Taipei's central square and exhorted them to war, crying, "Back to the Mainland!" as cheers rang and artillery sounded.

This spirit of war was all around me. My father had fought in World War II, had been an eyewitness to the attack on Pearl Harbor. My godfather was an Air Force major. As the Vietnam War escalated in the late '60s, our small American enclave in the hills above Taipei became home to the families of Army officers fighting there, their children my new playmates. When I was seven, the first GI I knew, George, gave my brother and me green berets from Saigon and took us to the Taipei zoo—this was on his last R&R visit before he was killed in the Mekong Delta.

War, then, came to seem like a natural phenomenon to me, a cyclical storm always massing on the near horizon. Eventually, I was sure, the right conditions would develop, the winds would shift, and war would come to where I was. Because this was in the natural order of things, I was not frightened; if anything, I awaited it with impatience. I looked forward to Double-Ten Day the way other children did Christmas, and each time I watched Chiang Kai-shek raise an enfeebled fist in the air and squawk his call to battle, I felt a shivering thrill and thought, "This time he means it, this time it's really going to happen."

But as fate would have it, war never did come to me. Instead, I had to go find it. I was twenty-four and it was August of 1983.

For five months, a girlfriend and I had traveled through Europe, hitchhiking and backpacking, slowly going through the money we had saved from a year of working in restaurants. In Athens, we were down to $300 and our return tickets to the United States. Neither of us wanted to go home yet, but we differed on how best to forestall it. She was leaning toward picking grapes in Italy or hanging out on a kibbutz in Israel. I was leaning toward Beirut.

Beirut had been in the news a lot that year. Since the Israeli invasion of Lebanon the previous summer, the city had sunk ever deeper into chaos, a free-fire zone for a bewildering array of armies and private militias. Four Western nations—the United States, Britain, France, and Italy—had sent in troops, the Multinational Peacekeeping Force, to restore order, and now they were being attacked as well; by August, the American Embassy had been torn in half by a car bomb that killed sixty-three, and a dozen-odd Marines had been killed or wounded at their isolated outposts around the city.

I'd heard vague stories about how news agencies and wire services were always looking for "stringers" in dangerous, newsworthy places, and Beirut seemed to fit the bill. Just what "stringing" entailed, I hadn't a clue, but I managed to convince my girlfriend otherwise.

From the moment we stepped off the plane at Beirut airport and I saw the shell-pocked terminal building, the ring of tanks and armored personnel cars, the soldiers holding back a huge throng of civilians desperate to find some way, any way, out of the city, I felt I was in a familiar place, the place of my childhood visions.

And, I must admit, it was just as thrilling as I always imagined it would be. At night, I lay in bed and listened to the crack of sniper fire and the peculiar feline scream of Katyusha rockets, the low

rumble of artillery from the battles taking place in the Chouf foothills some fifteen miles away. By day, I was a tourist of war. Most
mornings, I would leave the relative safety of our hotel on Rue
Hamra, a main commercial street of West Beirut, and walk the mile
down to the shattered old city center around Martyrs Square, inch
my way as close as possible to the firefights that periodically sprang
up along the Green Line, the no-man's-land separating Muslim West
Beirut from the Christian East. Walking the ruined streets, past
buildings that had been blasted so many times they resembled melting
houses of wax, hearing the occasional gunshot echo from some
unseen sniper, I felt exquisitely alive. It was as if I had supernatural
powers: I heard the slightest sound from blocks away, my vision
seemed telescopic, I could isolate the faintest scents in the air. And
through it all came a strange, ethereal quality, a sense that I wasn't
really there but viewing everything from a remove, through a lens;
and this quality rendered pedestrian issues—of self-preservation, of
what was bravery and what was stupidity—moot. I was invisible,
invulnerable; a bullet could not find me.

I could justify my tourism, of course: I was looking for a job.
As I made the rounds of the different news bureaus, I was greeted
with puzzlement, mixed, I imagine, with contempt—the same
contempt I would later feel when meeting dilettantes in war zones.
Some journalists urged me to leave Beirut. Others were quietly
encouraging—the level of violence was not yet to a point where
they needed another hand, but I was to check back if something
big happened.

I had been swept up in the madness of the place, but my girlfriend had not. To her, Beirut was just an ever-unfolding tragedy. The sight of the amputees hobbling along the waterfront
promenade, the white fear in the faces of the young Marines guarding the new American Embassy saddened her to tears, and after a
few days she stopped accompanying me on my walks, would stay
in the hotel reading books and writing letters.

One day, a firefight that had started down at the Green Line in
the early morning gradually moved up the hill toward us; by noon,
I estimated it to be about a half-mile away, the concussions causing the hotel room to shake. I had learned to temper my enthusi-

asm around my girlfriend—it disgusted her—and for an hour or so I pretended to read, trying to invent a plausible excuse to go outside.

"I think I'll check in with Reuters," I said, tossing my book aside. "Want to come?"

She looked up from her letter writing. She was not the least bit fooled. "Go ahead."

With guilty pleasure, I left the hotel and started down Rue Hamra, which was oddly deserted, in the direction of the shooting. When I came to Clemenceau Place, I stopped.

The small park had once been beautiful but had long ago been destroyed, most of its trees shorn to stumps by shellfire. I had walked through Clemenceau Place many times on my wanderings to the old city center, another half-mile on, and there were usually vendors and children, old men lolling on the grass. On this day there was no one.

The gunfire sounded very close, and I studied the buildings on the far side of the park for snipers. For the first time since arriving in Beirut, I felt a glimmer of dread, made stronger somehow by the bright sunlight and heavy stillness of the leaves in the few remaining trees. I decided to go back, but as I turned, I saw an Arab man standing perhaps twenty feet away. I was startled that I hadn't noticed him before. He wore a long white robe, appeared to be about forty, and he, too, was staring across the park, as if waiting for some sign.

I don't know who stepped first, but without words passing, we started through the park together. We walked at the same speed, separated by some twenty feet, and out of the corner of my eye I saw the white of his robe, and it encouraged me.

We had gone only a very short distance, maybe thirty paces, when the white of his robe slipped from my vision. I stopped and looked over to him. He was standing still, his head bent forward, and I saw that he was working his lips furiously, licking them, biting them, the way some insane people do. Then he began to walk in a small, tight circle, his left leg kicking out, his right dragging slightly, his lips still moving but producing no sound. After his second or third turn on the walkway, I noticed a small red spot on his robe, over his heart, and I saw how this spot grew each time he turned to face me. After five or six circles, he abruptly sat down on the concrete, the force causing his head to jerk, his legs splayed out before him. With the thumb and forefinger of both hands, he pinched the fabric of his robe on either side of the spreading red spot and pulled it away from his chest, as if it were a stain he did not want to have touch his skin.

I felt rooted to the ground. I knew that I should either go to him or run, get out of Clemenceau Place, but I was incapable of deciding. Then the man fell onto his left side, his hands not breaking his fall, his fingers still clutching the fabric, and I knew he was dead from the way his body settled on the concrete. I turned and walked back the way we had come.

As I returned to the hotel, I tried to find meaning in what had happened. I had just watched a person die, and I knew it had to mean something, but no matter how hard I tried, I simply could not imbue the event with much significance. We had walked together across the park, and a bullet had come, and it had found him and it had not found me, and he had died and I had not. That was all.

It took me some time to realize that this—the sheer lack of meaning in what had happened—was the lesson. War's first horror is not that people die for perverse reasons, for a cause, but that they die for no discernible reason at all. They die because they guess wrong. They seek shelter in buildings when they should flee onto open ground, they stay on open ground when they should hide in buildings, they trust in their neighbors when they should fear them, and none of it is knowable—nothing is revealed as foolish or wrong or naive—until it is too late. All that the death in Clemenceau Place meant was that the Arab man should not have attempted to cross the park that afternoon, and it was this very paucity of meaning that stunned me, that I wished not to see.

Others have likened the sound of an artillery bombardment to the sky being ripped apart. I don't know. What I can say is that after a time it no longer even seems like a sound but something animate. It travels through the ground, and you first feel the ache in your knees, then in your upper chest, and before long you can start imagining that it is inside you and will not leave. I wonder if this is why people go mad during bombardments; not the fear of a quick death, of a shell finding you, but the fear of a slow one, the sense that the constant thrumming through your body is inflicting violence from within. And in Chechnya, these thoughts are from eleven miles away, from perfect safety.

The courtyard I am standing in is an expanse of concrete enclosed by an eight-foot brick wall. Along the far wall is a fallow flower bed. I cross the concrete and step onto the bare earth. The vibrations are much softer here, barely noticeable. I lean my back against the wall, soothed by the stillness.

Ryan comes out of the house. I realize by the way he peers around the courtyard that he can't see me in the dark. For a moment I think he will go back inside, but then he sits on the steps, leans onto his knees.

I am not in the mood to deal with Ryan. He is twenty-two—a kid, really, considering where I have brought him—and a couple of years ago he left his native Southern California to scratch out an existence teaching English in Moscow. When I offered him $150 a day to come to Chechnya as my interpreter, he jumped at the chance. He is a good guy, intelligent and sweet-natured, but he left behind a pleasant life in Moscow, a girlfriend he wants to marry, and he has no idea what he has gotten himself into. I have not told him that he was chosen to make this journey simply because no one else would.

I should feel grateful to Ryan, but I don't. Rather, he irritates me. I have attributed this to his talkativeness, his fierce determination to fill every minute of his days with words. When we first arrived here, I tried to explain that the most important safeguard on a battlefield was to listen, but Ryan has either been unwilling or unable to heed this advice—and on this matter I have not been patient. Now I tell him to be quiet fifteen or twenty times a day, and the more he talks the less I do.

After some minutes, I step from the flower bed and walk softly across the courtyard. I'm only a few feet away when Ryan jumps, startled by my presence. "Whoa," he says. "Where were you?"

I don't answer.

He moves over on the step, clearing a space for me, but I remain standing, lean against the stair railing. I feel the ache in my knees again, the vibrations in the metal rail against my shoulder. "They're really blasting the shit out of it, aren't they?" Ryan says.

I don't answer.

"It's never been this bad before. Are they doing air strikes?"

"Tanks and artillery," I reply. "No planes."

I'm quite sure he doesn't like me—how could he like someone who tells him to shut up twenty times a day?—but Ryan maintains appearances. More than anything, I think he is impressed by how I watch and listen out here, imagines me to be something of an idiot savant when it comes to gauging danger.

He has no way of realizing that, in fact, I know very little. Even though it is elementary physics, I do not know, for example, if the sounds I hear, which I carefully count off each night, come when the shells are launched or when they explode. I don't know if the count is thrown off by wind or topography. I don't really know if what I am hearing are tank or artillery rounds. And I still imagine that knowing these things could be important, that knowledge alone might somehow keep us safe.

"Do you believe the stories about them burying people alive?" Ryan asks.

"They're rumors," I say.

"I know, but do you think they're true?"

He is apprehensive, of course, as we all are, and it would take very little from me to reassure him, to at least take the edge off.

"How would I know?" I say. "How in the fuck would I know?"

One night six weeks ago, I sat on the back of a houseboat on a Texas lake with the twenty-nine-year-old son of the man I have come to look for. We sat there for many hours, drinking beer and talking—about women and football and Mexico, only occasionally about his father. At around 4:00 A.M., after a long silence, both of us staring out at the black water, he turned to me.

"I don't want you to go to Chechnya," he said. "It's not worth it. My father's dead. It's not worth someone else getting killed."

The son had recently ended his own four-month search for his father in Chechnya, and over the course of a few days in Texas we had become close. Now he stared down at the beer can clasped in his hand, then took a gulp from it. "At least promise me you won't do anything crazy."

He was not used to talking to another man in this heartfelt way, and neither was I. I drank from my beer and looked out at the water. "I promise."

In the six weeks since that night, I have offered a number of variations on this promise. To my family and friends, it was that I would be careful, that I would not do anything foolish. To those who knew the details of the story, it was more specific, that I would not attempt to reach the village. I was asked to make this promise so many times that I began to deliver it preemptively—"well, I'm certainly not going to take any chances"—reinforcing the point with an incredulous little laugh, as if the very idea was bizarre. And the truth is, before I came here I believed my promises.

"What if they start shelling while we're there?" Ryan asks.

I turn to him. He is looking up at me, moon-faced. This is something I haven't considered. In the time we've been in Chechnya, they have never shelled the village during the day, always at night, and we have planned our journey to be well away before dark. But they've never shelled the village as they are doing tonight, and it finally occurs to me that it might be the prelude to a ground assault.

"Get into a ditch," I say. "If there isn't a ditch, get to a low wall, the closest low wall you see."

I think of telling him more—of explaining why he should go to a low wall instead of a high one, that if he can see the explosions it means that he is against an exposed wall and needs to get around to the other side—but I know he won't remember any of it if shells start coming in. I doubt he'll even remember the little I've said, and I have an image of him standing in the middle of a road—slack-jawed and paralyzed—as the world around him disappears.

"You have to understand something," I tell him. "You will be on your own. In an artillery attack, everyone is on their own. If you freeze and stay in the open, I won't come out for you, no one will come out for you. It's not like in the movies. Do you understand?"

Ryan nods, but in his eyes I see a hint of bemusement, as if he is trying to be respectful and suitably grave but not really buying any of it. I am reminded of what I must have been like at his age, politely enduring the lectures of the correspondents and photographers in Beirut. I'm sure I had the same reaction, the same expression. At twenty-two, you can't conceive of dying.

But this is a different situation than Beirut—Ryan is here because I am here, he is following me—and his expression means quite a bit more. In his eyes, he is saying, "I know you won't leave me out there, I know you'll come out for me," and that smugness, that juvenile conviction that I will protect him, angers me.

It is then that I understand the deeper source of my irritation with Ryan. I am irritated by how easily and blithely he left his girlfriend, his happy, pauper's life in Moscow, and placed his fate in the hands of someone like me for $150 a day. I cannot possibly blame him for this—I would have done the same at his age—but I am infuriated by his trust in me.

For a long time, I did not learn anything worth knowing by going to war, and then, finally, I did. It happened on a November evening in 1986 in Uganda, maybe an hour before dark, when, glancing out the window of a moving car, I saw an old man, thin and bare-chested, standing in an overgrown field, swinging a machete.

I think what I first noticed was the intensity with which he worked. In Uganda, as everywhere in the tropics, people laboring in the fields pace themselves for the heat, maintain a slow, steady rhythm, but this old man wielded his machete with a passionate energy, arcing it high over his head, swinging it down hard. I asked my driver to stop the car and, from the open window, watched the old man for a few minutes. Then I got out and started across the field toward him.

The grass was very high, almost to my chest, and I remember thinking it odd how uneven the ground was, how it kept crunching under my feet. Hearing my approach, the man stopped his work and watched me. I saw that he was not as old as I had thought, perhaps only forty-five or so, his face and body aged prematurely by peasant life. I couldn't read his expression—not friendly, not curious, really no expression at all beyond a steady stare. I came to the space he had cleared and saw the two piles he was making—one of clothing, another of bones—and I understood then that we were standing in a killing field, that the crunching I'd felt under my feet had been the breaking of human bones.

I had come to Uganda because my older brother, Jon Lee, and I were writing a book together. We had already collaborated on one book, and this time we decided to compile an oral history of modern war by spending a year going from one war zone to the next interviewing soldiers and guerrillas and the civilians caught between them. With a meager advance from a publisher, we packed our bags and set out, to Northern Ireland, to the Sudan, now to Uganda, where one cycle of civil war had recently ended and another had just started.

Beginning a few miles north of the capital of Kampala was the Luwero Triangle, a verdant patch of farmland that had once been home to one million members of the Baganda tribe. Between 1981 and early 1986, it had been the vortex of a civil war that drifted into genocide; the Ugandan military had sealed off the Triangle and tried to erase it from existence, razing villages, murdering an estimated quarter-million people, and sending the rest into the bush or to concentration camps. When Jon Lee and I arrived in October 1986, the old government was gone, the rebels were in power, and the survivors were starting to return. They came back to a place where nature had reclaimed the fields, where their shattered homes had settled to mud, and in every village they built a memorial to the horror that had been visited on them, a display of the bones and skulls of their fallen.

For several weeks, we made periodic sojourns into the Triangle, interviewing survivors, chronicling the atrocities, watching the harvest of the dead. Everywhere were people carrying bundles of bones on their backs, on their heads, hauling them to communal places, where the remains were laid out with mathematical orderliness—tibias in one row, spines in another, skulls arrayed in descending order of size. The survivors then walked among these displays, studying first one skull and then another, hoping, it seemed, that they might somehow recognize those that belonged to their own families. It was as if, in their state of suspended shock, they had reverted to what they knew: gathering from the fields, carrying to market, examining the yield.

With Jon Lee up north, tracking the newest cycle of war, I had decided to make one more trip into the Triangle. It was while leaving, heading back to Kampala with another tape collection of atrocities, that I noticed the man in the field with his machete.

There are things about that evening I cannot explain. The man and I never spoke, but I intuitively knew a good deal about him. I knew he had just returned to the Triangle, that the killing field was his land, that he was looking for his family. I began to help him.

This was not easy, because there is nothing mathematical or orderly about a killing field. Amid the weeds, bits of rotted cloth were strewn like garbage, tamped into the earth by the rains, and the bones lay scattered without pattern—a pelvic bone here, two skulls there. I remember thinking that it was pointless, that we would never be able to find what the farmer was looking for, but then I saw that he had a system. The bones he ignored, just threw them onto the pile: It was the clothes he studied. Each time his slashing revealed a piece of cloth, he would lift it with the tip of his machete and scrutinize it for a familiar pattern before throwing it on the pile and going on.

I found a stick and began to do the same. I would poke at the cloth until it came free from the earth or the bones it encased, then pick it up with the end of the stick and carry it to him. He would stop his labors to look it over, maybe scrape off some dirt to see the pattern, and then he would turn away without a word, and I'd drop the cloth on the pile and go back to my spot.

We went on like that for a long time, maybe thirty or forty minutes. The sun dropped to the tree line, and the land started to get that heavy gold light that comes to the tropics in the evening. I remember thinking how beautiful it was out there, how peaceful despite what had happened, as if the land were trying to heal itself, and then I realized I wasn't hearing the thrush of the machete anymore, and I straightened out of the tall grass and turned toward the farmer. He was about thirty feet away, standing stock-still and staring at me. A piece of brown and white cloth hung from the tip of his machete, and even from that distance I could see it was part of a woman's dress, that he had found his wife's dress. In his eyes was a hatred deeper than any I had ever felt, a rage without end, and I realized it wasn't passing through me; it wasn't as if I happened to be where his eyes were fixed: The hatred was directed at me, meant for me.

I didn't know what to do, so I didn't do anything. I didn't go to him, I didn't speak, I don't think I even looked sad for him. The most I could do was avert my gaze, stare off across the field. Then I turned and went back to the car and told my driver to take me to Kampala. I know I didn't look back, but sometimes I imagine I did, and in this false memory, the farmer is watching me go, the scrap of his wife's dress dangling from his blade, and across the expanse of the sun-struck field I feel the burn of his hatred.

And here, finally, was something worth learning. War is all about hatred, and the hatred between combatants is only the easiest kind. At that moment of discovery, I believe the farmer hated all the world, not just the men who had murdered his family; he hated me for being a witness, hated himself for having survived, hated his wife for dying and leaving him alone. After that evening, I understood that it is impossible to go through a war and not learn how to hate.

Every morning in Chechnya I awaken with a start, instantly alert, and this morning is no different. Out the window, I see the blue-black of dawn. I stare up at the ceiling and listen. Somewhere far off is the sound of a rooster. The shelling has stopped. I think of who will be making the trip today, three of us in this house, two others sleeping a half-mile away. I estimate the time to be 5:00 A.M. We are to leave at 8:00.

I go to the basin and throw water on my face, then walk through the house. All is bathed in the milky wash of first light. I pass Ryan. He is sprawled on the bed, snoring. Nothing interrupts his sleep.

The front room holds a table with four chairs and the narrow cot where Stanley sleeps. He is on his back, perfectly still, his hands folded on his chest. Every time I've seen him asleep he is in this position, as if he doesn't move at all during the night. Stanley is forty-six, ten years older than I am, an American living in Paris. He arrived in Moscow two weeks ago wearing an all-black outfit—black hiking boots, black jeans, black shirt, black jacket, black knit cap—and he has not changed out of it since.

Our first meeting was marked by a certain mutual wariness. I knew Stanley had a reputation for taking chances. He was a war photographer who liked to get as close as possible to his subject matter, and his manner at that first meeting—his low-pulse calm, the watchful stare of his eye—made me wonder if he might get us killed in Chechnya. I knew he was wondering the same thing about me. I think we both saw reflections of ourselves in the other, and this was both good and bad: We could count on the other to watch and listen, to know what to do in a bad situation, but it wasn't like there was going to be safety in numbers on this trip. Whatever affinity exists between us does not translate into a need to share personal information. What we talk about, when we talk, is the wars we have been to and where this one is headed.

Before we got to Chechnya, I had no intention of trying to reach the village; the journey was impossible, insane. But, as often happens in these sorts of situations, there occurred a confluence of events, of coincidences, that began to make it seem possible—and then, quite quickly, what had seemed merely possible began to feel like destiny. I happened to meet a rebel liaison who said the journey could be arranged, who even wrote out a coded message of introduction for me to present to the village commander. Then I happened to meet Alex, a relief worker with a four-wheel-drive ambulance and a stockpile of medical supplies, who agreed to attempt a "mercy mission" into the village, with us—Stanley, Ryan, and me—going along on the pretense of documenting the humanitarian effort. With such an extraordinary convergence of good luck, how could I not go?

Of course, riding this wave of good fortune meant overlooking certain details. The man I was looking for had also gone to the village with an interpreter and rebel credentials. He, too, had gone in an ambulance laden with medical supplies. And he had gone with an insurance factor I could not hope to arrange: two doctors who were known in the village. None of it had helped; the doctors and the interpreter had simply disappeared as well.

As the days here pass, though, it has become increasingly easy to forget all this. A kind of resignation has settled upon us. Events are happening of their own accord, momentum has built to such a degree that there are no longer any decisions to be made. Whether due to destiny or some kind of group psychosis, we are being propelled forward; the time for debate and reason has slipped away.

In the front room of the house, I quietly pull a chair out from the table. It makes a creak when I sit, and I glance over at Stanley. He is a light sleeper, given to popping up at the slightest sound, but the noise doesn't rouse him.

My notebook is on the table, and I flip through the pages until I find the encoded letter of introduction from the rebel liaison. It's not really a letter but one word written in blue ink on a yellow Post-it note, with a couple of odd, Arabic-looking symbols at the end of the word and three quick dots above it.

It suddenly occurs to me that the code's meaning is unknown to us, that our "safe passage" note to the village commander could actually say something very different, could even be our execution order. In this new light, I study what has been written. Why three dots? Maybe three dots mean "friend" and two mean "foe." Or maybe it's just the reverse. Maybe the liaison meant to make only two, but his hand slipped and left a mark that wasn't supposed to be there. Maybe the dots don't mean anything at all and what I should really be focusing on are the Arabic-looking symbols. I find it both remarkable and humiliating that my future might be decided by a word hastily scrawled on a Post-it note, but there is no choice in the matter and finally I give up.

I turn to a blank page in my notebook and take up my pen.

Many years ago, my brother, far more experienced in war than I, tried to teach me to calculate the risks before going into a battle zone, to arrive at a percentage chance that something bad might happen. "Your cutoff should be twenty-five percent," Jon Lee had told me. "If it's higher than twenty-five percent, you don't do it."

It wasn't a true equation, of course—just hunches and intuition, guesses contrived to look like math—and I'd never had much faith in my ability to weigh factors properly, but on this morning I try.

I try to imagine the chance that the Russians will attack the road while we're on it and decide on 10 percent each way: 20 percent. I try to imagine the chance that the rebels in the village will think we are spies. Here, at least, there is some empirical evidence to work with: those who have gone to the village and disappeared. I decide on 50 percent.

Seventy percent. I have never done anything anywhere near 70 percent.

I decide these numbers are way too high. I cross them out and start again. Five percent for the drive each way, 30 percent for the village: 40 percent. Still too high. Five percent total for the drive, 25 percent for the village: 30 percent. Out of curiosity, I calculate the odds of being unlucky at Russian roulette—a little less than 17 percent—and then decide the whole exercise is a waste of time, that either something will happen or it won't.

But my fatalism wavers. I stare at the two pieces of paper in front of me, the word in blue ink on the Post-it note, my calculations on the page. I turn in the chair and look at Stanley. Even though he is asleep, I am surprised that he cannot feel my stare, that some unconscious alarm doesn't trigger him awake. I slowly press against the chair back until it creaks. I wait for his eyes to snap open, for him to bolt up in the bed and meet my gaze.

I believe that if Stanley wakes up right now, I will tell him we're not going to do it. I believe I will show him the numbers in my notebook, explain that we might die over what is written on the Post-it note, tell him that it was a crazy idea, that I am frightened. But Stanley doesn't wake up, and I lack the courage to make him.

At some point, I began to take relics with me when going into war zones. It started unconsciously—a seashell here, a girlfriend's silver earring there—but my collection steadily grew until it filled a small plastic bag tucked into a corner of my rucksack. I think at first I carried these things because they reminded me of the world outside of war, small and lightweight links to my normal life; it was comforting to fiddle with an old Budweiser bottle cap or a Lion Brand matchbox or a familiar stone bead when I was bored or lost, when I was waiting for something to happen or something to end in a dangerous place.

Gradually, though, I saw that my relics were becoming talismans. I developed the habit of carrying some of them in the left front pocket of my trousers, occasionally replacing them with others from my plastic bag. I knew this was a bad sign, for it meant that I was inventing good luck to keep me safe, that my sense of immunity was gone.

Late one night in mid-January 1987, I lay on a deck chair beside the pool of the Galle Face Hotel in Colombo, the principal city of Sri Lanka, smoking cigarettes and staring up at the fronds of palm trees, thrashing and black against the sky. In my left front pocket was an American bicentennial quarter, the key to an apartment I no longer lived in, and a tiny anteater figurine made from yellow rubber. Behind my head was a stone seawall against which the Indian Ocean—turbulent and at high tide—rhythmically crashed.

The Galle Face, built at the height of the British empire, was a pile of mahogany and rattan, slow-turning fans and ocean breezes, but in 1987 the civil war in Sri Lanka was entering its fourth year and the tourists had long since abandoned "The Pearl of Asia." Now the Galle Face and the other luxury hotels along the Colombo waterfront were virtually shuttered, their lobbies filled with forlorn maids and bellhops and reservation clerks. On afternoons, my brother and I would sit by the Galle Face pool, the only charges for the five uniformed attendants there.

The first time I climbed the seawall and prepared to dive into the ocean the attendants beseeched me to stop. It was dangerous to swim there, they said, there were reefs and sharks, strong currents that could sweep me out into the shipping lanes. I looked out at the sea. The waves were high, cresting at eight or ten feet, and it was true that no one was in the water. I told the attendants I would be fine and dove in. On that first day, I went out only a short distance, maybe fifty yards, treading water and riding the swells, and when I turned, I saw the five of them in a row behind the seawall, staring at me. I waved and they all waved back.

It became a daily ritual, and each day I went out farther, out to where I could begin to feel the current pulling me away, and where I had to struggle a little harder to get back. And each day the attendants and I exchanged our reassuring waves across the water.

I could not explain to them that I went into the ocean because there I felt in control over what happened to me. At least in the ocean I knew the dangers I faced, and the effort to stay calm, to override the fear of riptides and sharks and deep water, was an act of free will and a measure of power. How could I possibly explain this to the attendants? For them, caught in a country at war, their futures and their children's futures becoming bleaker by the day, such a needless tempting of fate could be viewed only as an absurd extravagance. Better that they regarded me as an unusual athlete or a friendly fool.

Earlier that night, I had set out across the city in a restless search for diversion and had ended up at the former Hyatt Hotel. With its vast vacant atrium and ascending tiers of empty rooms, the hotel had the feel of a great mausoleum that no one visited, its gloom deepened by a spirit of desperate optimism. Piped Indian pop music—frenetic and reedy—rifted on the still air, and at various intervals in the hollow building teams of cleaning women rubbed its marble and gold to a high polish, as if preparing for a party.

There were four customers in the lounge, three Asian businessmen at a table and a white man sitting alone at the bar. He was in his mid-thirties, with short blond hair, and he perked up at the sight of me, as if he had been awaiting my arrival. I sat a few stools away, ordered a beer, and within seconds he was at my elbow, his hand extended.

"New in?" he asked. "Where are you posted?"

James was a thirty-year-old Briton, a mercenary pilot for the Sri Lankan government. It was an open secret that for more than a year the government had employed several dozen mercenaries—or "contract officers"—to run their air war against the Tamil Tiger guerrillas, and that it was now in the process of hiring more; James, in Colombo on a five-day R&R, had assumed I was one of the new arrivals. Although a bit disappointed to learn otherwise, he chose to make the best of it; it was not like he was going to find anyone else to talk to that night.

He told me that he flew a helicopter gunship and that his particular beat was the Jaffna lagoon on the northern tip of the island. It placed him at the center of one of the war's most crucial battlegrounds. The Tigers had held the narrow Jaffna peninsula for over three years and had repelled every army offensive against it, but they had one huge vulnerability: All their supplies, from food to bullets to medicine, had to come in by sea. A vital route was across the ten-mile expanse of the Jaffna lagoon. In the past year, James and his fellow contract officers had turned the lagoon's waters into a shooting gallery.

"Anything that tries to go over," he said, "we kill it."

My meeting James was serendipitous, for ever since arriving in Sri Lanka, my brother and I had tried to devise some way to get to Jaffna. With the army controlling the peninsula neck, we had been told that the only possibility was aboard a Tiger supply boat trying to run the lagoon, but we'd also been told that such a venture would be extremely risky now that the mercenary gunships were killing anyone they saw. After several beers that evening in the old Hyatt, James came up with a plan.

"Here's how we can work it," he said, putting his hand on my shoulder. "We'll set up a prearranged time for you to go over and come back, and I'll just stay out of that zone. It would have to be a very small window, of course, but as long as you keep to schedule there shouldn't be any problem."

There was something both touching and ironic about this offer. Watching James's earnest face as he awaited my reaction, I knew that even more than wanting to help me he wanted to protect me. But I also thought of all the things that could go wrong and throw us off schedule—a flat tire, a flooded boat engine, a long-winded interview in Jaffna—how the smallest misstep could set into motion a course of events whereby this lonely man in the cavern of a hotel bar would, through no fault of his own, slip down from the clouds to become our destroyer. Well, there's never a shortage of irony in war. As it was, all I could do was thank James for his offer and tell him I would consider it.

But walking back to the Galle Face that night, I had become aware of an odd discomfort in my chest. It was not an entirely new sensation, but on this night I felt it acutely, as one might feel the onset of a flu before it strikes. While lying in the lounge chair beside the darkened pool, staring up at the thrashing palm trees, I realized that I believed I might soon die.

At first, I was tempted to attribute this feeling to my conversation with James, my apprehensions about running the lagoon, but I knew it ran far deeper and had been with me for some time. It was why I had begun to carry talismans, perhaps even why I dove off the seawall to play with fate in the ocean's currents. It had to do with punishment.

I finally understood that I was not merely an observer of war and never had been. I had always been a participant—by my very presence I had been a participant—and war will always find a way to punish those who come to know it. I had watched people die. I had walked through killing fields and felt human bones break beneath my feet. I had picked up the skulls of murdered children and rearranged them with an eye to photographic composition. I had cajoled or intimidated or charmed scores of people into revealing their most intimate horrors, and then I had thanked them perfunctorily and walked away. If I was to be punished—and there were charms in my pocket to forestall this, there was an ocean behind my head to hasten this—it would be because I deserved it. God knows I deserved to be punished for the things I'd seen.

As it turned out, my brother and I did not attempt the Jaffna lagoon. Instead, we journeyed east, to the marshes and rice paddies along the windward coast, to the Tigers fighting there, to Athuma.

At 7:45 A.M., minutes before we are to set out for the village, I tell Ryan and Stanley that I am going to the town square for cigarettes and slip away from the house. The day has broken cool and the air is clear. By noon, the dust will rise to lie over the town like a shroud, but for now it is still wet with dew, and in the distance the snowcapped Caucasus mountains shine like glass.

In the square, the kiosk women are just setting up for the day, throwing open the wood shutters of their booths or laying out their wares on the sidewalk, blankets wrapped tightly over their shoulders. I buy three packs of Marlboros and push them into my coat pocket.

At one end of the square is a high school and, next to it, a small park, its entrance dominated by peeling portraits of men I do not recognize. I have passed the place often in the past few days, and on this morning I wander inside.

It is a very modest park and suffering from neglect—the paving stones of its path are shattered, and nothing has been pruned or trimmed in a very long time—but at its center I come to a massive, marble monument, a small eternal flame burning at the base. It is a memorial to the town's dead from World War II, and in the black stone are chiseled scores of names.

Standing before the flame and the list of war dead, I suddenly find that I am praying. I haven't prayed in twenty-five years and am not really sure anymore how it is done, if I'm supposed to preface it in some way or direct it to some god in particular. In any event, it is a selfish prayer: for the soul of my dead mother, for the safety of my companions and myself on this journey.

I hear laughter behind my back, and I turn to see two schoolgirls sitting on a nearby bench, watching me and giggling. I am embarrassed that they know what I am doing, that even though I haven't bowed my head or closed my eyes, they know I am praying. I stoop down to pick up a pebble from the path, then leave, finishing the prayer in my mind as I walk. In the left front pocket of my trousers is a fossilized shark's tooth from Florida, the keys to my apartment in New York, and a tiny 1973 two-kopeck coin I found in the gutter of a Moscow street. At the entrance to the park, I slide the pebble into my pocket, one more charm to keep me safe.

In my absence, the ambulance has arrived at the house, and my companions stand in the street, waiting for me. The relief worker, Alex, is a tall, rail-thin Hungarian in his early thirties, an Oxford divinity student, of all things, on leave to perform rescue work in Chechnya. There is something in his quirky, rather dandyish manner—his vaguely British accent and soft stutter, the long

woolen scarf he habitually wears—that seems both charming and
brave in its incongruity with this place. On this morning, he appears to be in high spirits—clean-shaven and jaunty—and he
bounds over the dirt road to shake my hand.

"Nice weather for it," he says, glancing up at the blue sky, "but
I suspect we'll find mud in the mountains." He turns to me, still
smiling his crooked smile. "In any event, perhaps we should take
a closer look at this note from the liaison. Wouldn't want to walk
into a trap of some sort, would we?"

Alex says this without any hint of real concern, and I take the
Post-it note from my back pocket. He studies the single word for
a moment, his fingers distractedly playing with the frame of his
horn-rimmed glasses, then hands it to Aslan.

Aslan reminds me of other young men I have known in other
wars, the native "fixer" hired by Western visitors—journalists, relief
workers—to get them in and out of dangerous places. He is in his
mid-twenties, with dark hair, sunglasses, and a black imitation-
leather jacket. Others have dressed differently, of course, have been
Asian or African or Latin, but what unites them all is a cocky
bemusement at our ignorance and bad ideas. Aslan glances quickly
at the note and shrugs.

"I don't know what it means. It's in code."

"Nothing for it, then," Alex says, merrily. "We'll just have to
go and find out."

And so we set off, the boxes of medical supplies—gauze ban-
dages, glucose solution, antiseptic wash—jouncing and sliding in
the ambulance bay. We follow the path of my imagination, over
the plain, into the foothills, and then there is the dirt track, the
river, and we are in the mountains. The day is bright, a blinding
light reflecting off the snowcapped peaks to the south, but the small
valleys below us are cloaked in morning shadow and fog. We are
still on neutral ground, but that doesn't mean much here, and out
of habit I watch the valleys, look for a flash of refracted light in a
dark recess, a sudden swirl in a fog cloud, for some sign that a troll-
ing gunship is rising out of the depths to meet us. But there is no
flash or swirl, and the only sounds are those of the wind and the
grinding of the ambulance engine. We pass no one on the track—

no cars, no homes—and we do not talk. It is as if each of us is making this journey utterly alone, each in his own private ambulance on a ridgeline at the top of the world.

About an hour after crossing the river, Alex, sitting in the front passenger seat, suddenly points down the hillside. We are skirting a mountain, somewhere near the unmarked frontier between neutral ground and war, and in the pasture below is a haphazard cluster of large, rectangular stones.

"They look like ruins," Alex says excitedly. "Old ruins."

As Aslan continues to steer along the track, the rest of us peer out the windows. It is a strange sight, this jumble of square-edged rocks in the middle of nowhere, but not strange enough to dispel our stupor of silence.

It was a very hot day. The air was still, and thick with the smell of paddy water and sweat, and when Athuma was led into the hut, the sun was behind her so that for a moment she was only a silhouette against hard light. That is how I remember it, how it looks when I return to it.

The day had started off very differently. In fact, it started the way I, as a child, had imagined war would be but war had never been: grand, cinematic. The night before, a messenger had come with our instructions, and at noon Jon Lee and I had walked into the marketplace of the government-held town and two Tiger guerrillas had suddenly appeared beside us on their motorcycles, motioning us to get on. There had been a wild, careening ride, down side streets and narrow alleys, dodging army roadblocks and personnel carriers, until finally we burst free from the town and were in the countryside, speeding past farmhouses and rice paddies and palm trees, and my life had never felt so much like an adventure.

The sensation lasted for a time, through the dash across the lagoon in the motorized canoe, through the half-hour drive on the other side, crammed in the back of a battered jeep with a half-dozen Tigers. It ended at an old farmhouse hidden in a grove of trees. It ended the moment I saw Kumarappa.

He was twenty-seven years old, the Tiger commander for the region, with a pistol on his hip, a potbelly, and dark, dead eyes.

His young followers—weighted down by weapons of every kind, ampules of cyanide hanging on leather thongs around their necks —gathered close to his side, as if posing for a group photo, as if mere proximity to him bestowed status. And because they were only boys, and because they had been living in the bush, the Tigers could not hide their excitement at our presence; they whispered animatedly to one another, smiled shyly in our direction. But not their leader. Kumarappa stared without expression, his eyes unblinking, as if we were not really there at all.

The Sri Lankan army was closing in on Kumarappa's group. In the last few days, they had launched a series of lightning assaults in the area, coming ever nearer to the base camp. Just that morning, helicopter gunships had swept in over the lagoon and killed several people caught out in the open. It was now only a matter of time—probably a very short time—before the army moved on the old farmhouse amid the rice paddies, and if his boy followers hadn't figured that out yet, it seemed that Kumarappa had; it was dying time, and Kumarappa was already there.

He motioned for us to follow him to the main hut, a long dark room with reed walls and a thatched roof. Four wicker chairs were arranged around a low table, and upon this table a young Tiger placed three bottles of warm orange soda.

Hunched in his chair, his weapon-laden boys gathered behind him, Kumarappa began to talk of death, of the cyanide ampules he and his Tigers would bite into when the final moment came.

"It's a good death. Yeah, it's a good death. Our soldiers do that. It's a very brave death. . . . I'm not afraid to die, you know?"

He talked of spies, of the spies who were all around him, in the villages, in the rice fields, even coming into the area from other places. They were trained by British intelligence or the Israeli Mossad, maybe even the CIA, and Kumarappa was always uncovering them, getting them to confess, tying them to lampposts and blowing off their heads as examples to others who would betray.

"Sometimes we put them on the lamppost," he said, cradling his bottle of soda. "Sometimes, you know, we have the explosive wire—just around the body—and then we detonate it. This is our maximum punishment. We do it sometimes. Two or three times we've done it."

And as he spoke, I felt Kumarappa was studying me. I don't know if this was true or merely my imagination, but every time his empty, dead eyes turned in my direction, I became more certain that I was the subtext of his rambling conversation, that in me Kumarappa was deciding if he had found his latest spy.

Once this conviction took hold, it became paralyzing. Even as I tried to meet Kumarappa's stare—and it is impossible to stare for as long as a madman can—I knew that the fear was registering on my face, that I looked, in fact, very much like someone with a guilty secret. I felt caught in a deepening trap, fear giving way to a panic I wasn't sure I could suppress. At last, I simply dropped out of the conversation, let Jon Lee take over all the questioning, while I busily scribbled in my notepad, peered up at the thatched ceiling as if in deep concentration, anything to avoid Kumarappa's gaze.

"We can show you one spy that we have caught," I heard Kumarappa say after a time. "Would you like to see a spy?"

It was impossible to not look at him then, and when I did, I saw that he was watching me, the hint of an indulgent smile on his lips. It was the first time he had smiled, and it was the first time in my life I was sure I was about to die.

I don't know how long this belief lasted—at most a few seconds—but then I looked down the length of the hut, down the passage that had suddenly formed between the gathered Tigers, and at the far end I saw the silhouette of a woman in the light, a silhouette being led toward us. That is when the belief left me, when I saw I was to live, and this filled me with such relief and gratitude that I felt transported, as if on this broken-down farm in the marshlands a hideous miracle had just occurred.

They sat her across from me, in the empty wicker chair beside Kumarappa. Her name was Athuma. She was thirty-six years old, the wife of a peasant farmer, the mother of seven children. Among the many events that had, no doubt, filled her short life, only the following were now important:

The Sri Lankan army had taken her husband and tortured him until he was a cripple. They had taken her two youngest children and given them to the sister of a Sergeant Dissayanake. And then the army had told Athuma that she could change the situation, that everything would work out, that there would be money for food and the children would be returned if only she gave Sergeant Dissayanake information about Kumarappa and his boy soldiers in the bush. And so, apparently, Athuma had.

But Athuma had not been a good spy—people who are coerced into it rarely are—and very quickly, before she was able to report anything of importance, the Tigers had found her and brought her to Kumarappa. That was two days ago. After two days of torture—revealed in the swelling on her face, her shuffling, lopsided gait as she walked toward us—Athuma had confessed to everything. There was now just a little more torturing to be done, and then it would be over.

"She knows very well the final decision," Kumarappa said. "She knows we are going to kill her."

And then Athuma began to beg for her life. It began as a soft whisper but gradually rose to a high-pitched chant, a disjointed blend of Tamil and English, and this pleading was not directed at Kumarappa but at us.

"Save me, save me, save me."

It continued for a long time, became a keen on the edge of hysteria. Kumarappa turned in his chair to watch Athuma, appeared both bored and amused as she leaned over the table, looking desperately between Jon Lee and me.

"Save me, save me."

And we tried. Slowly, gingerly, we felt around for some hidden corner in Kumarappa's heart. We went over the circumstances that had led Athuma into being a spy, the fact that she had not told the army anything damaging. We asked what would happen to her children, both the stolen ones and those here with their invalid father, if she were to die.

But Kumarappa, his hands folded over his little potbelly, remained unmoved by any of this. Instead, a suspicious light came into his eyes, and this time there was no ambiguity, no mistaking what it meant: He was asking himself why these two foreign men were trying to rescue this spy.

As if Kumarappa's paranoia was infectious, the mood throughout the room changed. The Tigers who were gathered behind him—friendly, unsophisticated boys a moment before—turned suddenly sullen and dark, their faces set hard against us.

"Save me, save me."

Athuma leaned out from her chair toward me, compelled me to look directly into her eyes—dark brown with flecks of yellow—and I remember opening my mouth to try one more time, but even while looking into her eyes, I felt the stare of Kumarappa and his boy killers, and I couldn't speak. I turned to Jon Lee, and in the gaze that passed between us was an agreement, an understanding that it was over, that we had tried and could not try anymore.

Athuma understood as well. As quietly as it had begun, her plea ended, and I will always remember the sound of her sitting back in the chair, the creak of the wicker, for it was the moment when all hope left her. I could bring myself to look in her direction only one more time. She was staring down at the table, her matted hair framing her bruised face, and she no longer seemed frightened, only sad and terribly tired. A few minutes later, they took her away, and she again became what she had been at first: a silhouette, limping and hobbled, this time receding, passing out into the light of day.

I was in New Delhi, eleven days later, when I learned of the assault on the farmhouse. The army had come in on gunships at dawn and encircled the area, then methodically worked their way through to the grove of trees, killing everyone they found. The Sri Lankan government was claiming twenty-three dead Tigers, including Kumarappa, while local residents were claiming nearly two hundred dead, mostly civilians; the truth was probably somewhere in between. Indian television ran a video of the aftermath and there was a slow pan of a dozen torn bodies in a row beside the ruins of the main hut. I looked for Kumarappa among the corpses but couldn't find him, only a couple of the boys I had talked to.

★   ★   ★

Jon Lee had flown on to Europe for a reunion with his wife, and in a week I was to join him in London before we moved on to our next war zone. I had told him I was going to stay in New Delhi for a few days to relax—maybe go down to Agra to see the Taj Mahal—but what I really wanted was to be alone. I didn't know how the incident with Athuma had affected him—we had barely discussed it before parting—but I believed that he was less bothered by it than I was; my brother was older, tougher, more experienced at war; he surely knew how to handle such things.

For me, it had brought a sense of shame deeper than I had ever thought possible. On an intellectual level, I understood I was not responsible for what I had felt in the hut—for either the fear or the relief—but no matter how many times I replayed that afternoon in my mind, told myself it was irrational, I could not be rid of the belief that Athuma and I had somehow traded places, that I hadn't really done all I could have to save her because if she had lived I would not have.

My first two days in New Delhi I didn't leave the hotel room. I ordered food and beer from room service and had it left outside the door, told the maids there was nothing for them to clean or straighten. I watched television, smoked cigarettes, paced, stared out the window at the people passing in the street. I relived being in the Tiger camp and conjured up different scenarios, different endings. I played back the tape of that afternoon, listened to all the places where I should have said something but didn't. Then on the third day came news of the attack on the farmhouse, and I felt better. Now I could distract myself by envisioning how the Tigers died.

I knew Kumarappa hadn't eaten his cyanide; in war, the glory of martyrdom is reserved for children and rubes, those who don't know any better. I envisioned him trying to make a break for it, leaving his boys behind to die, flailing through the rice paddies with his pistol, perhaps getting far enough away to start believing he had made it, that he was safe, before being cut down, and I hoped that his end had not been quick, that Kumarappa had died for a while.

I thought of one boy in particular, Shankar, a sweet-faced twelve-year-old with a beautiful smile and a Chinese sniper rifle, a boy so small he had sat on the lap of another Tiger when we interviewed him. I knew Shankar hadn't eaten his cyanide either. I envisioned him panicked as the soldiers closed on the farmhouse, lying wounded in the grass when the shooting stopped. I envisioned him crying for his mother and for mercy as a soldier approached, and I hoped the soldier had not been swayed, that he had put his gun to Shankar's head and pulled the trigger. What an awful thing, to hope for slow death, for quick murder, but it was these hopes, this hate, that enabled me to finally leave the hotel room and rejoin the life I had watched from my window.

It seemed that the world had changed in my brief absence; of course, it was I who had. Beginning the day I left the New Delhi hotel and continuing over the subsequent years, there was about me a new manner, a kind of taut gentleness. At one time, my pride had not allowed me to walk away from a fight. After Sri Lanka, I never showed anger, defused tense situations with an almost obsequious politeness. At one time, I had enjoyed going into the woods with a .22 rifle and shooting at birds and squirrels. Now I didn't want to kill anything, and even the feel of a gun in my hand was repellent. For a long time, I didn't want to go back to a war zone. When I finally did, it was only to "safe" battlefields—Belfast, Gaza—places where I was unlikely to look into the face of another Athuma.

There were other changes as well, a quirky, eclectic array. I discovered that I now had to live on the top floor of buildings, with large windows to view my surroundings. I was not comfortable in crowds or dark places. I no longer dreamed when I slept. I overreacted to sharp sounds. I felt nervous when helicopters flew overhead.

I understood that the incident with Athuma was not the cause of these changes but rather the culmination, the last link in all that had come before. I had been traveling a path ever since Beirut—perhaps ever since I first heard Chiang Kai-shek's rantings in the central square of Taipei—and at the old farmhouse in Sri Lanka the path had finally given way beneath me. I understood that it had always been only a matter of time before I met an Athuma.

What did not change was my reticence to talk about these things, about Athuma or anything else that had happened. Instead, I felt a keen desire to not do so, to partition off those memories as something that had no relevance to my new life. For some time, I seldom told new acquaintances I had written books, even more seldom the subject matter. To old friends who were curious about my apparent drift—why I wasn't working on another book, why I had moved to a seedy apartment in Baltimore, where I knew no one, or, later, why I spent two years doing clerical temp work in Boston—I offered the blandest of explanations, if any at all. Only to those closest to me could I talk about the farmhouse—and this only after four or five years had passed, only after I had extracted from them a promise of absolute secrecy. What also did not change were the returnings to that day, the sudden, always unexpected moments when I found myself back in the hut, Athuma coming toward me.

It was not until a number of years after Sri Lanka that I realized there was another force guiding my changed approach to the world. It was an unsettling force, one that I had briefly glimpsed in the New Delhi hotel and imagined to be temporary. Along with whatever other emotion had taken root—sadness, shame—now there was also rage, a well of directionless hate. If I had become a gentler person, it was at least in part because I was fearful of the alternative. I didn't get angry, I didn't fight, because I didn't trust what I would do. I wouldn't get near a gun because I was afraid I might use it. And in seeing this, the odd little set of neuroses I had developed did not seem so eclectic after all; guarding against the rage meant being vigilant and quiet, always in control, forever watching the horizon for signs of danger.

I found safe, discreet targets for my anger. Chief among them were those who advocated war or professed to understand it. In London, I watched leftist students, in sandals and patchouli, demonstrate in support of the Tamil Tigers. In the buildup to Operation Desert Storm, I watched Young Republicans at the University of Iowa conduct a mock trial and execution of Saddam Hussein, listened to them cheer and whoop when "Hussein" was made to kneel on the stage to be "shot" in the head. I listened to pundits and academics opine about why a war was or wasn't a religious conflict, an economic or constitutional one. I did not need to confront leftists, rightists, college professors, or yahoos holding forth in a bar; it was enough to loathe them in silence, and I nurtured this loathing as if it were something precious.

It was in the autumn of 1994, nearly eight years after Sri Lanka, that my brother and I talked about Athuma for the first time. We were sitting on the porch of our sister's home in Connecticut late at night. A week earlier, our mother, who lived in Spain, had arrived to visit me and my sister—the only two of her five children who lived in the continental United States. She had fallen ill suddenly, too suddenly for my brother, living in Latin America, or my two other sisters in Hawaii to reach Connecticut before she died. Now, the day after our mother's death, Jon Lee wanted to be told everything that had happened, the precise chronology of events in her rapid decline. Her passing had been a painful one, difficult to witness, but for several hours on our sister's porch I calmly, numbly, told Jon Lee all he wanted to know.

"I don't know why we couldn't save her," I kept saying. "It happened so fast, but I don't know why we couldn't save her."

After a time, though, my numbness wore off, replaced with the naked grief that tends to ebb and flow on such occasions, and amid this my sorrow expanded to encompass the other woman we hadn't been able to save, Athuma.

"Did we really do everything we could? Did we really?"

"Yes, we did," Jon Lee insisted. "We did everything we could, and it wasn't enough. We tried, and we couldn't try anymore." He said the right words, but in his eyes I saw that Jon Lee didn't believe them either, that he had remained haunted over the years as well.

And despite what is said, it is not always easier to grieve together. Sometimes it is easier to imagine yourself alone, to believe that others—stronger, tougher than yourself—have figured a way out and laid a trail that you might follow. Seeing the sorrows of my brother—the new one for our mother, the old one for Athuma— was not an easy thing. Along with tenderness, I also felt an anxious despondency: No one was strong or tough enough to emerge unscathed; there was no trail out.

A few months later, I decided I would return to Sri Lanka. I got the idea from watching television programs about American veterans who were returning to their old battlefields, to Okinawa, to Vietnam. I watched these programs closely, studied the faces of the veterans—especially those who, earlier in the programs, in their prejourney interviews, had let their masks slip, had lost their composure in a moment of bad remembrance—because I wanted to see whether they finally found some measure of reconciliation, of peace, in the happy playfulness of the children in villages they had once fought over. The results seemed mixed at best, but the journeys also appeared to be the only thing these old soldiers could do, and I decided to copy them; I would go to Sri Lanka and find Athuma's children, those who were still alive. I would tell them what had happened, how I had tried. I would apologize.

Instead, someone called to ask if I would go to Chechnya, to follow the trail of a middle-aged American man and his three companions who had disappeared there, and a different image came to mind: this man and his companions somewhere in the Caucasus mountains, captive, despairing, but alive, waiting for death or someone to save them.

And so, perhaps having not truly learned anything yet, I went to Chechnya.

When a person believes he is about to die at the hands of another, he does not look at all the way one might expect. He does not scream or cry. Rather, he becomes very quiet and lethargic, and his eyes fill with a kind of shattered sadness, as if all he wants to do is sleep. It is only like this with a certain kind of dying, I imagine, the kind where you have been given time to see what is coming, where you have tried to negotiate and reason and have failed.

In the front room of the farmhouse in the village, I see signs of this exhaustion in all my companions: Alex hunched forward on the couch, gazing miserably at the bare concrete floor; Aslan leaning against the wall, his arms wrapped about his middle, staring down at his shoes; Stanley's eyes fixed on the far white wall, distant and puzzled. Even Ryan seems chastened, his habitual grin gone, his eyelids heavy. I am reminded of looking into the face of Athuma that last time.

We had been stopped as soon as we reached the outskirts of the village, hustled out of the ambulance and led into the stone farmhouse that was the rebels' command post. They were startled to see us—the village was closed to civilians, the track in "restricted" —but at first we were treated more with curiosity than with suspicion; we drank tea and shared cigarettes, the rebels talked animatedly about the war and why they were fighting. It was when the commander arrived that everything changed.

He was in his forties, wearing a black leather jacket and strange, ankle-high boots. He shook each of our hands without smiling, then sat on the edge of the broken-down couch and leaned onto his knees, and in the long silence that ensued he seemed lost in thought, methodically massaging his fingers, staring down at the floor. At last, he sighed and looked up at me.

"You are not supposed to be here. No one is allowed here. How do I know you're not spies?"

The note from the liaison was gone. I had given it to one of the rebels who first stopped us, the one who seemed most senior, and he now made a great show of looking for it, rummaging through the various pockets of his fatigues and turning up nothing.

"I must have given it back to you," he said to me. "You must have it."

He was lying, but I didn't know to what end. Was he protecting us or doing the opposite? It was impossible to know, and there was no time to ponder or watch for clues.

In the absence of the note, the commander began his slow, calm interrogation of us. He asked why we had come, who had sent us, and studied our identity papers as if they were weighty evidence. To his questions we gave the most innocent of answers— that Alex had come to deliver relief supplies, that I had come to chronicle the mission—but nothing swayed the commander. Instead, it seemed that everything we said, every insistence of our simple intentions, served only to convict us more, lead us that much closer to a bad end. Everyone in the room knew what was happening—the rebels who a short time before had given us tea and cigarettes now looked away, refused to make eye contact— and it was the interminable slowness of our descent, our grinding inability to find an ally or the words that might save us, that finally led us into a crushing apathy, to this place where our strongest remaining desire is simply for the process to end.

And then I find the words that cut through. Or maybe it is not words at all but the way I look unblinkingly, guiltlessly, into the commander's eyes. Or maybe it isn't any of this but only a capricious shift in the executioner's heart—suddenly we find the interrogation is over and we are free. Still dazed by the speed and mystery of our deliverance, we are led to the ambulance, and the rebels gather around to shake our hands, to slap us on the back, to wish us a safe journey, as if we are close friends they are sad to see leave.

While driving back through the mountains, I remember the man I had gone to the village to find. I never asked the rebels about him. For the first time I grasp the colossal scale of my hubris. What had I expected? That I would stumble upon the American and his companions standing at the roadside? That I could go to the village, meet the men who had almost certainly murdered the lost group, and have them confide in me? What had I been thinking?

During the slow quiet drive away from the village, I am reminded again of what it is about war that has always tormented me, that I have never been able to reconcile. Although it has been proved in front of my eyes a dozen times, I have never truly accepted that what separates the living from the dead is largely a matter of coincidence, of good luck or bad, that in war men and women and children die simply because they do, and that there is no plan or reason to any of it. If a faith has guided me, it has been one of arrogance, the belief that I have power, that I can save, that vigilance will see me through.

Athuma was dead before I saw her, she was dead sitting across from me, and she was dead when I left. There was nothing I could have done to make it turn out differently. There was nothing I could have done to save the American man in the village, and there was nothing I could have done to save myself or my companions— no note, no talismans, no words. But this impotence is almost too much to bear. It is easier somehow to endure the self-tortures— of rage, of shame, of hope—that come with the belief that there is a pattern, that we can shape it.

Perhaps this is because of the greater powerlessness that lies beyond, the inability to ever go back. Returning to Sri Lanka and seeing Athuma's children would not have changed anything. Finding the American man in the village would not have canceled out Athuma in the farmhouse. If the goal is to reconcile, to "get over" what has happened, the self-torture will never end; grace can come only in knowing that the wounds never heal, that they have become a part of you and are to be carried. That you can't atone, that you must stop trying.

About an hour after leaving the village, while skirting a hillside, we come upon a Toyota Land Cruiser stuck in the mud up to the floorboards, its three occupants sitting dejectedly in the grass. It is the only other vehicle we have seen all day, and, following the etiquette of the mountains, Aslan stops the ambulance and starts to fashion a towline from a coil of rope. The rest of us step out to stretch our legs. By coincidence, we have stopped above the same small glade where Alex pointed out the unusual sprawl of stones that morning, and for several minutes, the four of us stand silently on the edge of the bluff, staring down the hillside at them.

I look to the far side of the road and notice that we are directly below the crest of a flat-topped mountain, a mesa. Most of the slope is dirt, but at the crest is a uniform, six-foot seam of rock, and I see that the square boulders in the pasture below are not old ruins but simply sections of the escarpment that have fallen away. I turn to point this out to my companions, but it is too late: Alex has begun running toward the rocks. I watch him go—an awkward girlish run, his scarf snapping in the breeze—and I am seized with a dread that, at first, I cannot identify. I clamber down into the mud, to where Aslan is busy with the towline.

"Is this area mined?"

Aslan looks up and seems to sniff the air, as if I've asked him if it might rain. He shrugs.

I climb back to the edge of the bluff and see that Alex has reached his destination. He is standing atop one of the immense stones, his hands on his hips, and although he surely knows now that his ancient ruins are only fallen boulders, he seems quite pleased with himself, a preening explorer.

I shout down to Alex, tell him to be careful, that there might be mines. Even across the long expanse of pasture, I can see the tension come into his body, and I know the weight that has dropped into his chest, the ringing emptiness that has replaced his thoughts. I watch him gingerly pick his way back up the hill, his shoulders stooped like an old man. I try to remember the way he was just moments ago—happily running through the meadow grass, exultant upon his rock—and I am held by the sadness of how he has changed, of how we all change out here.

# TO SEEM IS NOT TO BE

*Mary Kay Blakely*

Three years ago, shortly after publishing *Nobody Nowhere: The Extraordinary Autobiography of an Autistic,* Donna Williams met me in the lobby of Manhattan's Mayflower Hotel. That is, Donna avoided me. After emerging from the elevator, she immediately shielded her face behind a sheaf of papers—her written answers to the questions I had submitted—and quickly bolted out the door. Wispy blond curls around a prettily freckled face gave her a waiflike appearance, camouflaging the iron will that led her to liberty after more than twenty years in what she calls the prison and sanctuary of autism. Avoiding any brush with passersby, she fled down the street and headed into Central Park as I trotted breathlessly behind. Donna didn't have much use for people then. Even less for journalists.

I spent my first two hours with Donna trying to conduct an interview as she walked briskly through Central Park. Pacing reduced the terror of speaking to strangers and provided a rhythmic pattern for conversation. She didn't lower her defenses until she could be sure I had mastered the rules: no touching, no inflections, no fluttery gestures, no tape recorders, no changes in plan. Especially no eye contact. Interviews had to be conducted outside. Sentences had to be simple—subject, verb, object—until she got used to strange voices. Questions had to be drawn in pictures if words didn't work. Good-byes had to be speedy, without any emotion. These were the strict terms of Being with Donna.

Symptoms vary among autistic individuals—less than 1 percent of the U.S. population—and have been blamed on everything from demonic possession to bad parenting to sleep deprivation. Today, autism is known to be a neurological disorder in which sensory information floods the brain. It is, as Donna experiences it, "like having a brain without a sieve." When people speak to her, particularly excited people with booming voices, she sees only waving hands and hears only "blah, blah, blah." Overstimulation can trigger a "shutdown"—the catatonic stare and frozen body that Donna has said is like being "involuntarily anesthetized."

With obsessive concentration, another symptom of autism, she managed to write her first astonishing autography in four manic weeks. She had plopped the 500-page manuscript on the desk of a child psychiatrist at the London hospital where she was a temporary clerk, asking him "to read it and tell me what kind of mad I was." At age twenty-five, she finally learned that the massive confusion and mighty frustration she had been wiring around all her life had a name: autism. Despite severe sensory and neurological impairment, she is a high-functioning autistic individual with exceptional talents ("idiot savant" in psychological lore). The doctor passed the manuscript to a literary agent in London; it became a best seller in the United States and abroad.

Donna has now completed another memoir describing the obstacles she overcame to move from "Donna's world" to "the world." *The New York Times* described Donna as "prodigiously talented. . . . And oh, can she write. The windows through which she allows us to view her experience are metaphor, perfectly rendered details and wonderful surprising phrasing." *Somebody Somewhere* is an almost incomprehensible achievement for someone who never thought of words as her first language.

Throughout childhood, Donna communicated mainly through gestures and objects. Objects had life: "My bed was my friend; my coat protected me and kept me inside; things that made noise had their own unique voices which said vroom, ping, or whatever.

I told my shoes where they were going so they would take me there," she wrote.

Since words were meaningless strings of sound, she was never moved to ask the ubiquitous childhood question: But why, Mom? Why do I have to look both ways/turn off the TV/kiss Grandma good-bye? Instead of learning how and why people did what they did, she learned to copy conversation and behavior, exhibiting the echolalic and echopractic habits of autistic children. During her childhood in Australia, she memorized episodes of *The Brady Bunch*. Whenever a situation triggered this stored dialogue, she would become Marcia or Greg or Alice. She responded to questions at school or home with the answers she thought people expected: "I said a lot of yes, yes, yeses. Cups of tea arrived without any connections between their arrival and the yes that had brought them there."

"Life was just a great long game of strategies and battle tactics to hide the flaws, holes and deficits," she wrote. Information did not translate from one situation to the next. "If I learned something while I was standing with a woman in a kitchen and it was summer and it was daytime, the lesson wouldn't be triggered if I was standing with a man in another room and it was winter and it was nighttime," she explained.

Her alcoholic mother interpreted Donna's strange behavior as a sign that she was possessed by evil spirits. Aside from a weekly paycheck, her father largely absented himself from his troubled family. At age sixteen, Donna left home. She supported herself with routine factory jobs, but the next ten years were a constant struggle, including episodes of homelessness and unemployment.

Eventually she moved to London, where her exceptional ability to store facts helped her pass the entrance exam for college. (Donna has scored both genius and retarded on IQ tests.) Haunted by the constant threat of institutionalization, she hid her difficulties from most of her teachers and fellow students. After watching Donna for a few months, however, an observant classmate tried to confirm her hunch:

"Donna, you're different, aren't you?" she asked.

"I guess so," Donna said.

"Just how different are you?" she pressed.

"Put it this way," Donna replied. "I'm a culture looking for a place to happen."

Passing a London consignment shop on her way home from work one day, Donna saw a used typewriter and decided on impulse to buy it. She put in a sheet of paper and, four sleepless weeks later, had the book that "both saved me and destroyed me."

Dr. Lawrence Bartak, an Australian specialist in autism, offered to help Donna begin building bridges instead of walls between worlds. "I think I can now accept that I am disabled, with a very big abled and still quite a dis," she says.

While Donna had much to gain by joining "the world," there were excruciating losses as well—she learned that without a nervous system, inanimate objects could not think or feel. Her treasured objects lost their life with this concept. "I realized I'd lived in a world of object corpses. God has a curious sense of humor," she wrote. She braved the initial loneliness and shock because "I was in love with my own aliveness and completeness. The alternative was not to give a damn. I gave a damn bigly."

I had not imagined three years ago that this woman from another world would move me so deeply, introducing me to another way of seeing, another way of knowing. Donna and I stayed in touch after our first memorable meeting, by fax and phone and once, when she returned a year later, through a long weekend visit at my home in Connecticut. Conversations with her are often a humbling experience—though that is never her intention. "What have you been doing all summer?" I'd ask. Well, she'd learned French *and* German, written another book, composed a musical score for a movie, finished several paintings, and was preparing an instruction manual for teachers of autistic children. "What have you been doing?" she'd ask. Well, I was almost finished with the essay I started three months ago. One of us was once thought to be retarded and one of us was not—and all of us, it seems, should rethink the usefulness of labels.

Ours was not to be a conventional friendship. Donna is a wholly mature intelligence with a highly original take on life, questioning the meaning of everything and forcing me to do the same. Last year, as we were walking through my neighborhood, Donna looked up at the sky, stopped abruptly, and sang a tune I had never heard before. Did she write that song? I asked. No, she replied, the birds wrote it. She pointed to the telephone lines, where dozens of blackbirds were perched. At least I saw birds. Donna saw a musical phrase. The universe is full of unsung music most of us never hear.

A lot has changed in the past three years. She has gained greater insight into the ways of Red People (the "so-called normal people," who are like noisy, vibrating colors to her), and though one is never cured of autism, Donna now grasps more meaning from speech. "You don't have to speak so slowly now," she told me recently.

She's also found a way to reduce the distracting visual overload. Donna's earliest companions were bright spots of translucent color dancing before her eyes—a mesmerizing light show no one else seemed to notice. Much later, she learned that she wasn't hallucinating—the spots were real: Because of her acute vision, she can see air particles of reflected light that are invisible to Red People. Now, she has more visual mastery with a pair of special glasses that "provide context," minimizing the distracting details that could lock her attention for hours.

She has also ceased the tapping, pounding, beating behavior commonly observed in those with autism, "the outward sign of the earthquake nobody saw," Donna wrote. When her senses overloaded as a child, she would bite her flesh like an animal bites the bars of its cage, not realizing the cage was her own body. "My legs took my body around in manic circles as though they could somehow outrun the body they were attached to. My head hit whatever was next to it, like someone trying to crack open a nut that had grown too big for its shell."

Before she learned new strategies, the rhythmic tapping, pounding, and slapping also helped her keep track of where the edges of her body left off and the Big Black Nothingness began. In *Somebody Somewhere,* she describes the two painful extremes of autism, both of which obliterate any concept of self: "Autism makes me feel everything at once without knowing what I am feeling or it cuts me off from feeling anything at all."

Though human touch and emotions present the risk of shut-down, Donna discovered she could brave these hurdles between autism and intimacy with Paul, her new husband. She met Paul, a musician, in a London music store. After noting his shy mannerisms and abrupt conversation, she correctly concluded that "he is like me." She wrote her phone number on a piece of paper and gave it to him. Four weeks later, he rallied the courage to call.

For an autistic couple, the recognition of love is not a wholly pleasant sensation. As her emotions approached "five on a scale of one to five," Donna battled to keep the self she had worked so hard to uncover from submerging again.

"Something awful is happening," she told Paul. "I have a feeling I don't understand."

"Is it something you ate? Are you upset? Do you need to eat?" Paul asked.

She finally worked her feelings out on paper and wrote him a letter: "The safer and happier I feel, the more it will make me want to run and escape. Do you realize this? Do you care enough, have patience enough and understanding enough, to support my fight against this stupid compulsion? If you do not, it is OK. But it would just be too hard if you didn't understand."

He did understand. Together, they developed systems to keep the "self" from disappearing during frightening emotions—Donna into her characters, Paul into his "faces," both manifestations of memorized behavior that they had used previously to cope with everyday life. They established what Donna calls their "ongoing specialship, a place of belonging." They had to talk a lot about sexual desire—or the lack of it. They could both remember sexual experiences in their past when there was no "self" involved. An adult going through the motions of sex without a self, Donna said, feels much the same as a child who is "molested, abused, and confused." The worst part, they agreed, was having to pretend to feelings they didn't have because that's what the Red People expected. "We were a pair of comrades discussing a decade each of self-rape," Donna says, "a pair of prostitutes talking trade." The desire to touch came slowly, with respect for their acute sensitivities.

Conducting their courtship was tricky—the usual gift exchanges held no appeal for Donna, who rarely wants to own anything. The things she most enjoys are clouds, sunshine, trees, plants, flowers, wind and waves, a fire in a fireplace. How to wrap up the ocean? Paul once adopted the persona of man-romancing-woman and tried to buy a crystal Donna had admired in a gift shop. She told him to put it back—she didn't want it. "There was too much 'I want to please you' in the air," she wrote, "too much 'let me escape me by focusing totally on you.' I could accept nothing in this atmosphere." Such blunt honesty is crucial to their relationship. Maintaining the self—not characters, not facades, not routinized behaviors or patterns—was perhaps the first and most critial rule of specialship.

I felt my anxiety rising as I drove into Manhatan to meet Donna and her husband for the first time. Traffic was moving at a crawl after a blizzard had dumped a foot of snow on the streets. I was already an hour late that February morning when I parked outside the Lyden Gardens, hoping their rule against changes in plan was flexible during natural disasters.

Donna had always stayed at the Mayflower because familiarity was necessary to a sense of security. Whenever she enters a new room, she feels secure only after memorizing every detail: the windows, the blinds, the wallpaper pattern, the color of the furniture, the marks on the floor, and, of course, the position of the door. Change frustrates autistic people because this memorizing is hard work. If one item is moved, the whole room has to be memorized again. When Donna returned to the Mayflower last year and asked for the same room, she instead was given an identical room with exactly the same furniture, colors, paintings, floor plan. But it might as well have been a tent in Central Park. What was so different, the concierge wanted to know? The view from the window.

But this time, they had switched hotels so as to have a suite with a kitchen. Because of their multiple food allergies—to milk, cheese, wheat, onions, among many others—Paul preferred to cook their meals rather than risk eating unidentified ingredients in restaurants.

"Our suite looks like a biscuit," Donna had said over the phone, meaning that it was beige. "It gives me a floaty feeling." Strongly affected by color and light, she was unmoored by beige.

Donna opens the door when I ring the bell, then steps immediately back into the foyer. She hums softly, makes a chuckling sound, then hums again. I recognize this pattern as her way of reducing terror. Though we have spoken freely on the phone, the initial moments of being together again are still frightening.

"Hello-Donna," I say evenly, looking over the shoulder of her yellow sweater. She puts her fingers on her lips, as if deciding whether to bite her nails or invite me in. I stand still as she hums, chuckles, hums, letting her take me in peripherally through her dark, tinted glasses. Finally, she speaks.

"Please take off your hat," she asks in her flattest, most mechanical tone, like a voice in a car telling me to put on my seat belt. I realize she can't see me yet. Even with the special glasses that provide context, I am The Friend Donna Mistook for a Hat. I remove the obstacle and she smiles in recognition.

She introduces Paul, a slim, tall man standing very still in the foyer. He looks past me and says hello, then disappears. Behind his colored glasses, the lower half of his handsome face appears stoic and solemn. Paul seems ill at ease, which I attribute to the presence of a stranger, my being late, and their jet lag after a harrowing trip from London to New York. The blizzard had delayed their flight, the airports at both locations had been filled with frenzied crowds, and they were living in a biscuit that made them feel floaty.

When Donna sits on the carpeted floor and immediately begins talking to me, I sit down on the floor, too. Our plan for the morning had been to take care of business first—she had called the night before, greatly upset, because her printer wasn't working. Since Donna did her thinking on paper first, the broken printer rendered her mute, as it were, just as she was headed into a full week of media interviews. I had offered to take them to a computer store first, then visit for a while, then take a walk through Central Park together, blizzard or no.

Paul had picked up his coat as soon as I arrived, preparing to go out, then had put it down again when Donna and I sat down and began talking. He keeps walking in and out of the room. Half an hour later, his level of anxiety seems to escalate.

"Are you doing an interview?" he asks.

"Not really an interview," I explain. "We're just visiting." He gives no sign that he appreciates the difference, but my remark triggers a question about whether we want a cup of tea. Paul is the member of their team in charge of food and refreshments. We both say yes.

While Paul makes two cups of chamomile tea, a loud knock on the door abruptly halts all conversation, Donna, startled by the sudden sound, stares at the door as a key slips into the lock. The hotel maid materializes in the doorway.

"Stop!" Donna calls. "Don't come in!" Paul hollers from the kitchen. A clamor of raised voices—from Donna and Paul, from me, from the maid—fuse in mutual alarm. "We told them at the desk . . . do not disturb. . . . I'm sorry . . . thought you were out." The maid quickly disappears but all equanimity is destroyed in an instant, as if a teargas bomb had dropped into the room.

Paul delivers two cups of tea, then sits down on the couch away from Donna and me. Then he gets up. Then he sits down. He becomes absorbed in making a list of some sort. His jaw is set in grim endurance, as if he is lifting weights. Donna sees his distress, recognizes a case of the "jubblies" coming on—"the yukky, gripping things inside your stomach under stress."

"Paul, what's wrong?" she asks.

No response. Paul looks straight ahead, his face frozen. Emotional overload. Her words aren't getting in, so Donna steps over to the couch and gently bows, putting the crown of her head in Paul's face. Humming softly, she holds perfectly still for a few minutes, letting him smell and feel her hair. Then she reverses position, burying her face in his hair. This must be what they call a "jubblieectomy—a ritual to get rid of the jubblies." Paul's jaw finally unlocks.

Words now flood out. He reminds Donna of the plan—and how anxious she had been all morning about the broken printer. Having absorbed her anxiety, he was prepared to take action as soon as I arrived. Now here we were, sitting on the floor, acting like two talking heads. All order and structure had disintegrated. Donna apologizes for abandoning the agenda. My appearance had started a chain reaction of triggered behaviors—the compulsive speaking, the rote social questions, the automatic "yeses" that once more brought cups of tea seemingly out of nowhere.

In record time, we don our coats, get in the car, complete our chore. After a brief autistic tour of the city—noticing the honking horns and the loud behavior of the Red People, seeing how the air conditioners just outside of apartments form a pattern like black boxes in a crossword puzzle—we return to the hotel. Errand accomplished, everyone is more relaxed. I am invited to stay for lunch.

Quicker than I can make a peanut butter sandwich, it seems, Paul arrives with three plates of steak, broccoli, cauliflower, and beans.

"We don't talk while we eat," Paul informs me when I start to chatter. "If you start talking, Donna won't know what she's eating." We click knives and forks and "simply be." Occasionally, a hum meets a good bite or signifies a private thought.

I mention after lunch that Donna doesn't seem to be interested in "buzzing" on colors and sounds as much as she used to. I remembered standing under a pink streetlight with her late one evening, our faces turned up to catch the falling snow directly— it felt like we were speeding through space, rushing through a field of tiny pink planets. Did the willful control of autistic symptoms that imprisoned her also mean giving up the extraordinary pleasures of her acute sensory perception? What activities does she now enjoy?

She says the concept of "enjoy" is a whole new realm. She and Paul have "developed a checking procedure which gives us, for the first time, an ability to tell compulsion from 'want' or 'like.'" That was a huge breakthrough in autism terms; now that she knows the difference, she buzzes only when she "wants" to and not because the snow is there.

I put on my coat and prepare for terse farewells. The first time Donna and I parted company, she said "Good-bye" and closed the door. The next time, as if teaching herself to be more social, she said, "Good-bye . . . and thank you. You have been a great bagful of information."

Now, with the blunt honesty of her real self, she says: "I can't say I've enjoyed your company. But I didn't mind it." She means to be clear, but then worries.

"Did that hurt your feelings?" she asks. Red People have complicated feelings that are always cropping up unexpectedly, getting hurt unintentionally.

"No," I answer honestly. After three years, I understand that while I may be enjoying Donna, she is most likely enduring me.

After a week in New York with another week of interviews to go, Donna calls to ask whether she and Paul can come to Connecticut for the weekend. When I come to pick them up, Paul asks me to look directly at him before we leave. It's a necessary hurdle to surmount before he can move into close proximity with me. I make eye contact, which, just like loud voices and fluttery gestures, can cause sensory pain. He jumps, then laughs loudly, then shivers. "It's like being pelted with ice cubes," he explains. It hurts, but it's done. Now he can bear my company for the weekend.

Donna mentions that she and Paul have a firm house rule: No leaving soap suds in the sink after the dishes. Suds contain rainbows of color, and they can nearly paralyze an autistic person. If one of them happened by the sink, he or she could get stuck until the bubbles burst. I ask Donna if they have any other household rules. Here is a partial list:

*No reading newspaper headlines in gas stations or newsstands.*

*No watching Oprah Winfrey or Sally Jessy Raphael without checking first if I want to.*

*No making the fruit bowl symmetrical.*

*Attempt to keep track of your face and your body at all times.*

*Say, "It's important to me," instead of just going ahead and doing things when you face opposition and can't battle verbally.*

*Don't force yourself to stay in rooms or situations, eat food, or be with people that are allergenic or that force you to disassociate or overload.*

*Say "time" instead of throwing wobblies.*

*Don't talk or answer people in a triggered way—triggering gets out of control and the consequences are entirely out of your hands.*

*To seem is not to be.*
*No lining feet up with the furniture.*
*Scrub your underarms—just putting soap on your body is not washing.*
*Take your glasses off before dressing (and put them back on afterward).*
*Dare to mess.*
*Don't use stored voices, stored intonation, stored movements, or stored facial expressions.*
*Never buzz on a road.*
*Be nice to your body.*

I have instructed my son Ryan, who is home from college, on the basic rules of Being with Donna and Paul. He's a gregarious kid with a ready handshake and hearty laugh. I tell him to reverse all his usual instincts: "You'll make them most comfortable by ignoring them." When we enter through the back door that afternoon, he quickly turns off the TV and disappears so that they can get acquainted with the house. After depositing their copious luggage, computer equipment, and grocery bags in the guest room and kitchen, they begin feeling my house—touching objects, tapping walls.

"What's that noise?" Paul asks suddenly. I recognize the faint electrical hum of the refrigerator—which Paul hears reverberating off the walls, blasting his ears. When they are acclimated, I bring Ryan back into the kitchen to introduce him.

"Hello-glad-to-meet-you," he says, looking down at his feet and speaking like a robot. He stands awkward and still for a moment, like a rookie actor who doesn't know where to put his hands. Donna wonders whether he is autistic or well-educated. She asks: "Are you always this quiet?"

Simultaneously, we answer, "Never" and "Sometimes." I mean that Ryan is not autistic; he means that he can handle the rules. Getting a straight answer from the Red People is a trial.

Ryan and I go out for lunch to give Donna and Paul the kitchen to themselves. When we return, they have cooked, eaten, done the dishes, and are now outside in their snowsuits. My yard, front and back, is filled with exquisite snow sculptures: a perfect cat, with thin twiggy whiskers; a penguin on an iceberg with a fish at its webbed feet; a large snail with antennae. Their masterpiece is a two-story cottage landscaped with shrubs and trees; Paul is placing lighted windows in the second story. He asks if it was okay to take a few yellow Post-it notes from my office.

Without a word, Ryan goes to the front porch and picks some flakes of chipped concrete off the steps. As Paul puts the last Post-it in a second-story window, Ryan makes a flagstone path to the front door. Donna hums. "There are other ways of communicating besides language," as she often says.

Aware of their food allergies, I ask whether Paul would like to cook dinner. Paul freezes at the suggestion. I don't know what part of my question has thrown him. Donna, reading his expression, calmly begins what I now recognize as a familiar litany of questions:

"Does Paul want to cook?" No response.
"Does Paul not want to cook?" A faint smile.
"Do Paul's defenses want to cook?" No response.
"Does Paul want Mary Kay to cook?" A faint smile.
"Does Paul want Ryan to cook?" A big smile.
So now we know.

As we get into the car the next day, Paul says, "Look, Donna! The big black arm is swinging back and forth instead of around in a circle!"

"Oh, yes!" she says, like a tourist spotting a cultural peculiarity in a foreign country.

I look up from the ignition to see what they're talking about. What black arm?

"There." Paul points to the house next door. I look at the broad white exterior, the windows, the shrubbery. I see no arms.

"In the electric meter," he explains. I squint and focus, finally spotting a tiny black dot moving along a slotted opening. Even with perception glasses, Paul and Donna take in every minuscule movement. I start to understand Paul's earlier comment that 80 percent of the information overload is visual. I have lived next door to the big black arm for four years and never noticed it.

Donna's agent has invited us all to her country house for Sunday brunch. It qualifies as a "dinner party," which is never fun—but Donna knows Ellen will appreciate the effort and she chooses to go. She and Paul have established their decision as a "want to" and not a compulsion to be polite. ("Mary Kay can take care of the 'blah, blah, blah,'" Paul says.)

During lunch as Ellen and I talk, Donna overhears a remark that gives her a new insight.

"So you don't just sell books for the money—you keep them for a while and make them better. You have feelings about the books?" Donna asks. "You care about them before you sell them?"

"Yes, that's right," Ellen clarifies.

"So, you are like a babysitter of books?"

"Yes," Ellen says, smiling broadly. They connect.

Ellen walks us to the car after lunch. "Good-bye, Donna," she says warmly. "I'll miss you."

"Good-bye," Donna says, and closes the car door.

We drive in silence for a while. "Why did she say, 'I'll miss you'?" she asks. I explain the concept of missing.

"Why didn't she keep that feeling to herself?" There is no accusation in her questions—she is merely consulting her bag of information, trying to understand the mysterious ways of the Red People. We like to blah-blah, we get attached, we love and enjoy, we miss.

After dinner Sunday night, we realize we are getting close to our own good-bye. Donna starts twirling a napkin on the table, buzzing on the spin. "Stop that, Donna," Paul says, then looks toward me. "She's doing that to make you irrelevant," he states matter-of-factly. Donna laughs her real laugh. She is delighted to be understood so perfectly, to be called on her "autie" behavior.

When a similar exchange occurred the day before, Paul wondered if I had taken his comment as criticism of Donna. He explained their agreement to help each other this way, to recognize autism and assist each other in controlling it. Several times throughout their visit, one or the other had issued a reminder—"Don't use 'voices' when you tell a story". . . . "That's a 'stored dialogue,' not a 'conversation'".... "Build a sculpture but don't 'perform' for people." The No. 1 rule: Be your real self. Which means you have to have a self.

Donna can mesmerize audiences with her ability to recite whole books on the subject of autism—and just about anything else—but Paul recognizes that those compelling speeches are not always what she means to say. Her own conversation is much more of a struggle. Much harder, but authentic. "It's like if someone you knew could walk sat down in a wheelchair and wouldn't get up," Paul explains. "You could push her around, but that wouldn't be good because you know she really wants to walk." He sees his role as her companion walker.

Donna now looks directly at Paul. "I think you are a good man," she says. It is a whole, emotional speech. His real smile lights up as he simultaneously laughs and cries in soft, quiet gulps. It's painful, but he stays with the emotion. He doesn't overload.

I realize then that their rules for an autistic marriage would be useful to all married couples: Pay attention to details—they matter; don't aggravate each other with compulsive, thoughtless habits; don't assume you understand—check feelings out with each other; be tolerant of self-comforting quirks; teach each other what you are learning about the world; get out of your wheelchair and walk on your own two feet.

My sister hopes that Donna will write another book, called "Everybody Everywhere," a kind of etiquette manual that would teach people to be more sensitive and less presumptuous about the rules and expectations we impose on other people.

"I am an accidental educator," Donna says when I tell her she has taught me a lot about my own life. She had no choice about instructing the Red People in the ways of autism if she wanted to come out of her private world. Now that she has, maybe she doesn't need to write any more books. All she wanted, for nearly thirty years now, was to find a specialship where she could belong—a place where her culture could happen.

I drive my odd couple to their next destination. Then, after speedy good-byes, I drive home, numb with exhaustion. Being a chauffeur to two autistic people in love—explaining, learning, running interference between small planets—I feel like I'm approaching overload myself. I recognize shutdown not as an absence of emotions but too many at once. A surge of affection rises, a fierce yearning for happiness and safety and cosmic understanding. The two small red taillights from the car ahead disappear around a bend and my mind goes blank.

# A DAY AT
# THE DOGFIGHTS

*Harry Crews*

His name was Skete. I never knew him by any other name. He never said and I never asked. It would have been bad form because Skete was a breeder of pit bulldogs, bred especially to fight, bred for ferocity, tenacity, quickness, and strength. Fighting dogs in a pit, or anywhere else for that matter, is against the law—a felony if the breeder takes his dog across state lines to fight. I'd met Skete through a girl I'd known about four years before. In the middle of the night the girl called me up and asked if I'd like to go to a fight being held in South Florida. She knew, as everybody does who knows me at all, that I love blood sports. Not a particularly admirable trait, but one that I've always had and one I've never tried to suppress or find the reasons for.

"You think Skete would let me come with him?" I asked over the telephone.

"I told him about you. He said he'd take my word you were a stand-up guy and would cause him no trouble."

"I'd want to write about it."

"I told him you'd never burn down his proposition."

The girl, Monica, nicknamed Money, had worked for a long time in carnivals, and in a carnival nobody has a job, he has a "proposition." And if you put him out of business, by using the law or anything else, you are said to "burn down his proposition."

"You know the people and things I've written about," I said, "and I've never burned anybody. Nobody gets hurt letting me watch and letting me write."

"I know," she said.

I talked to Skete the next night on the telephone to confirm the invitation. The conversation was short.

"Nobody hurts me and mine with impunity," he said. "Come, if you can live with that."

Impunity. Skete was not without an education. In his late twenties, Skete already owned a hotel on the Gulf Coast of Florida. I suspect—I *know*—he must do a lot of things most folks would not approve of. Money knew him because she worked in the bar of his hotel.

"Then it's done," I said.

"Done," he said. And hung up.

I was supposed to meet him in Naples, Florida. To get there, I had to fly from Gainesville, in the middle of North Florida, where I live, to Miami, and then across the state to the Gulf of Mexico. He met me in a Dodge van. Money was with him. So was Skete's Pryde, or, more formally and correctly said, Mr. Pryde. They'd driven up from Skete's breeding kennel fifty miles south of Naples. It was then about ten-thirty at night and we'd been told the fight would be held at five-thirty in the morning in Boca Raton, which was all the way back across the state. Both of us knew the fight was not going to be held in Boca Raton, nor was it going to be held at five-thirty in the morning. Those were simply the instructions Skete had, the place to go, the motel to check in to. From that point on, we would wait for a telephone call telling us where to bring the dog and when. Nobody knows where a pit fight is going to take place except the promoters. Skete had already signed a contract with a breeder from Arkansas. Pit contracts always include the money the breeder will forfeit if his dog loses. He also loses the money if he does not show up at the appointed hour and place. I did not know how much money was in the contract, nor did I ask. Again, it would have been bad form. But I've seen contracts written in such a way that $30,000 was at stake. The promoters hold the money bet in the contract; they also hold any side bets made during the fight. And between the whiskey, and the blood, and the sweat, the most frantic betting in the world goes on at dogfights, much more so than at cockfights, and the betting at cockfights is something out of a madman's dream. Mr. Pryde rode sweetly with us in the van, giving no hint that he was about to fight to become a grand champion. He had already won four fights, one more than enough to make him a champion; five wins would make him a grand champion, and he would be retired to stud, never to fight again. He was five and a half years old and had not fought in two years. He was going to fight a dog that was also fighting to become a grand champion. They were fighting at forty-eight pounds, and like prizefighters, they had to come in at or under the appointed weight. Mr. Pryde was gentle, almost like a puppy, his long, slender tail continually wagging. He never barked or growled—no pit bull ever does when he's fighting, and rarely does he ever bark or growl at all. He was utterly beautiful, conditioned down to nothing but bone and muscle and ligament.

But when we checked into the motel in Boca Raton and Skete took out a pair of scales and hung them on the shower rod in the bathroom, Mr. Pryde became noticeably agitated, the hair got up on his back, and his long, thin tail whipped into a blur of speed. As soon as he saw the scales he knew he was going to fight. Skete lifted him to the scale and the needle swung and held like magic on forty-eight pounds. It was then about four o'clock and a boy had arrived whose name was—or at least he was called—Little Brother. He would be Skete's second at the pit. Money was there to operate a hand-held moving picture camera. Many breeders photograph their dogs fighting, just as a football coach photographs his football team. The breeder is looking for errors, for gameness— which cannot always be seen in the frenzy of a fight—looking for any idiosyncrasy the dog might have developed since he fought last. Mr. Pryde was, in fact, the sire of Skete's kennel, and he would continue to be even if he lost.

There are probably more misconceptions about dogfighting than about any other blood sport. In the March 1976 issue of *Harper's Magazine,* somebody named Edward Meadows, who writes a

column called "Political Economy" for a newsweekly in Colum-
bia, South Carolina, has about as many errors packed into a piece
called "An American Pastime" as he could possibly manage. The
fact is the English Staffordshire bull terrier was bred to a variety of
bulldog bloodlines and game, aggressive breeds to develop the dogs
that are most often fought at the pits today. The English bull terrier is small, about eighteen inches at the shoulder, very quick,
and will clamp on to almost anything it can take hold of. The
American pit bull is much heavier, more courageous, and has much
stronger jaws. In the pits, a one-hundred-fifty-pound German
shepherd, for instance, has no chance against a forty-eight-pound
pit bull. A shepherd has comparatively weak jaws (a pit's bite is at
least twice as strong), and the configuration of the pit's teeth makes
its bite far more lethal.

Here is Mr. Meadows on pits when they are what breeders call
"in keep," which means when they are in training for a fight:
"Proper training of a bull terrier for the dogfighting pit requires
two dozen live kittens a week. Each kitten is tied unceremoniously
to a stick and dangled in front of the dog to whet his lust for killing. A good pit bull will quickly tear the kitten's front legs off.
Then, excited by the kitten's blood and its agony, encouraged also
by his trainer's bloodthirsty yells, the true fighting dog will rip the
kitten's head off. After perhaps eight weeks of kittens . . . the dog
is graduated to the killing of puppies and small dogs. He learns
well the taste of their blood. . . . The dog is forced to run for hours
on a treadmill to build his muscles." Later, Mr. Meadows says that
during the actual fight, "cut-rate prostitutes work the sweaty,
darkened pit rooms, even though the fans' wives and children are
present."

I could go on with this sort of thing, but the above is more
than enough. I am not defending fighting dogs. I just wonder why
we can't tell the truth about blood sports, which would go a long
way toward telling the truth about ourselves. We are a violent
culture. We like to see the two dugouts emptied at baseball games
and the players—armed with bats or anything they can put hand
to—break each other's heads. We are thrilled at the spectacle of a
football player going off the field on a stretcher or a race-car driver

losing it against a retaining wall and being fried alive, trapped in his car. Do we read with shivers of pleasure or of horror about such things as Indian Red Lopez fighting David Kotey for a world featherweight championship and beating him so badly that it took some three dozen stitches to close up Kotey's face? If the shivers are not of pleasure, why are the results set down in a special section of your newspaper where you can easily find them and read them over your morning cornflakes?

But back to the pit bull. I've been around dogfights all my life and I've never seen a dog killed in the pit. I don't say it doesn't happen, just that I've never seen it. But didn't Emile Griffith kill Benny "Kid" Paret in the ring, beat him to the doors of death with a full house screaming for him to do it? Every fight between pit bulls I've seen—and I've seen 'em all over the country—has been fought by what are called Louisiana rules, which means the dog does not have, as breeders say, "to take his killing." All he has to do is "cur out." If he turns from the other dog, or won't leave his corner, the fight is over.

The four of us were sitting in the motel room in Boca Raton, Mr. Pryde asleep in the middle of the bed, his head on Skete's lap. We were waiting for the call that would tell us where the fight would be held.

I asked Skete about how he trained his dog in keep and also the business about making the dog aggressive and savage by letting him tear up kittens and puppies.

"Bullshit," said Skete. "You can't train gameness, or any other fighting qualities, into a pit bull. It sometimes takes years to find the right sire, and sometimes even longer to find the right bitch. If you don't find the right bitch, you'll never have a world-beating kennel."

"How do you find the bitch?"

"By watching them fight and then paying what the winning bitch is worth or, more often, buying one of her bitch pups."

"I've never seen two bitches fight," I said.

"You ought to," he said. "You haven't seen a dogfight until you do. I think bitches are the finer animals."

I didn't know if I was pushing too hard or not; you never do, but I wanted to know: "What did you pay for Mr. Pryde?"

"Seven hundred dollars as a pup, and flew him all the way from California." He stroked the dog's head, the ears of which were chewed down to little more than nubs. "He's a great dog. He's already sired three champions. He retires after this match, win or lose."

"What would you sell him for?"

"He's not for sale."

"I hate to sound like something out of a Grade B movie, but everything's for sale. This is America, where money's more serious than death."

"I wouldn't sell him."

"What *could* you get for him?"

"I've never thought about it. He's not for sale."

It was the tone of his voice that changed the direction of the questioning.

"When he's in keep, how do you train him?" I mentioned running on a treadmill.

"Some breeders apparently do it, but I've never known one that did. Running a dog's no damn good. These are fighting dogs, not greyhounds. For five weeks before a match, I walk him twenty miles a day. I cheat and ride, but he walks. I never run him. He eats almost entirely protein in a mixture I made up myself."

"What kind of mixture?"

He smiled. "If I told you, then everyone would know, wouldn't they? Every breeder has developed certain things he believes in and he doesn't give those things away. To anybody."

I knew that cockfighters pump their birds up with vitamin K to retard bleeding. Did he?

"No, because I don't believe it works. You bring the dog in as dry as you can because the less water he's got in him, the less blood he'll lose. But that's a delicate thing nobody can teach you. You just learn over the years how much water he has to have to come in strong but not so much that he'll lose blood for nothing. Besides, a breeder doesn't notice the blood and neither does the dog. Blood doesn't mean a thing unless he starts pumping."

But I already knew that. You never hear a bull make a sound in a fight, even when he's covered with blood. If he starts pumping, though, he's cut an artery and there isn't much a breeder can do—short of stopping the fight—to save him. That's why a leg dog is one of the worst to fight. The artery in the hind leg is too easy to cut, but a good fighter will recognize immediately that he's up against a leg dog and will instinctively protect that quarter of himself. There are throat dogs and stomach dogs and chest dogs and there are rider dogs—dogs that will take hold in the top of the shoulder much the way collegiate wrestlers ride each other. A rider dog simply maintains the top position until he wears his opponent down, until not even the gamest dog will have the strength to continue. Each breeder knows the breeder he's coming up against but not which of the breeder's dogs his own pit will have to fight.

"Mr. Pryde has always been a face dog," said Skete. "In the same way you can't train a dog for gameness, you can't train one to fight a certain way. You can try, but you'll end up making him a poorer fighter than he would have otherwise been. These dogs live to fight." He leaned forward. "Listen, I don't want my dog hurt. I love him. But he's not happy unless he's in the pit." He sighed. "There's a lot of guys breeding who don't know the first thing about it."

"What kind of fighter you hope you face this time out?"

"I don't care. Mr. Pryde doesn't either. I've done everything I can for him. He's ready."

He took some pictures out of an attaché case. They were of Mr. Pryde swinging on the knotted end of a thick hemp rope hanging from the limb of a tree. "Pryde's always loved to swing on the knotted end of a rope. It's a game to him. It's also as good a thing as you can do to strengthen his jaws, toughen his gums, thicken his neck. Mr. Pryde's got a muscle high between his shoulders like a fighting bull. I've seen him lift a dog that weighs as much as he does entirely off the ground and shake him like a doll. But a dog is either a rope dog or he's not. Making a pit do something unnatural to him ruins him. Like his weight, for instance. Every pit has a weight that's his natural fighting weight. You have to try to find out what that weight is and bring him in at it. You try to make him heavier or lighter than that and you only put him at a disadvantage."

The phone rang. Skete took it, talked little, made notes on a pad, and hung up without a good-bye.

"The fight's twenty miles this side of Stuart. I know the place. Let's leave a call and get some sleep." Skete and Money slept in one bed with Mr. Pryde between them. Little Brother, who hadn't said a word since he got to the room, slept in the other bed with me.

Ah, it was good to be back among my people again. And I'm not talking about southerners. I'm talking about Americans. *Naked* Americans. In the parking lot there were cars and pickups with tags from as far away as Illinois. The fight was being held in an enormous building that must have once been a paint and body shop of some sort, a building large enough to accommodate at least five hundred people. There were as many women there as there were men, but no children that I could see. The building was closed and blue with smoke. If there was a hand there that didn't have a whiskey bottle or a beer can in it, I didn't see it. Money was everywhere, balled in fists and folded between fingers and hanging from shirt pockets. There were men standing in $400 suits and others in overalls. There were lacquered women who didn't seem to sweat at all and other women who would have sweated if you'd shucked 'em down and put 'em in a deep freeze. There was an incredible din, the noise of violence, viciousness, and the lust for blood and money. The *naked* American. Nothing fake here. Life insurance and retirement plans were forgotten, children were forgotten, there was no future, only the moment, and the moment was savage. Here was the faith that brought the black man from Africa, the faith that still kicks the shit out of American-born Mexicans in Texas, the faith of the officer saying in his laconic but believing voice, "We had to destroy the village in order to save it." It was so ugly, it was beautiful. It was mine and I would no more deny it than I would my own blood. And disguise that faith how you will, it lives, breathes, and gets fatter every year in this great country of ours. Give us the world and this would be the paradigm we'd use to remake it.

In the center of the building was a sixteen-foot-square pit made of plywood about thirty inches high. Everybody in here had paid the promoters $20 to howl and scowl and bet their last penny on the blood of dogs bred for the sole purpose of spilling it.

That night there were to be four fights. Mr. Pryde was going to fight first. The dog he was going against was a throat dog, three and a half years old, with great configuration of head and body. Pits are bred with a face shaped in such a way that they can take a really deep bite and still breathe. Mr. Pryde's opponent had a classic head for doing just that, a mouth and nose so formed that he looked like he could go in five inches and still breathe comfortably.

Both dogs were in a rage now that they had seen each other. They only had to be put into the pit and the fight would be on. The rules are simple to the point of ritual. Each breeder washed the other breeder's dog, washed him with a clear solution and dried him good, all under the watchful eye of the seconds. The washing was necessary because there is a chemical you can put on your dog that will cause the other dog to refuse to bite him. Money was operating her movie camera. Little Brother stood just outside Mr. Pryde's corner with a towel he would use to fan Pryde when the dogs broke. But the towel could never touch the dog. If it did, he would be disqualified and the fight would be over. There was a sponge and bucket of water in each dog's corner. But the single rule central to the entire proceeding was this: Once the fight started, *nothing* that was outside the pit could enter it, and *nothing* that was inside the pit could leave it. Any violation of that rule was an automatic disqualification. There were three men allowed in the pit—the two breeders to handle their dogs, and a referee. Each breeder lifted his dog into his corner of the pit. The dogs strained to get at each other. Each breeder held his dog by the nape of the neck and by the heavy skin of his back. The referee stood in the center of the pit. Side bets were already being made and Little Brother—it was part of his job as second—covered every bet that came down against Mr. Pryde. I don't know how much money Skete had brought with him, but it had to be thousands. The promoters kept track of the bets and held the money.

"Pit 'em!" cried the referee, and each breeder released his dog. The dog can only be released; he can't be shoved toward the other dog. If he does not charge on release the fight's over.

The dogs slammed together in the center of the pit, both of them on their hind legs, their heads together, fighting for a hold, Pryde in the face, the other dog in the throat.

The breeders can get as close to their dogs as they like, down on the floor with them, talking to them, hissing in their ears, but they cannot touch them. As long as the dogs are locked, as long as one or both dogs have their teeth buried in the other's flesh, the breeders cannot touch them. But if they break apart, each breeder snatches his dog up and carries him to his corner, where he is fanned and sponged and mucus is sucked from his nose at times, or blood from his throat. The breeders turn the dogs so they cannot see each other. This calms them down so they can be ministered to. The screaming bets continue right through the match to the end. After thirty seconds, the referee cries again: "Pit 'em!" The breeders turn the dogs and they charge to the center of the ring.

For some reason Skete couldn't understand, Mr. Pryde started going down when the two dogs collided, fighting from his back, which allowed the other dog into his throat. Curiously, the dogs fought without making a sound, but their tails wagged constantly, wagged so furiously that at times you could hardly see them.

The fight lasted forty-six minutes, which is about average for a dogfight, though it is not unheard of for a fight to go for two or three hours. Once the other dog was buried in his throat, I thought surely Mr. Pryde would be killed or at least give up. But he'd come to fight, and he continually shook the other pit out of his throat and went for his face. Even at that, the other dog must have been in Mr. Pryde's throat twenty minutes. But at about the forty-minute mark, it was obvious the other dog had had enough. He was still fighting, had not turned, but I knew Mr. Pryde was about to do what he'd come to do and I wanted to see it.

An enormous man had moved in front of me. I touched him on the shoulder and told him I'd paid $20 to see this and since he himself had a clear view of the pit, would he mind getting the hell out of the way. He turned and caught me in the throat with what felt like brass knuckles, and when I went down he came down on top of me. I didn't see Mr. Pryde's victory. I woke up in the back of the Dodge van with Mr. Pryde lying beside me, snoring away. He had been given a shot of Demerol and a shot of cortisone and had all his wounds covered with some secret concoction of Skete's that was black and had the consistency of tar. By the time we got back to the motel, I'd passed out from a slight concussion. My vision was blurred, and I had more lacerations and blood on me than Mr. Pryde.

All in all, it had been a grand evening.

# MISSING ALICE

## *Pete Earley*

*M*idway across Ohio, the man beside me on the DC-10 asked where I was going.

"Fowler, Colorado. A little town of about a thousand near Pueblo."

"Why would anyone go to Foouuller?" he asked, grinning as he exaggerated the name.

"A death. My sister."

"Sorry," he mumbled and turned away.

*I was relieved. I didn't have to explain that my sister had been dead nineteen years.*

Alice was killed when I was fourteen. She was two years older and we had been inseparable as children. I couldn't talk about her death at first. My voice would deepen, my eyes would fill with tears. My parents would cry at the mention of her name, and we rarely spoke of her. Then it seemed too late. After I left home, my mother would phone me each February 13 and remind me that it was my sister's birthday. Year after year, I would forget—and find myself angry with my mother's insistent reminders.

It was just before last Christmas, as I shuffled boxes in the basement, that I ran across Alice's picture and a clipping describing her death. "A tragic accident Tuesday, June 14, about 7:05 P.M., took the life of Alice Lee Earley. . . ."

I sat down on the concrete floor, closed my eyes, and tried to picture her. I couldn't. I tried to focus more sharply: Alice eating Sugar Pops beside me at the breakfast table, Alice washing the green Ford Falcon, Alice stepping on my toes while singing in church. The events I recalled vividly. Alice's face I recalled not at all. I could only see the girl in the photograph—an image I had never liked, the face being without joy or expression. But in my mind I found no other. For the next week, I seemed to think of Alice constantly.

One night I awoke in bed, turned to my wife, Barbara, and said: "Alice, are you there?" It took me an instant to realize what I had done. When I called my parents, now living in South Dakota, and told them I was returning to Fowler, my mother said: "Good, everyone always acts like Alice never existed."

I was at church camp when Alice died. The camp director shook me awake in the middle of the night and said my father was in his office. I padded barefoot on the barrack's cool concrete floor toward a yellow sliver of light escaping from beneath a closed door. Inside, my father was crying. I had never seen him cry.

I liked camp and I hated to leave, but I rode home quietly in the front seat between my parents. My mother sobbed. My father was silent, though once he smacked his palm fiercely atop the steering wheel. I tried to remember the last thing I had said to Alice, but I couldn't. So I thought of the girl I had met at camp the day before, about how I had hoped to sit next to her at evening vespers tomorrow, about how my friend, Eddie, would take my place. I knew the camp director would announce at breakfast that my sister was dead: Everyone would feel sorry for me. Maybe the girl would write me a letter.

On the way home we stopped at the house of the woman driving the car that had struck Alice. Flora Ledbetter came out of the bedroom in a white terry cloth robe, her eyes red. She sobbed. My father, a Disciples of Christ minister, said she was not to blame. Mr. Ledbetter put his arm around my shoulder. My mother hugged Mrs. Ledbetter. I felt sorry for her.

People came to the parsonage all that day. With each new wave, my parents repeated how Alice had died. "This is part of some greater plan," one woman offered.

I escaped to the garage, where I found my Honda 50—its front wheel bent, its spokes snapped, its battery case cracked. Alice's blood dotted the gas tank. I loved that scooter. On summer mornings, I would slice through the steam above the warming country blacktop, my shirt unbuttoned and whipping my back. The Mexicans picking cucumbers, cantaloupes, and watermelons in the fields would pause and glance as I passed at full throttle, 45 miles an hour.

When my father found me in the garage, I'd cleaned off everything but the blood and was trying to straighten the mangled wheel with a hammer.

"I think I can fix it," I said. The next day it was gone.

Fowler is nine miles west of Manzanola, eighteen miles west of Rocky Ford, and twenty-eight miles west of La Junta. No planes, no trains, no bus stations. The Arkansas River keeps the flat, rocky land around Fowler, population 1,241, rich for watermelons, sugar beets, sweet corn, and cantaloupes. Fowler is nine blocks square. I think of it as home.

My family had moved six times by my fourteenth birthday, the year we arrived in Fowler. The constant migration made Alice and me close, as did the nearness in our ages. Our brother, George, was six years older than I. Alice was alive for only the first year we lived in Fowler, and most of my memories of the town do not include her. But walking the streets of Fowler again helped me remember: Alice working behind the soda fountain at Fowler Drug, mixing me 15-cent cherry Cokes, Alice walking to the Fowler swimming pool with me on hot afternoons, Alice assisting me in my incarnation as Dr. Sly, child magician and escape artist.

I remembered the time she and I convinced our Sunday school teacher that all of the students should read their favorite Bible stories aloud. The others read David and Goliath or Noah. I read Judges 5, Verse 26, how Jael pounded a tent peg into the head of Sisera, the heathen. Alice read Second Samuel 11, how David spied

Bathsheba naked and dispatched her husband to the front lines to be slaughtered.

I drove to Fowler's First Christian Church, where my father had been pastor. The four chandeliers my parents donated in memory of Alice still hang from the white roof of the sanctuary. My mother's painting of a girl lighting candles at an altar still decorates the east wall.

I sat in a wooden pew and stared above the communion table at the stained-glass window of Christ praying in the Garden of Gethsemane. I had taken collections, said prayers, and read announcements beneath that window a hundred times. They called me "the little preacher." I closed my eyes:

*I am lanky boy with buzz-cut hair and glasses mended with Scotch tape. My mother wears her most colorful hat and we walk down the church aisle together holding hands as the mourners' heads turn in unison at our passing. We step to the first row in front of Alice's open coffin. She is in heaven and we are witnessing: "Alleluia! Where O Death Is Now Thy Sting?"*

"I did the first portion of your sister's funeral service," said pastor Charles Whitmer when I asked him for his memory of the funeral. "When I finished, your father walked up next to the casket and began talking about Alice. He talked about his relationship with her and how much all of you loved her and he kept his composure the entire time. I remember thinking that no one could do that, no one could have kept his composure like he had, unless Christ was with him."

*During the prayer, I search for Flora Ledbetter, who sits near the back of the church. She is sobbing. Her husband sees me and lowers his eyes. She is not to blame, my parents had said. I look at my mother, my father, my brother. Their eyes are closed. My parents are holding hands, tightly. I look at Alice. They have put too much makeup on her. She hates makeup. I had kissed her good-bye, the night before, and her skin felt hard. My father had called her "Our Sissie." I raise my head and look at the window of Christ in the Garden. The morning sun has turned his robe blood red. Alice's faith was always so complete. She had once promised that if the Communists took over, she would die a martyr.*

I opened my eyes, walked to the altar, and knelt to pray, but I couldn't. I waited, and it didn't come. I looked up at the stained-glass window of Jesus.

"Damn you!" I whispered. They were the words of a fourteen-year-old boy.

I drove to Jones Corner from Fowler by the route Alice had taken that night. Then I drove Ledbetter's route, three times. On the last trip I jammed on my brakes, imagining that I had just seen Alice on the scooter. The car swerved as it entered the intersection, its headlights cutting a swath across an empty field. I got out of the car and began pacing. In the four years I lived in Fowler after Alice died, I had never visited Jones Corner.

I stepped from the road into the ditch where Alice had been thrown. It was steeply sloped, several feet deep, patched with snow. I stepped on a beer bottle. An old magazine was frozen to exposed grass. I tried to picture the scene: Ledbetter's car in the center of the road, my motor scooter thrown sixty-six feet to the side, my sister at my feet.

"I remember your sister was lying in the bar ditch about here," Wes Ayers, Fowler's deputy sheriff, had told me earlier in the day as he marked the spot on a piece of paper. "At the time, state troopers filed reports only if there was a fatality, and I asked the state trooper if he was going to do a report on your sister. He said, 'No.'

"'Don't you see that big cut on that little girl's leg?' I asked. 'Well, it ain't bleeding at all and that can only mean one thing: She's got to be bleeding inside.' After I told him that, he got out his clipboard."

The thought of Alice lying among strangers as they speculated about the odds of her living enraged me. It had taken almost an hour after the accident to get Alice to the thirty-seven-bed Pioneer Memorial Hospital, only twenty-two miles away. The emergency room report, brief and routine, didn't explain the long time gap; it said she died of shock. She arrived at 8 P.M., awake and complaining of pain.

"Pt ventilating when first seen. BP 90/60—gradually dropped. Given Demerol 75 mg. for pain. Pt went into shock & coma." After Alice lapsed into unconsciousness, they finally started IVs in her right arm and ankle, suctioned her throat, massaged her heart, gave her adrenaline. "Pt never regained consciousness. Expired 9:30 P.M."

Years before my sister died, I shot a rabbit a few yards from the Fowler Cemetery, east of town and set amid towering Chinese elm trees. I had spooked the cottontail from a woodpile and it ran up an embankment, where it froze. I blasted its entrails across the snow. I thought about the rabbit and my clear memory of it when I drove into the cemetery. But I could not recall a single detail of my sister's graveside service.

It was almost midnight and the moon illuminated the tombstones. It was snowing gently. I walked to the headstone I believed was my sister's, but it wasn't. I slowly walked row by row, examining each headstone, seeing the names of people I had known in Fowler. Clouds began to block the moonlight and it seemed to get colder.

It is embarrassing to say, but I suddenly felt afraid, as if I were intruding. For two decades I had lived without thinking of Alice. I thought: "I knew her only fourteen years. She has been here for nineteen. They are her family now."

I couldn't find the headstone, so I shined my car's headlights into the cemetery. It was so cold now that I began to speed up my search. It struck me that Alice would not let me find her! I ran, faster and faster, glancing at each name. A sense of desperation shot through me. Suddenly, I caught myself. The image of me, frightened and racing through the Fowler Cemetery at midnight, was ludicrous. I would return tomorrow.

That night, voices outside my motel door awakened me from a dream. I lay in bed afraid to move, an emotion I had not felt since childhood. In my dream, I had been jogging. It was dark and a car began to follow me. It forced me down an alley blocked by a tall chain link fence. A gang of boys got out of the car. They pulled knives from their coats. I scrambled up the chain link fence, but as I reached the top it curled backward, slowly lowering me toward them. Just as they were about to reach me, they turned and grabbed someone else from the shadows. They stabbed and stabbed and stabbed, until the person was dead. Then they turned and pointed their knives toward me.

I found Alice's grave without trouble the next day.

"Alice Lee Earley. Feb. 13, 1949. June 14, 1966. A lovely Daughter."

I wanted to talk to her, but I felt foolish. If all there ever was of Alice was still in that grave, she would not hear me anyway. If life and death are miracles, though, I could have talked to her as easily from Washington as Fowler. I placed a bouquet of daisies before her headstone. A farmer drove by in a pickup. He glanced at me; I was ashamed at my embarrassment.

I stood for the longest time. I wanted a sign. Some little miracle—hearing Alice's voice in my head, perhaps. But I heard only the silence that reaffirmed her refusal to welcome me. I thought that the daisies would freeze that night. I hoped the caretaker would leave them at least through tomorrow. "Alice gets flowers so seldom," I thought.

A sadness came to me: My trip was for nothing. But as I returned to the car, the anger rose in me again—this time anger at Alice. I walked back to her grave and placed my hands on the stone. I drifted between talking and thinking. "Okay, you died, but things weren't so great here either."

I did move into your room. I got your dresser. I got your guitar. But things changed after you died. Night after night I lay in your bed listening to Mom and Dad cry: "If only we had bought her a car!" "If only we hadn't bought the Honda!" When they started the tranquilizers, I was terrified they too would die.

"You left me, Alice!" You died on my motorcycle! You always were so careful! I was the reckless one, everyone knew that! Why didn't I take the Honda's keys with me to church camp?

I began to cry: "Why did you have to die, Alice? Why not me?" I turned to leave, but as I walked to the car I felt a calm. I returned to the grave and sat in the snow. Eventually, I began to talk. I told Alice that I had left Fowler for college, that I had married at twenty. I talked of the newspapers where I had worked, my house in Herndon, Virginia, my three children. I said my oldest son, Stephen, had scored four points in last Saturday's basketball game.

I told her that I teach Sunday school, but that the "little preacher" had died with her. Even today, I think of her and a naive rage at God wells up. My faith is unclear to me. I told her that my three-year-old daughter, Kathy, looks a lot like her, which makes me happy. At the times when I have been the happiest, however, I've looked at Kathy and felt sad at the inevitability of despair.

I talked until I had nothing left to say and then I sat. I reached down and touched her grave marker. It wasn't enough. I kissed the stone. "I love you, Alice. I always have."

I tracked Flora Ledbetter to the western slope of the Rockies. She and her husband, a teacher at Fowler High, had left Fowler a year after the accident. He was later killed in an airplane crash. Her second husband died of cancer. She married again and moved here. I wondered if her husband knew.

"I don't know if you will remember me or not," I said.

"I remember you," she answered. "What do you want?"

What I wanted from Ledbetter was remorse. I wanted her to say she was sorry. I wanted her to accept the blame I had assigned to her for nineteen years. It turned out that she wanted absolution from me. The accident had devastated her at the time, she told me. She wondered why she had lived and Alice had died. She sobbed for days; she couldn't sleep. Three days after the accident, she returned to Jones Corner. By then a stop sign had been installed on the road Alice was traveling.

"If anyone was to blame," Ledbetter said, "it was your sister. That's where the state put the sign, didn't they? . . . The worst part was that your parents sued me. The Bible says Christians shouldn't sue each other. Your father knew that. I didn't care about the money, but they were trying to prove that I was responsible. That wasn't fair."

I had not expected this. Like me, Ledbetter was angry—but at the state, at Alice, and at my parents for filing a $25,000 wrongful death suit against her. Suddenly, I was on the defensive. I told her my parents sued because her insurance company had harassed them repeatedly and claimed that Alice's life was worth only $500. The case was eventually settled out of court for about $10,000, without Ledbetter admitting or denying guilt. I still remember the talk around town: My father, the minister, profiting from Alice's death. "Blood money," one Fowler gossip called it.

"The state trooper told me that this was one of those truly unavoidable accidents," Ledbetter said. "Your folks sued me anyway."

My tone changed. "I drove to that corner," I said coldly. "I retraced your steps and I could see *perfectly*."

"There were weeds there and a big mound of dirt back then that made it hard to see. I think there was an irrigation well, too. I can't remember."

"I hated you when I was growing up. I covered your husband's photograph in the school yearbook with white tape."

She was quiet. "How do you feel now?"

I hesitated. "I don't hate you anymore. It was an accident. I guess it was no one's fault."

"I'm glad we talked," she said. I went to a bar.

My mother had put the family scrapbooks out for my arrival. She was eager to talk about Alice. My father was reluctant. Late that night, we finally began.

"We were in the emergency room with Alice," my mother said. "She kept saying to me, 'Mamma, Mamma, I'm gonna die. It hurts. I'm gonna die,' and I said, 'No, darling, it's okay. They are going to save you. You are going to be okay.'" My mother took off her glasses and wiped her eyes.

"They didn't do a thing for her," my father said. "They cut her foot and put some kind of line in it, but it was leaking out all over the floor. Then they got into an argument because one of them didn't want to put a tube down her throat. She would have been just as well off if they had left her in the ditch, maybe better.

The ambulance ran out of gas on the way to the hospital." That explained the delay in Alice's arrival at the hospital.

I thought of my parents standing helpless as Alice died. "Why didn't you sue them?" I demanded.

"Who?" asked my father.

"All of them!"

"I'm sure that they did all that they could," said my mother. "They didn't know as much then as they do now."

"But you sued the Ledbetters."

There was a long silence. "The last time I saw Mrs. Ledbetter," my father said, "she said it was 'God's will' that Alice died."

"It was just so unfair," my mother said. "Here was this big insurance company and we were so little. . . . Do you know when Ledbetter's first husband died? He was killed February thirteenth—on your sister's birthday. When I first heard it, I felt it was retribution. Your father never felt that way, but I did. Then I decided that was wrong."

"Everything that could have gone wrong did," my father said. "Both doctors in Fowler were out of town that night."

"Alice was supposed to be at work," my mother said. "But she had traded hours with another girl. I got so mad at that girl that I couldn't stand seeing her. I was mad at the Ledbetters. I was mad at the superintendent's wife because she didn't come to the funeral. I was mad at the sheriff's wife for not calling us when the accident happened so we could have gotten there in time to send Alice to Pueblo. I was mad at the doctors. But after a while, you realize that it doesn't help. Nothing can bring Alice back."

"How about God?" I asked. "Did you blame Him?"

My father shook his head. "No, I never felt that way."

On my first night home in Herndon, Kathy woke me in the night and I carried her downstairs to the rocking chair. We sat long after she fell asleep and I thought of Alice.

"She's gone," my mother had said. "What's the use in blaming?"

I had told Flora Ledbetter that I didn't blame her for Alice's death. And I had meant it. Still, if she had left a minute earlier,

taken a different route, Alice would be alive. I don't blame Ledbetter, but I do blame Ledbetter.

Job demanded of God: Why are the innocent slaughtered?
"Then the Lord answered Job . . . Where were you when I laid
the foundation of the earth? Tell me, if you have understanding."

"I don't," I thought. "I don't understand."

I closed my eyes and thought of Alice: *My mother, father, brother,
Alice, and I are in our backyard in Fowler. It is a summer Sunday night,
near dusk. My mother sits in the brown lawn chair next to my father in
his folding chaise. I sit with my brother a few steps away in the long grass
holding our dog, Snowball. Alice stands at the grill, her back to us. She
wears navy-blue shorts and a white blouse. She is barefooted. Smoke and
the scent of cooking hamburgers rise from the grill. Alice turns. The sun
has reddened her face. The wind has uncurled her hair. She looks at me,
and she is laughing.*

# THE ENDLESS HUNT

## Gretel Ehrlich

A young Inuit friend asked if I had come to Greenland from California by dogsled. He had never traveled any other way and didn't realize that the entire world wasn't covered by ice. At age seven, he had never seen a car or a highway or been in an airplane, and he assumed the world was flat. He is part of a group of Polar Eskimos in northwest Greenland who still share in an ice-age culture that began more than four thousand years ago, when nomadic boreal hunters began walking from Ellesmere Island across the ice to Greenland. Many of their ancient practices—hunting with harpoons, wearing skins, and traveling by dogsled—have survived despite modernizing influences that began at the turn of the century, when the explorer Robert Peary gave them rifles. The Arctic cold and ice have kept these hardy and efficient people isolated even today.

I began going to Greenland in 1993 to get above tree line. I was still recovering from being struck by lightning, which had affected my heart and made it impossible to go to altitude, where I feel most at home. In Greenland, I experienced tree line as a product of latitude, not just altitude. I had already read the ten volumes of expedition notes of Arctic explorer and national hero Knud Rasmussen, and when I met the Greenlandic people, my summer idyll turned into seven years of Arctic peregrinations that may never end.

This latest journey is taking place in April; I am traveling to Qaanaaq, the northernmost town in the world, where I will join two Inuit subsistence hunters—Jens Danielsen and Mikile Kristiansen, friends with whom I have been traveling since I first came to Greenland—on their spring trip up the coast to hunt seal, walrus, small birds called dovekies, and polar bear.

Despite their Danish names (Greenland, once a Danish colony, is now largely self-governing), Jens and Mikile are Eskimos, descendants of hunters who walked the Bering Land Bridge from Siberia to Alaska, across the Canadian Arctic, and, finally, to Greenland, following the tracks of polar bears, the migration of caribou and birds, the breathing holes of seals, the cracks in the ice where walrus and whales were found.

Greenland is 1,500 miles long and is crowned by a 700,000-square-mile sheet of ice whose summit is 11,000 feet high. The habitable fringe of land that peeks out from this icy mass is mostly rock, to which houses are bolted. No roads connect villages; transportation is by dogsled or boat, or the occasional helicopter taxi that can be summoned at a formidable price, weather permitting. The closest town to the south would take one and a half months to reach by dogsled from Qaanaaq.

The ice came in October and now paves the entire polar north—rivers, oceans, and fjords are all solid white. Like old skin, it is pinched, pocked, and nicked, pressed up into towering hummocks and bejeweled by stranded calf ice sticking up here and there like hunks of beveled glass.

The arrival of a helicopter is still an event in any Arctic village. Snow flies as we land, and families and friends press forward to greet their loved ones. Qaanaaq, a town of 650 people and 2,000 dogs in the northwestern corner of Greenland, is built on a hill facing a fjord. Down on the ice, there is always activity: Sleds are lined up, dogs are being fed or harnessed, hunters are coming home from a day's or month's journey or are just taking off. It's said that the Polar Eskimo begins and ends life with traveling. Even at home, they are always preparing for the next journey.

Jens Danielsen comes for me in the morning. Tall and rotund, he has a deep, gentle voice and a belly laugh that can make the ice shake. He wears sweatpants and tennis shoes despite biting cold. Almost forty, he's already beginning to gray at the temples. Jens estimates that he travels more than 3,500 miles a year by dogsled while hunting for food for his family. When not on the ice, he is a politician, heading up the Avanersuaq hunting council, a job that requires him to go below the Arctic Circle to Nuuk, Greenland's capital city. There, he testifies in front of Parliament in an effort to preserve the traditional lifestyle of northern hunters. So far, they've been able to restrict the use of snowmobiles (in Qaanaaq, one is owned by the hospital for emergencies), limit the number of motorized boats in the summer so as not to disrupt the hunting of narwhals using kayaks, and dictate the means by which animals are to be killed. Rifles are used to hunt seals and polar bears. Harpoons are used on narwhals and walrus.

A northern hunter's year could be said to begin when the new ice comes in late September or early October. They hunt walrus by dogsled in the fall. After the sun goes below the horizon on October 24, the dark months last until February. By moonlight, seals are hunted with nets set under the ice. Spring means bearded and ringed seals, polar bears, narwhals, rabbits, and foxes, and when the dovekie migration begins around May 10, hunters climb talus slopes and catch the birds with nets. In summer, narwhals are harpooned from kayaks.

To say that Jens, Mikile, and the other villagers are subsistence hunters is perhaps stretching the truth. A couple times a year, in late summer when it can make it through the ice, a supply boat comes and delivers goods from Denmark: wood, building supplies, paint, heating oil, and other necessities. It is also possible to buy small quantities of imported Danish foods—brought in by helicopter—at the tiny, sparsely stocked grocery store, but most villagers can't afford to live on Danish lamb and chicken, and, furthermore, prefer not to. During bouts of bad weather, no supplies come at all. These are hunters who, at the end of the twentieth century, have chosen to stay put and live by the harpoon, gun, and sled.

At the last minute, Jens's wife, Ilaitsuk, a strong, handsome woman a few years older than her husband, decides to come with us. "*Issi,*" she says, rubbing her arms. Cold. Before getting on the sled, she and I change into *annuraat ammit*—skins. We pull on *nannuk,* polar bear pants; *kapatak,* fox-skin anoraks; *kamikpak,* polar bear boots lined with *ukaleq,* arctic hare; and *aiqqatit,* sealskin mittens. Then we prepare to head north in search of animals whose meat we will live on and whose skins Jens, Mikile, and their families will wear.

Mikile has joined the hunting trip because he needs a new pair of polar bear pants. He has already packed his sled and has begun harnessing his dogs. In his mid-thirties, Mikile is small and wiry, with a gentle demeanor and face. He is traveling light and carries only one passenger, photographer Chris Anderson.

Thule-style sleds are 12 to 14 feet long, with upturned front runners and a bed lashed onto the frame. Jens lays our duffels on a tarp, and Ilaitsuk places caribou hides on top. The load is tied down, and a rifle is shoved under the lash-rope. The Danielsens' five-year-old grandson, Merseqaq, who is going with us, lies on the skins with a big smile. The dogs, which are chained on long lines when not being used, are anxious to get to work. Jens bends at the waist to untangle the trace lines—something he will do hundreds of times during our journey. As soon as the dogs feel the lines being hooked to the sled, they charge off out of sheer excitement—there is no way to stop them—and the wild ride begins.

We careen down narrow paths through the village. Bystanders, children, and dogs jump out of the way. Jens leaps off as we approach the rough ice at the shoreline. Walking in front of the team, he whistles so they will follow him as Ilaitsuk steadies the sled from behind. We tip, tilt, and bump. The dogs are not harnessed two by two as they are in Alaska but fan out on lines of varying lengths. This way, they can position themselves however they want, rest when they need to, or align themselves with a friend. Ilaitsuk and Jens run hard and jump on the sled. I've been holding the little boy. Soon, we bump down onto smooth ice. Jens snaps the *iparautaq* (whip) over the dogs' heads as they trot across the frozen sea.

We head west, then straight north past a long line of stranded icebergs that, in summer, when there is open water, will eventually be taken south by the Labrador current from Baffin Bay to Davis Strait, then into the North Atlantic. In winter, the icebergs are frozen in place. They stand like small cities with glinting towers, natural arches that bridge gaping portholes through which more icebergs can be seen.

Jens snaps the whip above the dogs' backs. "*Ai, ai, ai, ai . . . ,*" he sings out in a high falsetto, urging them to go faster. Snow-covered ice rolls beneath us, and the coastline, a walled fortress, slides by. On a dogsled, there is no physical control—no rudder, no brakes, no reins. Only voice commands and the sound of the whip and the promise of food if the hunt is good, which is perhaps why these half-wild, half-starved dogs obey. A dogtrot—the speed at which we move up Greenland's northwest coast—is about four miles an hour. Dog farts float by, and the sound of panting is the one rhythm that seems to keep our minds from flying away.

Half an hour north of Qaanaaq, the snow deepens, and the dogs slow down. They are already pulling 700 pounds. We follow the track of a sled that is carrying a coffin. Earlier this week, a young hunter died in an accident on the ice in front of Qaanaaq where schoolchildren were playing. Now his body is being taken home to Siorapaluk, a subsistence hunting village of a few dozen people up the coast from here. Some say the hunter was suicidal. "There are troubles everywhere. Even here," Jens says, clasping his tiny grandson on his lap at the front of the sled. "*Harru, harru!*" (Go left), he yells to the dogs. "*Atsuk, atsuk!*" (Go right). When his grandson mimics the commands, Jens turns and smiles.

We stop twice to make tea. The old Primus stove is lit and placed inside a wooden box to shelter the flame from the wind. Hunks of ice are chipped off an iceberg, stuffed into the pot, and melted for water. Danish cookies are passed. A whole frozen halibut, brought from home, is stuck headfirst into the snow. Mikile, Ilaitsuk, and Jens begin hacking at its side and eating chunks of "frozen sushi." The dogs roll in the snow to cool themselves, while we stand and shiver.

The closer we get to Siorapaluk, the colder it gets. Jens unties a dog, which had become lame, from the front of the sled, and throws him back into the pack. Appearances count: It wouldn't look right to arrive in a village with an injured dog. We slide around a bend, and Robertson Fjord opens up. Three glaciers lap at the frozen fjord, and the ice cap rises pale and still behind snowy mountains. Where one begins and the other ends is hard to tell. On the far, east-facing side of the fjord, the village comes into view. It has taken us eight hours to get here.

We make camp out on the ice in front of the village, pushing the two sleds together to serve as our *igliq* (sleeping platform) and raising a crude, bloodstained canvas tent over them. When I look up, something catches my eye: The funeral procession is winding up the snowy path above the houses. Six men are carrying the hunter's coffin. We hear faint singing—hymns—then the mourners gather in a knot as the wooden casket is laid down on the snow, blessed, and stored in a shed, where it will stay until the ground thaws enough for burial.

When the sun slips behind the mountains, the temperature plummets to 18 degrees below zero. All six of us crowd into the tent. Shoulder to shoulder, leg to leg, we are bodies seeking other bodies for warmth. With our feet on the ice floor, we sip tea and eat cookies and go to bed with no dinner. When we live on the ice, we eat what we hunt—in the spring, that means ringed seals, walrus, or polar bears. But we did not hunt today.

The sound of three hundred dogs crooning and howling wakes me. I look across the row of bodies stuffed into sleeping bags. Jens is holding his grandson against his barrel chest. They open their eyes: two moon faces smiling at the canine chorus. There are gunshots. Mikile sticks his head out of the tent, then falls back on the igliq, grunting. "They shot at something but missed," he says. "At what?" I ask. "*Nanoq, immaqa*" (a polar bear, maybe), he says, smiling mischievously.

Bright sun, frigid breeze. It must be midday. We sit in silence, watching ice melt for tea water. "Issi," Ilaitsuk says again. Cold. My companions speak very little English, and my Greenlandic is, well, rudimentary. Some days we talk hardly at all. Other times we pool our dictionaries and enjoy a feast of words. I try to memorize such useful phrases as: "*nauk tupilaghuunnguaju*," which means "you fool"; and "taquliktooq"—"dark-colored dog with a white blaze over its eye." But often, I fail, which just makes for more merriment.

Today, we break camp quietly. The pace of the preparations is deceptive: It looks laid-back because Inuit hunters don't waste energy with theatrics or melodrama. Instead, they work quietly, steadily, and quickly. Before I know it, Jens is hooking the trace lines to the sled. I grab the little boy and make a flying leap as Ilaitsuk and Jens jump aboard the already fast-moving sled. Jens laughs at his grandson for not being ready, and the boy cries, which makes Jens laugh harder. This is the Eskimo way of teaching children to have a sense of humor and to pay attention and act with precision—lessons that will later preserve their lives.

Snow begins pelting us. "The weather and the hunter are not such good friends," Jens says. "If a hunter waits for good weather, well, he may starve. He may starve anyway. But if he goes out when conditions are bad, he may fall through the ice and never be seen again. That's how it is here."

Snow deepens, and the dogtrot slows to a walk, On our right, brown cliffs rise in sheer folds striped with avalanche chutes crisscrossed by the tracks of arctic hares. "Ukaleq, ukaleq," Ilaitsuk cries out. Jens whistles the dogs to a stop. Ilaitsuk points excitedly. The rabbits' hides provide liners for kamiks (boots), and their flesh is eaten. We look: They are white against a white slope and bounce behind outcrops of boulders. No luck. On the ice, there are no seals. What will the six of us plus thirty dogs eat tonight?

As we round a bend and a rocky knob, a large bay opens up. We travel slowly across its wide mouth. Looking inward, I see a field of talcum powder, then a cliff of ice: the snout of an enormous glacier made of turquoise, light, and rock, carrying streambed debris like rooftop ornaments. My eyes move from the ice cap above to the frozen fjord below. Bands of color reveal the rhythm of ablation and accumulation for what it is: the noise and silence of time—Arctic time—which is all light or all dark and has no hours or days. When you're on a dogsled, the twenty-four-hour day turns into something elastic, and our human habits move all the way around the clock; we find ourselves eating dinner at breakfast time, sleeping in the all-day light, and traveling in the all-light night. What we care about is not a schedule but warmth and food and good weather as we push far north of the last village and see ahead only cold and snow and a growing hunger that makes us ache.

We change course. The going has been torturously slow. Instead of following the coastline straight north, we now veer out onto the frozen ocean; we follow a lead in the ice, looking for seals. The snow comes on harder. The cowl of a storm approaches, crossing Ellesmere Island, pulling over the hundred-mile-wide face of Humboldt glacier. Wind whips the storm's dark edge; it fibrillates like a raven's wing feathers, and as it pulls over, the great dome light of inland ice goes dark.

There are breathing holes all along the crack, but no *uuttuq*—seals that have hauled themselves out on ice—which are usually common in the spring. We keep going in a westward direction, away from the historic camping sites of Neqi, where we will sleep tonight, and Etah.

All afternoon and evening, we travel in a storm. I remember a hunter once telling me about getting vertigo. "Sometimes when we are on our dogsleds and there is bad fog or snow, we feel lost. We can't tell where the sky is, where the ice. It feels like we are moving upside down." But today we aren't lost. "We can tell by wind direction," the same hunter told me, "and if we keep traveling at the same angle to the drifting snow, we're okay."

All is white. We stop for tea, pulling the two sleds close together and lashing a tarp between for a windbreak. We scrounge through our duffels for food. Chris finds a jar of peanut butter. I'm dismayed to see the words "reduced fat" on the label. Never mind. We spread it on crackers, then drink tea and share a bittersweet chocolate bar. Bittersweet is what I am feeling right now: happy to be in Greenland among old friends but getting hungrier with each bite I take.

It's easy to see how episodes of famine have frequently swept through the Arctic, how quickly hunting can go bad, how hunger dominates. Before stores and helicopters, pan-Arctic cannibalism was common. After people ate their dogs and boiled sealskins, they ate human flesh—almost always the bodies of those who had already died. It was the key to survival, repellent as it was. Peter Freuchen, a Danish explorer who traveled with Knud Rasmussen for fourteen years, wrote of the practice: "At Pingerqaling I met a remarkable woman, Atakutaluk. I had heard of her before as being the foremost lady of Fury and Hecla Strait—she was important because she had once eaten her husband and three of her children."

Freuchen went on to describe the ordeal. Atakutaluk's tribe had been traveling across Baffin Island when a warm spell hit and it became impossible to use a sled. There were no animals in the area. When they ran out of food, they ate their dogs, then the weaker people in their hunting party. When Freuchen met Atakutaluk, she said, "Look here, Pita. Don't let your face be narrow for this. I got a new husband, and I got with him three new children. They are all named for the dead ones that only served to keep me alive so they could be reborn."

We head north again, crossing back over a large piece of frozen ocean. Rabbit tracks crisscross in front of us, but we see no animals. The edge of the storm frays, letting light flood through. Snow, ice, and air glisten. Ilaitsuk and I tip our faces up to the sun. Its warmth is a blessing, and for a few moments, we close our eyes and doze.

There's a yell. Ilaitsuk scrambles to her knees and looks around. It is Mikile far ahead of us. He's up on his knees on his fast-moving sled: "Nanoq! Nanoq!" he yells, pointing, and then we see: A polar bear is trotting across the head of a wide fjord.

Jens's dogs take off in that direction. Mikile has already cut two of his dogs loose, and they chase the bear. He releases two more. "*Pequoq, pequoq,*" Jens yells, urging his dogs to go faster. It is then that we see that there is a cub, struggling in deep snow to keep up. The mother stops, wheels around, and runs back. Mikile's loose dogs catch up and hold the bear at bay. Because she has a young one, she will not be killed: An abandoned cub would never survive.

Now we are between the cub and the she-bear. Repeatedly, she stops, stands, and whirls around to go back to her cub. The dogs close in: She paws, snarls, and runs again. Then something goes terribly wrong: One of the dogs spies the cub. Before we can get there, the dog is on the cub and goes for his jugular. We rush to the young bear's rescue, but the distances are so great and the going is so slow that by the time we make it, the dog is shaking the cub by his neck and has been joined by other dogs. Mikile and Jens leap off their sleds and beat the dogs away with their whip handles, but it is too late. The cub is badly hurt.

We stay with the cub while Mikile catches up with the mother. The cub is alive but weak. A large flap of skin and flesh hangs down. Even though he's dazed and unsteady, he's still feisty. He snarls and paws at us as we approach. Jens throws a soft loop around his leg and pulls him behind the sled to keep him out of the fray; then we let him rest. Maybe he will recover enough for us to send him back to his mother.

Far ahead, the mother bear starts to get away, but the loose dogs catch up and slow her progress. Near the far side of the fjord, the bear darts west, taking refuge behind a broken, stranded iceberg. Mikile cuts more dogs loose when the first ones begin to tire. The bear stands in her icy enclosure, coming out to charge the dogs as they approach. She doesn't look for her cub; she is fighting for her own life.

The sun is out, and the bear is hot. She scoops up a pawful of snow and eats it. The slab of ice against which she rests is blue and shaped in a wide V, like an open book whose sides are melting in the spring sun. The dogs surround her in a semicircle, jumping forward to snap at her, testing their own courage, but leaping back when she charges them.

Five hundred yards behind Mikile, we watch over the cub. If we get too close, he snaps. Sometimes he stands, but he's weak. He begins panting. His eyes roll back; he staggers and is dead.

Jens ties a loop around his neck, and we pull the cub like a toy behind the sled. Mikile turns as we approach. "Is the cub dead?" he asks. Jens says that he is. The decision is made: Mikile will shoot the mother. I ask if killing her is necessary—after all, she is a young bear that can have more cubs—but my Greenlandic is unintelligible. I plead for her life using English verbs and Greenlandic nouns. Jens says, "It is up to Mikile."

Mikile, whose polar bear pants are worn almost all the way through, listens, then quietly loads his rifle. We are standing close to the bear, close enough for her to attack us, but she has eyes only for the dogs. Standing on her toes, she lays her elbow on top of the berg and looks out.

Silently, I root for her: Go, go. These are the last moments of her life, and I'm watching them tick by. Does she know she is doomed? Once again I plead for her life, but I get only questioning looks from the hunters. I feel sick. Peeking over the top of the ice, the bear slumps back halfheartedly. She is tired, her cub is gone, and there is no escape.

Ilaitsuk covers Merseqaq's ears as Mikile raises his rifle. The boy is frightened. He has seen the cub die, and he doesn't want to see any more.

The bear's nose, eyes, and claws are black dots in a world of white, a world that, for her, holds no clues about human ambivalence. She gives me the same hard stare she would give a seal—after all, I'm just part of the food chain. It is the same stare Mikile gives her now, not hard from lack of feeling but from the necessity to survive. I understand how important it is for a hunter to get a polar bear. She will be the source of food, and her skin will be used for much-needed winter clothing. It is solely because of the polar bear pants and boots that we don't freeze to death. Nevertheless, I feel that I am a witness to an execution.

The bear's fur is pale yellow, and the ice wall is blue. The sun is hot. Time melts. What I know about life and death, cold and hunger, seems irrelevant. There are three gunshots. A paw goes up in agony and scratches the ice wall. She rolls on her back and is dead.

I kneel down by her. The fur is thick between her claws. There is the sound of gurgling. It's too early in the year for running water. Then I see that it is her blood pouring from the gunshot wound that killed her.

Mikile ties his dogs back in with the others. Knives are sharpened. Tea water is put on to boil. We roll up our sleeves in the late afternoon sun. Ilaitsuk glasses the ice for other animals; Merseqaq is on the snow beside the bear and puts his tiny hand on her large paw.

The bear is laid out on her back. Jens puts the tip of his knife on her umbilicus and makes an upward cut to her neck. The fine tip travels up under her chin and through her black lip as if to keep her from talking.

Soon enough she is disrobed. The skin is laid out on the snow, and, after the blood is wiped off, it is folded in quarters and laid carefully in a gunnysack on the sled. Then her body is dismembered, and the pieces are also stowed under the tarp, so when we put away our teacups and start northwest toward Neqi, she is beneath us in pieces and we are riding her, this bear that, according to Inuit legends, can hear and understand everything human beings say. We travel the rest of the day in silence.

We cross the wide mouth of the fjord and continue on to Neqi, a camp used by Inuit hunters and European explorers for hundreds of years. There is no village, only a cabin, low and wide, set at the tip of a long thumb of land sticking out from between two glaciers. The cabin looks down on the frozen Smith Sound. The word "Neqi" means "meat," and this was a place where meat caches were laid in for hunters and explorers on their way to the far north of Greenland or to the North Pole. We push our sleds up through the hummocks to the cabin. The meat racks are crowded with walrus flippers, dead dogs, and bits of hacked-up seals. Half sanctuary, half charnel ground.

We stand on the ice terrace in front of the cabin. Looking out at the wide expanse of frozen ocean, we salute the rarely seen sun. Its warmth drives into us, and for the first time, we relax. A hidden beer emerges from Jens's duffel bag and is passed around.

The strangled cry of a fox floats out over the frozen bay where we shot the bear. Now a band of fog rises from that place, a blindfold covering the labanotations—the script of the bear's death dance: where she stopped, wheeled around, attacked, and kept running; the hieroglyphics of blood and tracks; and the hollows in the snow where the dogs rested after the chase. I'm glad I can't see.

A Primus is lit, and water is put on to boil. Then the backstrap of the polar bear—the most tender part—is thrown in the pot.

It's so warm, we take off our anoraks and hats. Jens passes paper plates. "Nanoq. Nanoq," he says in a low voice. "The polar bear is king. We have to eat her in a special way. We boil her like the seal, but we pay special respects to her so her soul shall not have too much difficulty getting home."

After twenty minutes, chunks of meat are doled out. They steam on our plates. "*Qujanaq,*" I say, thanking Mikile, Jens, and, most of all, the bear. The meat is tender and good, almost like buffalo.

Later, we get into our sleeping bags and lie on the igliq. It is still warm, and no one can sleep. Jens and Ilaitsuk hold their grandson between them as Jens begins a story: "A long time ago, when shamans still flew underwater and animals could talk, there was a woman named Anoritoq who lived on that point of land north of Etah. The name Anoritoq means 'windswept one.' This woman had no husband, and her only son was killed by a hunter out of jealousy, because the young boy had no father but was becoming a great hunter anyway. After her son died, a hunter brought the woman a polar bear cub, which she raised just like a son. The bear learned the language of the Eskimo and played with the other children. When he grew up, he hunted seals and was very successful. But she worried about him. She was afraid a hunter might kill him, because he was, after all, a bear, and his skin was needed for clothing. She tried covering him with soot to make him dark, but one day, when some of his white fur was showing, a hunter killed him. She was so sad, she stopped eating and went outside and stayed there all the time and looked at the sea. Then, she changed into a stone. Now when we go bear hunting in that area, we put a piece of seal fat on the rock and pray for a good hunt."

Morning. We follow the coast north to Pitoravik. It's not a long trip. From there, we will determine our route to Etah—either up and over part of the inland ice or following the coast if there is no open water or pressure ice. A wind begins to blow as Jens and Mikile take off to investigate the trail over the glacier. They are gone several hours, and when they come back, they shake their heads. "The drifts are too deep and the crevasses too wide, and the snow hides them," Jens says. "Down below, the ice is badly broken with open water. Too dangerous. We'll wait until morning. If the weather is good, we'll try to go over the top. If not, then we'll go to the ice edge out there, toward Canada, and hunt walrus and narwhal."

In the morning, the weather is no better. A continuous, mesmerizing snow falls. "I think the hunting will be better out there," Jens says, using our vantage point to look out over Smith Sound. Beyond, Ellesmere Island is a blue line of mountains with a ruffle of white clouds. We descend and go in a southwesterly direction toward the island of Kiatak.

For three or four days, we travel in weather that keeps closing down on us. When we stop to rest the dogs, Ilaitsuk, Merseqaq, and I play tag on the ice to keep warm. The child never complains. When his feet get cold, he merely points to his toes, and Ilaitsuk puts on the over-boots she sewed together when we were in the cabin at Neqi. Then he sits at the front of the sled, windblasted and happy, echoing his grandfather's commands, snapping the long whip, already becoming a man.

Patience and strength of mind are the hunter's virtues. Also, flexibility and humor. Jens shoots at a seal and misses. Another one catches his scent and dives down into its hole. He returns to the sled, laughing at his failures, explaining to Mikile exactly what he did wrong. Later, he reverts to winter-style seal hunting, called *agluhiutuq,* hunting at the *agluq* (breathing hole). But even this fails.

We continue on. "*Hikup hinaa,*" Jens says. The ice edge. That's what we are now looking for. There we will find plentiful seal, walrus, and narwhal. My stomach growls, and I think of the legend of the Great Famine, when winters followed one after the other, with no spring, summer, or fall in between. Jens says that this last winter and spring have been the coldest in his memory. Ironically, colder weather in the Arctic may be a side effect of global warming. As pieces of the ice cap melt and calve into the ocean, the water temperature in parts of the far north cools, as, in turn, does the air. Maybe global warming will cancel itself out, I say. Jens doesn't understand my "Greenenglish." "Issi," he says, rubbing his arms. Cold. "Maybe we will have to eat each other like they did in the old days," he says, smiling sweetly.

For the Eskimo, solitude is a sign of sheer unhappiness. It is thought to be a perversion and absolutely undesirable. Packed tightly together on the sled, we are fur-wrapped, rendered motionless by cold. It's good to be pressed between human bodies. We scan the ice for animals. Shadows made by standing bits of ice look like seals.

Then we do see one, a black comma lying on the alabaster extravagance.

Jens and Mikile stop their dogs. Jens mounts his rifle on a movable blind—a small stand with a white sailcloth to hide his face. The snow is shin-deep, but the wind is right. He creeps forward, then lies down on his belly, sighting in his rifle. All thirty dogs sit at attention, with ears pricked. When they stop panting, the world goes silent. As soon as they hear the muffled crack of the gun, off they go, running toward Jens as they have been trained to do.

We stand in a semicircle around a pool of blood, backs to the wind. Quickly and quietly, Jens flenses the seal. He cuts out the liver, warm and steaming, holds it on the end of his knife, and offers it to us. This is an Inuit delicacy. Eating the steaming liver has helped to save starving hunters. In gratitude, we all have a bite. Our mouths and chins drip with blood. There is a slightly salty taste to the lukewarm meat.

Ilaitsuk folds the sealskin and lays it under the tarp alongside the polar bear skin. Jens cuts a notch through the back flipper for a handhold and drags the pink body, looking ever more diminutive, over the front of the sled. Lash lines are pulled tight, and we take off as snow swirls.

We are still traveling at ten-thirty in the evening when the storm breaks. We watch the dark edge pull past, moving faster than the sled. Under clear skies, the temperature plummets to somewhere near 20 degrees below zero.

One seal for thirty dogs and six humans isn't very much meat. We stop at an iceberg and hack out slabs of ice, then make camp. As Ilaitsuk and I unload the sleds, Jens and Mikile cut up seal meat.

The dogs line up in rows, avidly waiting for food. It has been two days since they've eaten fresh meat. A chunk is flung through the air, then another and another. Jens's and Mikile's aims are so perfect, every dog gets its share, and the faster they eat, the more they get.

Jens cuts up the remaining seal for our dinner. Inside the tent, we watch as lumps of meat churn in brown water. As the hut warms up, we strip down. Merseqaq's tiny red T-shirt reads "I love elephants," though he has never seen one and probably never will.

We eat in silence, using our pocketknives and fingers. A loaf of bread is passed. We each have a slice, then drink tea and share a handful of cookies. After, Ilaitsuk sets a piece of plywood in a plastic bucket and stretches the sealskin over the top edge. With her *ulu*—a curved knife with a wooden handle—she scrapes the blubber from the skin in strong, downward thrusts. When the hide is clean, she turns to her *kiliutaq*—a small, square knife used to scrape the brownish pink oil out of a fur.

Ilaitsuk lets me have a try at scraping. I'm so afraid I'll cut through and ruin the skin, I barely scratch the surface.

Later, lying in my sleeping bag, I listen to wind. Jens tells stories about the woman who adopted a bear, the hunter who married a fox, and the origin of fog. His voice goes soft, and the words drone, putting us into a sweet trance of sleep so pleasurable that I don't know if I'll ever be able to sleep again without those stories.

In the next days, we search for the ice edge, camping on the ice wherever we find ourselves at the end of the night. We travel straight west from the tip of Kiatak Island out onto the frozen ocean between Greenland and Ellesmere Island. On the way, Jens teaches his grandson voice commands and how to use the whip without touching the backs of the animals. "Will Merseqaq be a hunter, too?" I ask. Jens says, "I am teaching him what he needs to know. Then the decision will be up to him. He has to love this more than anything."

When we reach a line of icebergs, Jens and Mikile clamber to the top and glass the entire expanse of ice to the west. It feels like we're already halfway across Smith Sound. Jens comes back shaking his head. "There is no open water," he says incredulously. "It is ice all the way to Canada." This has never happened before in any spring in memory. It is May 8.

We turn south to an area where sea currents churn at the ice. Maybe there will be an ice edge there. Down the coast at Kap Parry, we meet two hunters who are coming from the other direction. As usual, there is a long silence, then a casual question about open water. They shake their heads. No ice edge this way, either.

That night, I lie in my sleeping bag, squeezed tightly between Mikile and Ilaitsuk. "I feel as if we are stuck in winter," Mikile said earlier, looking frustrated. He has a big family to feed. Along with Jens, he is considered one of the best hunters in Qaanaaq, but even he can't kill enough game if spring never comes. We lie awake listening to wind.

At midday, we climb an iceberg that is shaped like the Sydney Opera House, to see if the ice edge has appeared. Jens shakes his head no. As we climb down, Mikile yells and points: "Nanoq." Far out, a polar bear dances across the silvered horizon, blessedly too distant for us to hunt. A mirage takes him instead of a bullet, a band of mirrored light floating up from the ice floor. It takes his dancing legs and turns them into waves of spring heat still trying to make its way past the frigid tail end of winter.

Finally we head for home, traveling along the east side of Kiatak. Walls of red rock rise in amphitheaters; arctic hares race across snow-dappled turf and grass. A raven swoops by, and a fox floats its gray tail along the steep sidehill. Near the bottom of the cliff, icicles hang at odd angles from beds of rock. We pass over a floor of broken platelets that look as if they'd been held up like mirrors, then tossed down and broken, making the sled tip this way and that. Some pieces of ice are so exquisite that I ask Jens to stop so I can stare at them: finely etched surfaces overlaid with other layers of ice punctured by what look like stars.

The dogs bring me back. They fight and fart and snarl and pant. One of them, Pappi, is in heat, and the other dogs can think of nothing except getting to her. Pappi slinks behind the others, clamping her tail down and refusing to pull. Then the males fall back, too, fighting one another, and the sled eventually comes to a stop. Jens unties Pappi and fastens her behind the sled, but this doesn't work, either. She falls and is dragged and can't get up.

Finally Jens cuts Pappi loose. There's a moment of relief, as if she had been freed from a tight world of ice and cold and discipline. Ilaitsuk looks at me and smiles. Her face is strong in the late evening sun. The boy is ensconced in his grandfather's lap, wearing dark glasses. We have failed to bring home much meat, but Jens shrugs it off, reminding me that worrying has no place in the Arctic. He and all those before him have survived day by day for four thousand years, and one bad hunting trip won't set him back. There is always tomorrow.

Now Pappi is running free and happy. Jens urges her to go on ahead. The snow is hard and icy, and the sled careens as the dogs give chase. Sometimes when we are airborne, flying over moguls, little Merseqaq gets on his hands and knees and squeals with delight. The cold and hunger and terrible hunting conditions are behind us now, and as we near Qaanaaq, the dogs, ever optimistic, run very fast.

# JOURNEY TO THE CENTER OF MY MIND

*Stephen S. Hall*

At a few minutes after 4:00 on a Sunday afternoon in January, when most of New York was tuning in to the playoff game between the Jets and the Broncos, I had something else on my mind. More precisely, I had something around my mind, namely the 1.5-ton magnet of the magnetic resonance imaging (M.R.I.) machine at the Memorial Sloan-Kettering Cancer Center. I wasn't there for medical reasons; I was there to embark on an adventure. My journey would take me no farther than this laboratory on the Upper East Side of Manhattan, and yet I was going somewhere very few people have been.

Of all the frontiers that await exploration, perhaps no other is more intriguing than the terra incognita that lies between our ears. There, in a three-pound pudding of neurons and wiring, lie the keys to the kingdoms of memory, of thought, of desire, of fear, of the habits and skills that add up to who we each are. It is an especially daunting frontier because even after you have entered the realm of the brain, it's still necessary to locate a second, far more elusive boundary that separates the mere hardware of neurology from that elusive quality known as the mind, the "I" that hovers in the background of all conscious mental activity. I had hopes of getting a glimpse of that I—my mind—in the course of my travels.

My Virgil on this journey through the dark wood of cognition was Joy Hirsch, a voluble, cheerful scientist with dark bangs over her forehead and inch-long nails. Hirsch directs the Functional Imaging Laboratory at Sloan-Kettering and is a professor of neuroscience at the Weill Medical College of Cornell University. I'd become interested in her work several years ago when her group published a paper in *Nature* suggesting that you could tell whether a person learned a foreign language early or late in life by pinpointing the exact location of the speech center in the brain. When I proposed taking a tour of my own brain, Joy saw it as an opportunity to extend her research into some new areas.

The premise was simple. I would undergo a series of brain-imaging sessions using the technology of functional M.R.I.—like diagnostic M.R.I., except that it also measures brain activity. These scans would, for the most part, be customized, almost autobiographical studies that would probe thoughts and emotions related to my personal history and work as a writer and editor. My journey, I understood, would be unscientific—no study of one individual holds statistical significance. But even as a neural picaresque, it wasn't without value. We designed exercises with reasonable experimental controls and, whenever possible, in ways that might complement published studies. We set out to investigate, among other things, the use of figurative language, the neural residue of emotional memories, the seat of humor, the source of sentence composition, and even the cognitive headwaters of storytelling.

Before setting out, I consulted several prominent brain scientists; Steven Pinker, the cognitive scientist at M.I.T., provided the most sage advice about the proper frame of mind for doing experiments in an M.R.I. machine. "Focus is essential," he said. "You almost have to be a Zen master." Easier said than done.

### The Lay of the Land

For the first session, Joy Hirsch set up fourteen scans, designed to sketch out a rough map of the auditory, visual, touch, motor, and language systems of my brain. "This is like a tour of the building before we start to talk to the individual departments," Joy said. This kind of mapping was pioneered by Hirsch's team at Sloan-

Kettering to provide a guide for neurosurgeons so that they can avoid speech, hearing, and other critical centers when removing brain tumors. (One condition for my participation was that patient scans always took precedence.)

As I lay flat on my back, about to enter the narrow bore of the scanner for the first time, Joy and a technician, Greg Nyman, sandwiched my head between cushions, placed a piece of tape across my forehead, and slipped a plastic cowl over my head. "We're going to put you in," Joy announced as I felt myself slide about four feet into an aperture 23 inches wide and only 17 inches high. Staring up at a mirror above my head, I could look out of the tube, where the vista included two familiar shoes forming a nervous V in the air. Each "run," Joy explained, would last 144 seconds; the machine divided my brain into about 185,000 units, or voxels, and measured the activity in each every four seconds. The huge, room-size magnet allows the machine to detect subtle changes in blood flow in each voxel, changes that are believed to reflect levels of brain activity.

Science is never quite as seamless as it appears in the pages of journals. The first few runs went fine—a flashing checkerboard pattern excited my visual cortex, as planned, and Joy rubbed an ordinary five-and-dime pot-scrubber over my right hand, to stimulate the tactile (or somatosensory) part of my brain. I had great difficulty seeing and hearing, however. I couldn't wear my glasses inside the machine—the powerful magnetic field would turn them into a ballistic missile. The prescription goggles on hand in the lab provided just enough visual acuity to turn an exercise where I named objects into a Magooish misadventure. I mistook a tennis racket for a globe and a canoe for a comb. Later, straining to hear words through earphones, I could make out only a couple over the din of the machine, which sounds like the loudest, most emphatic busy signal imaginable. Again, I resorted to pure conjecture. At this rate, I began to fear we were using our precious M.R.I. time to pinpoint nothing more than the neural headquarters for Guesswork.

Finally, we made our first tentative sortie into the land of cognition. Joy knew I spoke Italian, and I was curious to see where the "Italian speech module" was located in my brain. I had learned the language in my mid-twenties while living in Rome, but I thought there might be a chance I'd picked up a smattering of Italian as a child, since my maternal grandparents spoke it almost exclusively. It turns out that all languages learned early in life cohabit the same neural real estate, whereas a foreign language learned as an adult usually occupies a distinctly separate region. Would the conversations in Italian I had overheard as a child have left a neural residue?

To find out, Joy asked me to perform a task that formed the basis of the group's 1997 *Nature* paper. I had ten seconds to tell a little story in my head in response to a series of visual prompts—a picture showing either sunrise, noon, or night. During the first run, I would think up a scenario in English; the second time, in Italian. The morning scene, for example, elicited the following: "I woke up around eight o'clock, had a bite to eat, put on my coat, and walked to the subway, which I took to work." All I can say in my literary defense is, you try being clever with a deadline of ten seconds and 110-decibel honks in your ears about five times a second.

Lying stock-still in a horizontal phone booth might not sound like much of a physical adventure, but after fifty minutes I felt exhausted by the effort of inactivity. You're supposed to keep your head as steady as a statue, and just as empty. But any active, imaginative intelligence is apt to daydream, worry, have idle thoughts—all forms of mental static. Thoughts kept crashing through the artificial quietude of my empty head. "What's the Italian word for joke?" "Wonder how the Jets are doing?" "Man, is my mouth dry!" Theoretically, each of those errant thoughts has its latitude and longitude, its little magnetic wrinkle destined, perhaps, to show up in the raw data and fog this high-tech mirror in which I hoped to see something of myself.

## All Roads Lead to . . . Broca's Area

When I met with Joy to go over the results from the first session, we sat at a round table in her office, with twenty-one cross-sectional slices of my brain up on the light box, a brain atlas open on the table, and small printouts of each cross-section in front of her, marked by yellow Post-it arrows pointing to the predominant landmarks of my neural anatomy. She had carefully compared the lay of my brain to a standard atlas and, slice by slice, walked me through the basic landscape. "I love looking at brains," she confided at one point. "They're very beautiful, very intimate." Everything looked normal. "This is a beautiful, textbook brain," she said with obvious enthusiasm. But I almost didn't hear her. I was mesmerized by the beauty of this hidden landscape.

Now that I was on a guided tour of my own brain, I began to appreciate just how precise the convoluted geography of the brain actually is. Like a lot of laypeople, I thought the whorls and folds on the surface layer of the brain, known as the cortex, varied by individual like so many fingerprints. In fact, the patterns are basically the same in everyone. As I could see in Joy's atlas, each bulge (or gyrus) and each crevice (or sulcus) is as precisely plotted as any topographic map. All the cognitive action happens in those whorls; everything else is scaffolding, underground cable, antique structures handed down by evolution from reptile and early mammalian brains.

The first departments we checked were the somatosensory and motor regions. The touch of the pot-scrubber caused a small section of the postcentral gyrus on the left side to light up, as expected, while the finger-tapping exercise caused a herd of neurons just across the deep neural ravine from the tactile center to become active.

"This is very typical," Joy said. "In fact, it's particularly nice. Some brains have a little bit less specific activity. One of the nice things about the activity patterns in your brain is that they are very localized. Your brain just goes and gets the job done. It doesn't waste a lot of energy going other places."

I'd been concerned about my inability to see and hear stimuli during the first session, but those difficulties actually made the results more interesting. When I was straining to make out images during the object-naming task, my visual cortex looked like the wall-of-napalm scene in *Apocalypse Now*. "I'll tell you, this little

brain was working mighty hard to get that information," Joy said
with a laugh. The same evidence of effort showed up in the auditory map—the place in the midbrain that "listens," called the trans-
verse temporal gyrus, was screaming in Technicolor, even though
I could only make out one or two words.

Finally, we looked at my basic language centers. Language, of
course, is normally located on the dominant side of the brain, which
in right-handers like me is on the left side. When I spoke to myself in English, therefore, a small patch of cortex on the left side
lighted up. This is known as Broca's area, after the French patholo-
gist who first identified it.

The data from the Italian-speaking exercise unfortunately were
ambiguous. The image was filled with green blotches that signi-
fied movement. As anyone who watched Roberto Benigni at the
Academy Awards knows, Italian is a particularly kinetic language.
"The only time you moved your head the whole time was when
you were speaking Italian!" Joy cried, explaining why she couldn't
definitively say if my Italian was learned early or late. With prodding, she pointed out a tiny gap between the areas that lighted up
when I spoke to myself in English and Italian. "If I had to call it,"
she said, "you have Italian sitting above the English, and both of
them are pinned together here in Broca's area." That tiny gap,
about five millimeters, suggested that I'd learned Italian as an adult,
not as a child.

If there was a lesson from this first expedition, it was this: In
terms of neural architecture, we all live in Levittown. Every brain
is pretty much like the next. What makes each unique is how we
decorate them, as it were, with experience and memory and habits and skills. Staring at these voluptuous, serpentine folds of cortex, I was struck by the strange commingling of inert anatomy and
transcendent human qualities. Buried in those headlands and crev-
ices, I knew, were mental images of grandparents no longer alive,
of my mother trying to explain death to me for the first time, the
sound of loved ones' voices, my father encouraging me as we
played catch, of Roberto Clemente whirling and throwing a baseball, as well as the state capital of Vermont, the square root of 81,
and the narrative line of three books I've written. The vastness

and steadfastness of those memories, all nestled and synaptically etched in this bland gray and squishy landscape, was a miracle impossible to capture on film and perhaps beyond the grasp of our very modest experiments.

But we could try. We decided to devote the next session to exploring things that might be unique to me as a writer and as a person. We would search for the headwaters of storytelling, and we'd try to see if the brain reacted differently when it encountered family and friends as opposed to the faces and voices of strangers.

## To the Source of the Narrative

Joy and Diana Moreno, an Argentine graduate student in her lab, devised a plan to watch my brain in action as it invented a story. They would provide me with a set of narrative prompts—either a sequence of simple images (like a dog or a tree) or, using a different sensory route to the same destination, a sequence of distinctive sound effects (a honking horn, a crying baby). While the M.R.I. was blasting away, I'd ad-lib a running story in my head.

The results were fascinating. We saw the visual cortex light up as expected. But we also saw many small, discrete precincts of the frontal lobe activated on the right side of the brain, with particularly intense activity in an area called the inferior frontal gyrus— what might be called the storytelling area. "This is not a subtle effect, Steve," Joy pointed out. "In this business, this is big." It seemed to cover at least 1.5 cubic centimeters—about the size of a sugar cube. I asked her what might account for its size, and she replied that it could be a combination of things: a natural predisposition to use the right side of my brain (nature) and probably my frequent use of it (nurture) in the course of a lifetime.

There were other areas involved; they formed a network, actually. But Joy seemed particularly taken with the notion that the brain parceled out two related capabilities—one to create stories and the other to articulate them in speech—in essentially the same place in the two hemispheres, for my storytelling area was the mirror image of the site on the left, dominant side of the brain that controls speech.

Next we compared familiar voices and faces to unfamiliar voices and faces. When I had suggested the idea of looking at familiar faces while in the machine, I thought it might serve as a back road to memory and feeling; the difference between the perception of an unknown and known face should be the neural residue of recognition and familiarity. Once again, we were in for some surprises.

As the M.R.I. beeped around my head, I was shown a series of fifty-two photographs over the course of four runs, thirteen per run. During the first two runs, none of the faces were familiar— or, at least, they weren't supposed to be. One picture happened to be a spitting image of the girl—I'll call her D.—I had a crush on in high school and whom I'd asked, unsuccessfully, to the senior prom. As I processed this image, I experienced what felt like an Etna of neural activity somewhere in my cranium.

During the next two runs, I was shown only familiar faces— indeed, painfully familiar in the case of images of myself as Sullen Adolescent and Alienated Hirsute Expatriate. My wife, Mindy, had sent Joy's lab photographs of practically everybody I knew: my parents, Mindy giving birth to our son, my nephews, the college friend I bummed around with in Europe, old family friends, even my old landlady from Rome, as well as six photos of my younger self, including a high school graduation picture of me looking so clueless that I wouldn't have gone to the prom with me.

When we reviewed the brain scans a few days later, I had the thrill of witnessing a unique feature of the physical world for the first time. During the familiar-faces experiment, we saw activity in the visual cortex; no surprise there. We saw activity in the hippocampus. No surprise there, either; the hippocampus, a structure deep in the interior of the brain, is thought to be involved in the storage of long-term memory. "Your whole hippocampus is screaming!" Joy said. We also saw activity in a structure adjacent to the hippocampus known as the fusiform gyrus; this too, was not a surprise, at least not to Joy. Recent research on face recognition has identified this as the key area in the brain for the specialized task of perceiving faces. What was a surprise was that the most excited sector in my brain as it viewed familiar faces was, once again, the "storytelling area."

Next, we performed the same exercise using familiar voices: Relatives and friends provided the lab with taped monologues addressed to me. Unfortunately, I had the same difficulty making out the voices as in the earlier session; the only voice I could identify unambiguously was that of my wife. I guessed—correctly, as it turns out—that other voices belonged to my father, mother, and daughter, although I didn't learn until later what they had actually said. My father recalled going to the 1966 All-Star game in St. Louis and meeting the Cub infielder Ron Santo on the plane home. My mother invoked memories of what she called the "friendly persuader" of my mischievous childhood (the wooden spoon). And my three-year-old daughter, Micaela, had chattered, "Testing, one-two-three, Daddy, I love you, testing one-two-three." I didn't hear any of it.

But, remarkably, my brain apparently did. The scans showed the exact same far-flung network of parts fired up as when I was looking at familiar pictures—including the storytelling region in my right brain. It was almost as if I subconsciously filtered out the background noise and heard what I needed to hear. And not only that, simply hearing familiar voices activated the visual cortex, as if I mentally pictured the people whose voices I heard.

Joy used that all-purpose, noncommittal, scientifically discreet word to describe this effect: interesting. Exercising the layperson's right to speculate, I was immediately taken by a literary notion: the role of narrative in memory. What the data seemed to suggest to me was that part of what makes a face or a voice familiar to us is that the brain attaches it to a narrative. Perhaps we "tag" people with narratives to help us remember them. The image or voice (and perhaps even the taste, touch, or smell) of a familiar person summons up from our memories the story we've woven them into. That madeleine of Marcel Proust's seems less like a literary conceit and more like a brilliant scientific insight—but then Proust understood at least as much about memory as any modern neuroscientist.

## The Land of Metaphor

To map the creation of sentences in my brain, Joy showed me a series of words—highway, dawn, border—and asked me to use them in the most elaborate sentences I could think of, all in ten seconds. One that stuck in my mind was "The border between here and there is uncertain, and moving further into the future even as we speak."

Joy was particularly amused when she showed me the results of this exercise. The areas of activity were small, relatively discrete, and, unlike virtually all of the other creative tasks I performed, well-represented on the left as well as the right side of the brain, indicating, she said, excellent mental economy.

I reverted to my right-hemisphere bias on two other tasks: creating metaphors and synonyms. I suppose there might be something socially redeeming about spitting out a metaphor on cue, every four seconds, but after shoveling out ten examples of figurative language in forty seconds, it began to feel like an aerobic activity. The cues, once again, were simple illustrations: a globe, a wreath, a canoe, a snail, a tennis racket, a seahorse, and so on. Considering some of my responses—"Up the creek without a paddle" and "You've got quite a racket going on," to name two—I worried that we'd overshot Metaphor Mountain on the map and landed in the Slough of Cliché.

Not so. During this task—and to a great degree, during the Great Thesauric Expedition (as I now call the synonym task)—the right side of my brain lighted up like a neon sign on a cheap diner. Almost all the usual suspects were on display: parts of the visual cortex, the language area, that interesting storytelling area in the inferior frontal gyrus, and a spot toward the top of the brain, the medial frontal gyrus, that Joy believed was organizing and coordinating high-level activity on a number of tasks. With Joy's help, I was beginning to recognize a network I seemed to use over and over again.

As we reviewed the results, it occurred to me that we had begun to exhaust the usefulness of the geographic metaphor—and perhaps that was the real point of the entire exercise. The more complex the task, the more dispersed the brain's activity. The pattern in the scans stopped looking like a landscape with a few isolated peaks and more like a circuit with an extravagant number of relay points.

The potential link between circuitry and consciousness became especially clear when we went looking for the seat of humor. Joy showed me Gary Larson cartoons, first with neutral, unfunny captions and then with their proper punch lines. Perhaps because of the circumstances, one cartoon in particular had me struggling to suppress a laugh. It showed a group of doctors in the midst of brain surgery. The neutral caption read, "Operating Room"; the Larson caption had one of the surgeons exclaiming: "Wow! His brain still uses vacuum tubes!"

In response to this and other cartoons, my brain looked like those aerial shots of Southern California during brushfire season: There were little embers of neural activity all over. The hippocampus lighted up, suggesting the involvement of memory; the thalamus on the right side became active (the first time we'd seen that in any of our experiments), suggesting sensory processing; and we even detected a little activity in the sensorimotor cortex, which normally controls physical movement. Joy immediately thought "smile," and I thought "laugh." Like a Chopin impromptu, my "humor network" hit a great many notes, high in the brain and low, and did so with lightning rapidity: visual processing, language processing, memory, the perception of a cognitive disjunction, and all of it seemingly wired to trip a laugh instantaneously. Moreover, this network began to suggest something more complex than mere cognition—something like consciousness, for humor is very personal, turning as it does on such idiosyncratic traits as one's sense of irony, cognitive dissonance, and Schadenfreude. The network we were seeing, with its unique linkages, represented my sense of humor.

## There Is No Center There

As I look at my brain again, slice by slice, holding the film up to a window in my study, I am struck once more with the everyday wonder of the landscape—the shadowy lines of sulci running like streams to nowhere from the interior of the cerebrum, the peninsular gyri, each plump with purpose and secrets, and, like a river running through it all, the midline separating right hemisphere from left. And more than ever, I realize that the organizing metaphor for this expedition—a journey to the center of my mind—has been misleading. As task after task demonstrated, there is no center of activity, only way stations in a circuit, winking at each other in milliseconds, churning in some mysterious neural communion. And the notion of mind? We didn't make much progress penetrating that mystery. Perhaps it's nothing more than the heat given off by our personalized circuits, everywhere and yet nowhere.

If, as Joseph Conrad once said, the most interesting places are the empty spaces on a map, the prefrontal cortex must be an especially fascinating place for brain scientists. We were puzzled by the general dearth of activity in my frontal lobe; although it is supposed to be the real crucible of human thought, none of our exercises seemed to tickle it into much activity. Indeed, there were many questions I wished to ask that we couldn't approach for reasons of practicality or time, or an inability to even formulate a workable experimental question. I was interested, for example, in exploring skills more particular to an editor than a writer, like fixing ungrammatical sentences. I would have liked to probe emotions more intently, especially things we feel every day like anger and insecurity and sexual arousal, but it turns out they are exceedingly difficult to test in a meaningful way. I would have also liked to see what the brain looked like as it wrestled with a moral dilemma.

Brain scientists would like to know the answers to many of those questions, too. But as Joy, whose great-grandmother traveled the Oregon Trail, likes to point out, we're still in the "covered wagon" phase of mapping brain function. "When the real pioneers started their journey, they had no shortage of ideas about what Oregon was going to look like." she said. "And similarly, we have no shortage of ideas about mind and consciousness, even though we really haven't gone very far into the frontier." Even a modest journey like mine, however, hints at the territory ahead. "We have been able to observe several of the interconnected systems in your brain and perhaps have glimpsed some of your consciousness at work, even if it was only a snapshot of a brief instant of your life."

In our age-old struggle to understand the mind, we have always been empowered—yet oddly constrained—by the vocabulary of the moment, be it the voices of the gods in ancient myth, buried conflicts in the idiom of Freudian analysis, or associative memories in Proustian terms. But as psychology and neuroscience begin to converge, brain imaging may actually provide a new, visual vocabulary with which to rethink, and perhaps reconcile, some of these older ideas of mind. A common thread of both the Freudian and Proustian worldviews is the associative quality of recollection—the odd word or sight that connects to a deeper trauma, the odor that connects to a more extensive memory. Association requires connections, and as I saw, a brain scan of humor, for example, can actually depict a rich skein of associations in a diagram of neural connections. Preposterous as it may seem, I can imagine a day in the distant future when the M.R.I. replaces the couch, when the therapist uses words or odors or pictures to excite and pinpoint circuitry and then the neuroanatomist translates the images into explanations of behavior. Of course, there is always the possibility that after decades of exploration in search of mind, we'll still find ourselves, metaphorically speaking, knee-deep in a swamp of neurotransmitters that may bring us no closer to a biological understanding of "mind."

It's odd to put it this way, but I may know more about how my brain works than almost any human who has ever lived, and yet that knowledge has won nothing more than a beachhead on a vast, uncharted continent. That is no small achievement, though my journey makes clear that these are early days in the brain-mapping business. I cannot say what in my genetics or upbringing might have contributed to the hive of activity we observed in the right side of my brain. Or why I remember everything about the moment when my friend D. agreed to go to the prom with me thirty years ago but nothing about the moment when she changed her mind. Given the insecurities of adolescence and the uncertainties of affection, it seemed at the time like one of those watershed moments of my life, and even now it can still produce a wince, but it appears to have eluded the gaze of the M.R.I. machine. For when we went back and examined the scans taken in the moment when I thought I'd been shown D.'s face, the data had been subsumed in a stream of average responses. It didn't leave a trace.

# A FAMILY PORTRAIT IN BLACK & WHITE

*Walt Harrington*

My journey begins in the dentist's chair. The nurse's fingers are pressing dental dough into my lower incisors, and she and the doctor are playing dueling banjos with funny stories about their kids, when in walks another dentist, dropping by to say hello. "I've got a good one," he says cheerfully, and then he tells a racist joke. I can't recall the joke, only that it ends with a black man who is stupid. Dead silence. It's just us white folks here in the room, but my dentist and his nurse know my wife, who is black, and they know my son and my daughter, who are, as they describe themselves, tan and bright tan. How many racist jokes have I heard in my life? Five, maybe ten thousand, at least. But today—for the first time, for who knows exactly why—I am struck with a deep, sharp pain. I look at this man, with his pasty face, pale hair, and weak lips, and I think: "*This idiot's talking about my son!*"

I want to shake him, shove him against the wall. I say nothing. Quickly, my dentist grabs a tool, the nurse extracts the dough, and the idiot leaves. But I remain behind in suspended animation. It isn't the joke. It isn't the tension in the air. It isn't even the idiot. It is my recognition: I've crossed a line, and I know I have, and I know that for an instant I've traveled to a place where white Americans don't go. I feel revulsion and anger at this man. I feel fear and anguish for my children. I feel helpless. Am I, I wonder, feeling like a black man?

A memory: A long time ago, when I was eight, maybe nine, I sat with my grandmother on the steps of her house in the country outside Chicago, snapping fresh beans. My grandmother was a large, stern woman with a baritone voice, round wire glasses, and gray hair swept up in that old Gibson Girl fashion. I called her Big Grandma with fear and respect. That day, she told me she'd been to "the city"—Chicago Heights, Illinois, which in the 1950s was an industrial town of about 35,000. Big Grandma said she'd seen "coloreds" everywhere. Then she said this: While standing in line at the Walgreen drugstore, she'd heard one colored lady tell another colored lady, "I *always* carries a razor in *my* purse." Big Grandma said this with a dramatic inflection, a shiver, and a kind of rage, but I missed her complex meanings.

"*Coloreds,*" I thought, "what in the world are *coloreds*?"

I had no idea. But from her tone, I knew not to ask. Instead, I decided that *coloreds* were people whose skin, for mysterious reasons, resembled a concoction of melted crayons stirred into a weird, beautiful swirl. I remember this thought so clearly because of my later amazement when I went to Chicago Heights with Big Grandma and she pointed out a "colored." I was disappointed. They weren't *colored* after all.

Three decades later, sitting in the dentist's chair, I'm struck by how much I am still like that little boy who believed he understood what he absolutely did not. Ten years of marriage to a black woman, two children, years of visiting my wife's family in rural Kentucky, years of births and deaths, years of hunting with my father-in-law, Alex, his brother Bobby, and their friend Carl, years of shared bottles of Old Forester, shared jokes, lies and hunting knives—years of what I believed was a life lived across the color line . . . Yet only today, for the first time, have I felt, *felt,* the intimate intrigues and confusions of race in America.

Only today, for the first time, have I crossed the line.

My wife's father, Alex, slips the rubber band off the large, tightly rolled paper, uncurls it, smooths it on the coffee table, and then begins tracing the antecedents of his life. He starts in the upper left-hand corner, touching each name with the fingertips of his left hand: Tyler, Otha, Lou Emma, Annie, Beulah, Effie, Pratt, Samuel, Dollie, and Shed, who was his father. He then follows the branches of the handwritten family tree to his mother, Stella, through the names of his four brothers, to his own name, to those of his two sons, to that of his only daughter, Keran, who is my wife, and beyond to my name and those of our children, Matthew and Kyle. For this genealogical tour, for a tour of another world, I have come to my in-laws' farm outside Glasgow, Kentucky, where Alex grew up.

Thank the idiot in the dentist's office: His callousness has made me realize that what I know—about my wife and my children, about this thing called *race*—is really nothing at all. I'm here for a simple and complicated reason: My children share a heritage that I may understand historically and intellectually but for which I have no intuitive, no emotional, grasp. I hope, somehow, to change that.

I think of Alex as a friend. He's a soft-spoken man who cannot, to my mother-in-law's constant consternation, be hurried no matter what the occasion. At fifty-eight, he's still handsome, lean, and youthful. His sideburns and sparse mustache are sprinkled with gray. My children describe his complexion as brown-tan. He wears low-hanging Rustler jeans and a red-plaid flannel shirt over a crew-neck T-shirt, and he gently pads around the house in white socks. He's—how shall I say it?—something of an eccentric: He fries bull gonads for breakfast. (Served with well-seasoned brown gravy, they taste like tender chicken gizzards.) He maintains an antique Model A Ford, an antique Coke machine, and an antique Seeburg jukebox. He drives a hundred miles for a bottle of moonshine whiskey to share with his friends. Posted at his driveway is a classic jockey-boy statue—except that Alex has painted him bright white and named him Joe Zeller, after an old white friend. Alex is a country boy who left the country at fifteen, lying to the Air Force recruiter about his age. He had pure motivation to lie—he was just a hot-step ahead of the law for having sold a few illegally garnered gasoline stamps during World War II. He laughs: It's hard to believe more than four decades have passed. A few years ago—after serving in the Air Force in West Germany, England, France,

California, Washington, and Illinois—Alex and his wife, Celeste, retired to Glasgow.

"I gotta die somewhere," he says, smiling.

This morning, Alex and I are up at six-thirty and on the road, a twisting, two-lane stretch of blacktop called Kentucky 90. We are driving to Alex's beginnings, on the only road that runs the forty miles from Glasgow, a town of 12,646 people in southwest Kentucky, to Burkesville, a drab little burg set down in lavish forest along the Cumberland River. It's cold this morning, 35 degrees, but the Burkesville sky after dawn is so blue that it seems to disappear into itself, and the air is as clean as freshly washed glass. A hundred years ago, Burkesville—or rather a place called Lawson Bottom eleven miles northeast of Burkesville—was home to Alex's mother's family. Lawson Bottom was even named after her family, quite an accomplishment and quite an anomaly in the South of those days.

Alex didn't grow up in Lawson Bottom. His mother had migrated to Glasgow as a young woman, and Alex visited the farm only sporadically as a boy. Yet he has always seemed to have Lawson Bottom in him, carried its memory proudly, in a way that my wife and her brothers do not. As we make the final turn onto Lawson Bottom Road, Alex—for at least the hundredth time—tells me the story of taking his fiancée, Celeste, who was a college girl from a nice family of schoolteachers, to visit the farm in 1951. When they arrived at Lawson Bottom that first time, folks were so happy to see them that one of Alex's aunts called for a feast: "*Paee*-tehr," she yelled to her son, as Alex recalls with an exaggerated *Cain*-tucky accent, "go out and kill a *chai*-kin." Peter did—shooting its head off with a single rifle shot. From somewhere deep inside, Alex laughs so hard that his car swerves briefly to the left. He loves that story. It inevitably makes city folks cringe, and it inevitably reminds Alex of how far he and his family and his race have come.

These days, the Lawsons are long gone from Lawson Bottom—except for Alex's cousin Reid, a sixty-six-year-old man who has lived away from the "holler" only six months of his life. When Alex and I pull into the drive, Reid is outside hefting the wooden top off the well. The pump has stopped, but he's unconcerned.

Lawson Branch, a tiny mountain-fed stream, runs only twenty feet away, and it is an "everlasting" stream, as they call it, meaning that it never runs dry. If Reid must, he'll simply dip water from the branch for washing clothes or even for drinking, as the Cherokee Indians might have done two hundred years ago. But that won't be necessary. Alex was a master sergeant and an airplane mechanic in the Air Force—at least he was once they stopped dumping blacks into kitchen, janitorial, and paper-shuffling jobs in the '50s—and for the cost of a $4.50 electrical switch, he'll have Reid's pump whirring in a couple of hours.

While Alex works, Reid leads me toward the house, walking deliberately with his hands stuffed deep into the pockets of his old green coat. He's a tall man, only slightly stooped with the years. He has been lean all his life, and only recently has he put on a little weight around the middle. He wears jeans, leather boots, and a tan work shirt. On his head rests an orange hunting cap: "Burkesville Fertilizer." The hat sits back, angled to the right atop a full shock of chalk-white hair. "Let me put a dry stick in the stove," Reid says, heading back out the front door for five huge pieces of split cedar. I sit in a creaking chair, one of only three, and survey the single room in which Reid lives. It's as if I'm inside an old, sepia-toned photograph: the "Warm Morning" wood stove in the center of the room, the bare lightbulb hanging overhead, the long on-off string running from the light and tied to the bedpost, the dog-eared Bible, the brown cross painted on the unpainted drywall, the strong and—to my own weak, city-dweller nostrils—nauseating smell of dead mice in the walls, a cold-weather condition that can't be avoided on the farm. Reid is like a movie frame halted in time, the living embodiment of where Alex's family began a century ago.

Through the clouded window next to his bed, Reid points to a tuft of young trees, mostly elm, just across the drive on this side of Lawson Branch. There stood the family homeplace, the house of patriarch Berry Lawson—born 1865, died 1915. The legend of Berry Lawson has been handed down in the family for generations, and I have heard it not only from Reid but from my wife's grandmother, Stella, before she died and from my wife's great-aunt

Minnie, a short, eighty-one-year-old wisp of a woman with light, soft skin and wavy gray hair. She's known to everyone as Aunt G, after her middle name, Glatha.

There are no pictures of my wife's great-great-grandfather Berry, only the memories of his children, who say Berry Lawson was small and strong—and nearly white, with muted African features and straight, jet-black hair. "Good hair," as Aunt G still calls it. Berry's parentage, like that of so many in the simultaneously Jim Crow and miscegenational Old South, was fuzzy. He was raised by a white bachelor farmer named Billy Mayes and his spinster sister, Sally. Everyone assumed Berry was Billy's son by a neighboring black woman, a Lawson, who died when Berry was five. When Billy Mayes and Sally died, they left Berry the 250-acre farm. Reid says blacks and whites always got along in Lawson Bottom, but a black man—even a half-black man—owning so much land didn't sit well with everybody, particularly one rich white farmer who complained that no colored man should be allowed to own such fertile land.

But Berry did, and he set about raising his family with his wife, Ada. Their log cabin was magnificent against the shacks and shanties of other blacks. The house sat snugly between Lawson Bottom Road to the front and a 900-foot forest ridge to the rear. Its rough-hewn logs were sealed with wattle and daub and its roof was covered with foot-long split hickory shakes. Inside, the house was dominated by its massive, gray stone fireplace—five feet high with a hearth big enough for a six-foot backlog and guarded by heavy dog irons that Berry Lawson had tempered in his own blacksmith shop in the barn.

The Lawsons had plenty, little cash, but plenty. They had nice clothes, and my wife's grandmother Stella would give her old dresses to poor blacks—even to poor whites. For the winter, Berry Lawson stored mountains of 100-pound sacks of flour from wheat grown in his own fields. He grew corn, hay, and tobacco; he raised cows, hogs, horses, mules, chickens, and ducks. Each year, he put up ten 50-pound stands of lard. "Not even white folks had that much lard," Aunt G boasts. What the farm didn't produce, the steamboats on the Cumberland River delivered for barter—candy, coffee, and Red Rolling Fork whiskey packed four quart bottles to the cardboard box. Such affluence among blacks didn't go unnoticed.

As a girl, Aunt G once picked up the phone—yes, the Lawsons had a phone—and overheard two white women gabbing on the party line: "What're you eatin' tonight?" one white woman asked the other. "I don't know," came the reply. "The only person who's got anything is Ada Lawson. She's got everything." Aunt G laughs at the memory, a joyful little cackle that she mutes with a hand put discreetly to her mouth. "Of all the Negroes over there," she says, "we was the only ones with land and horses and wagons. All the others would be walkin', and we'd be ridin'." She laughs again. "They said we thought we was better, rich, because we were Berry Lawson's kids." Well, truth is, Aunt G *did* think she was better than the other Lawson Bottom blacks. "I thought it was their fault they were poor," she says with uncertain contrition. "I don't guess it was, lookin' back."

Even then, polite whites referred to blacks as "coloreds," which was Aunt G's preference. But for all her affluence, when some "poor white trash" would call her a "nigger" or a "blackbird" or a "darkie," there was nothing she could do about it, except seethe. Black and white children played together and ate lunches at each other's houses, became good friends, but it was a rare white child who didn't, when angered, resort to his ultimate weapon, racial slurs. The black kids would respond—calling the white kids "peckerwoods," a slur against whites that they had often heard their parents use privately. But it never had the same sting: Without raw power to back it up, a slur is only a pinprick.

Aunt G especially hated the name-calling. She was so proud of her light skin and straight hair, and she hated being called a darkie. "I'd rather have been called a 'nigger,'" she says bluntly. "We had lots of white blood." Aunt G's grandmother—my wife's great-great-grandmother—was the light-skinned child of a slave–slave master union, but she married a very dark man. Sadly, Aunt G says, "All her kids had nappy hair. They had bad hair. She'd say, 'I don't know nothin' about combin' those nappy-headed children.' She made Grandpa tend their hair." It was a sentiment Aunt G would carry into her generation: "I just had a horror of little black children, just thought I couldn't tend to them. I don't know why. It's something within me." Aunt G says this matter-of-factly, without guilt or self-reflection. For her, as for so many, race and social class and skin color were hopelessly intertwined. For Aunt G, light skin became a stand-in for the respectability she craved, just as surely as other blacks' resentment of her light skin was in part a stand-in for their resentment of her prosperity.

It is time for Reid to go to work. Outside, the sun has warmed the morning and I unzip my coat as we walk to the tobacco barn several hundred feet toward the ridge—past overturned and rusted trucks and automobiles, ancient and abandoned farm equipment, oil tanks and feeding troughs. In the barn, made of vertical, un-painted splinter wood, sweet-smelling tobacco stalks hang, curing, from three layers of crossbeams. Reid says, "Be sure to duck," but I hit my head hard anyway. He lights the kerosene heater and begins stripping the "trash" and the "lugs" from the three-foot-long tobacco stalks, leaving the lowest-quality leaves—the "tips"— for me to strip and bale for the burley market, where tobacco is bringing $1.67 a pound. "Ain't been much changed up here," Reid says finally, his breath hovering like a cloud in the windless barn. "Except whites and blacks go to school together and eat together." He laughs and hands me another stalk: "We'll make a farmer out of you yet." Reid and I strip and bale, strip and bale silently for a long time, until Alex has the well pump running again. Then Alex and I say good-bye, see you soon, Reid, and drive off, back into the twentieth century, leaving the last Lawson in Lawson Bottom in the cold barn, still stripping tobacco.

I have no memory of ever talking to a black person until I was re-cruited to play with an all-black baseball team from Chicago Heights. I remember that, despite Big Grandma's biases, my working-class parents preached right-thinking attitudes about race: People are people and everyone should be treated the same. It was easy to think right on race in my Midwestern surburban hometown—with no blacks, no Hispanics, maybe an Italian or two. As far as I knew, the platitude that people were people was correct—people *were* people just like us, like me. I vaguely remember fat southern cops and vicious dogs on TV. I remember the Rev. Martin Luther King Jr. being pelted in Cicero, which was only an hour's drive away. I remember thinking those Polacks were really ignorant.

Despite learning all these proper notions, though, I also discovered that I could make my parents vaguely uncomfortable if I spouted off too liberally about race. My sister even recalls a time in high school when I asked my mother, "So what would you do if I married a Negro girl?" I don't recall the taunt, but it sounds like me. I remember also that when Moses Turner, the coach of the all-black Chicago Heights baseball team, asked me to play for him the summer I turned sixteen, I was happy to agree. Big Grandma thought I'd gone mad. But I relished the renegade image I got playing on Moses Turner's team. I loved it when an umpire from my suburban league pulled me aside and asked angrily, "Why are you wasting your time with these niggers?" My little step across the color line seemed to make everybody uncomfortable, which I enjoyed immensely.

But that summer, I also learned something else. I became friends with the team's 6-foot-4 pitcher, Pee Wee—a dark, strong kid who was an imposing athletic hero in his neighborhood. I often drove Pee Wee home after the games, and I can still see his street: wide and tree-lined and gray, with mangy dogs and broken bicycles, with grassless yards, tar-paper roofs, unpainted picket fences, and missing screen doors. Kids were everywhere. The summer was 1967, and all around Chicago racial violence was breaking out. It was an angry time, and one day, as I turned onto Pee Wee's street, he said, in a voice husky and slow, "Whatever you do, don't hit one o' these kids. There won't be nothin' even I can do for you." This wasn't a threat, but good advice, and you have never seen a person drive more carefully. After Pee Wee got out, I drove around the block and back to the highway so slowly people were staring at me. I smiled and nodded. I think I held my breath.

After that, I wasn't so eager to give Pee Wee a ride home.

★   ★   ★

The signs on the gas pumps at the Gulf station in downtown Burkesville read: "You may have won a BMW." Driving past the station into town, it seems that nothing could be more out of sync with Burkesville. It's a town of pickup trucks, of old men with leather faces and weathered jackets standing outside the county courthouse across from the Dollar Store. When I stop a delivery man to ask directions, I see a large knife and a holstered pistol on the dash of his truck. Nope, this is *not* BMW country.

Alex has suggested I stop in Burkesvile to talk with his cousin Nell, because at fifty-five she's the last Lawson Bottom native of her generation still in town. I've met Nell before, at Alex's home, and I'm embarrassed to admit the prejudices I revealed that day. Nell wore modest clothes, and her hair was parted in the middle and turned up with simplicity. She said, "Hello, nice to meet you." At least I suppose she did, because I couldn't understand a word. She was, it seemed to me, strictly backwoods. I imagined her as a character out of Alex's story about Lawson Bottom: "*Paee*-tehr, go out and kill a *chai*-kin."

Only after Nell left did Alex tell me she was a schoolteacher with a master's degree. I felt stupid, though in my defense, it also was the beginning of my realization that what I had assumed was poor, uneducated, *black* Kentucky dialect was simply Kentucky country dialect. As meeting Nell had reminded me, things aren't always as they seem. Tonight, as I sit down with Nell and her twenty-five-year-old daughter, she is about to remind me of this again.

I ask innocently, "Who was your father?"

With hesitation and a deep breath, Nell says: "I'll be honest with you. My father was white and he never did pay me any attention. He would come to my mother's father's house and sit out, and I'd jump flips, but he paid me no attention." His attitude, Nell says, was "'Yes, I did this to your daughter and there's nothin' you can do about it!'" Nell's white daddy, it turns out, was the same rich white man who complained that no "colored" should be allowed to own land as fertile as Berry Lawson's. "I remember a kindly, round face with dark reddish hair," Nell says. "Maybe your height and a little chubby. When my father died, I didn't even go see him. I thought: 'If you don't care, I don't care either.' But I did care. I still do."

She pauses and no one speaks.

"I guess I didn't realize I really cared about my father just until you asked. I guess he's still controlling me from the grave. He never even spoke to me. I think he could have at least done that. I was called 'half-white' and 'bastard' by my own people. I don't know which was more painful. Just not being accepted by anyone, really. I've got a white half-brother right here in this town, and he does not acknowledge me. I've thought sometimes about calling him, but some things you just have to keep in the closet."

Nell's eyes are filled with tears now, as are mine. What to say? I think of good-hearted whites I know, even young affluent blacks, who would like this *race thing,* this ever-present *race thing* to disappear, go away, because life is different now, changed, better. Yes? Then I look at Nell, who is only fifty-five, but who—like any abused or beaten or abandoned child—will carry this *race thing* forever. And beyond . . .

"I tell my daughters to stay away from white men," she says. "I'd be afraid they'd be using them the way we were done."

"But what about me?" I ask. "I'm a white man."

"I knew you were different," Nell says. At first, I think she's talking about my wife and me. But as she speaks, I realize she's talking about someone else too. "I knew that you wouldn't be ashamed to be seen walking down the street with me, that you'd do more than take me behind closed doors. You married her." I look at Nell's daughter, Donna, who is only twenty-five. She says, "White men usually want one thing." What to say? Normally, this attitude would strike me as quaint, a throwback to another time and another place.

But not tonight, not in this town, this room, not in Nell's house.

I went to college in 1968 thinking I didn't have a racist bone in my body. Then this happened: At the height of the Black Power movement, black students circulated a petition to turn a little-used building on our small Midwestern campus into a meeting place for black students, which meant they'd be the only social group on campus with a building of their own. I didn't speak against this idea. I didn't campaign against it. But I did decline to sign the petition when it came my way, because I thought the idea was unfair to everyone else. I did not think this was a big deal. I was wrong.

Overnight, the several black members of my dormitory basketball team—with these guys we were expected to be campus champs—announced they wouldn't play as long as I was on the team. Shell-shocked and embarrassed, I offered to quit. But the team captain—a big white guy with definite racist tendencies—declared I would not resign. *We* would not be bullied! *We* would play without *them*! And that's what *we* did. To keep the peace, the college broke its own rule and allowed the black guys from all the dorms to form a team and play in the dormitory league. It was something of an event when my dorm played them, with me as point guard. We won that game, although it was little consolation. I'd been tarred as a racist, which was, I believe even twenty years later, too simple. I didn't know then that most blacks see the world as black *or* white, one *or* the other, and that to them the whole campus belonged to white students, while all they were seeking was one small, ramshackle building.

I was guilty, all right, but of believing people were people—just like us, like me. I was guilty, all right, but of seeing the world through my own eyes, guilty of not yet knowing that justice isn't always fair.

Lewis Street in the Kingdom . . .

The black places are gone today—King's Restaurant, the Royal Cafe, Mr. Troop's barbershop, the pool and dance halls, Kurd's cab stand, and, of course, the little gypsy restaurant Alex's father, Shed, ran in a tiny wooden trailer on rubber-and-spoke wheels near Lewis and Brown streets. In dry Glasgow in dry Barren County, Shed sold hooch from that trailer, as he also did from his kitchen half a block away at 506 Lewis, as his teenage sons Alex and Bobby later did on the streets. Shed's house has fallen to a modern brick funeral home today, and vacant lots and a B-Kwick Food Mart have replaced the rest. Alex can't help but be saddened by these changes. But he doesn't get too nostalgic, because the rats—bold rats made fat and healthy at the feed mill on the corner of Lewis and Back streets—also are gone. So is Red Row, a dozen or so leaning and dilapidated board and batten shacks, desperate even by Depression standards, that sat across and just up Back Street.

But the old Kingdom, the nickname for Glasgow's original few square blocks of black neighborhood, was the world as my children's mother's father's family knew it after they migrated from Burkesville to Glasgow in the 1920s. My children's great-grandfather was king of the Kingdom's bootleggers. Whites and blacks, rich and poor, visited Shed's kitchen with the devotion of churchgoers—especially on Saturdays, when Glasgow's town square, only a few blocks north, would be packed with gawkers and talkers in from the fields. Shots of moonshine cost 3, 5, or 10 cents; pints 35 cents. Demand was great and Alex's job was to wash the Pepsi bottles, the old ones with the brown and green paper labels, so they could be filled with bootleg beer. Shed was a short man with a confident look in his eyes. He wore a skimmer hat and string ties. He told his sons he was a blacksmith, but Alex can recall seeing him with a horse only once. He worked as a janitor, a busboy, a carpenter, a bellhop, and, for a long time, as a dishwasher at the Spotswood Hotel on the square.

But always, Shed was a bootlegger—until the day Alex, eight years old, watched as the police lugged jug after jug from beneath the house. Shed went to prison. He died soon after his release. For a time, my children's great-grandmother, Stella—radiant, kind, gentle, religious Stella—took over the family enterprise. "I got these five boys," she told Aunt G. Finally, Stella retired from the business to do what respectable blacks did in her day: She worked as a housekeeper and nanny and as a maid in Glasgow's hospital. Before she died in 1981, Stella soberly described her predicament by telling me this story: A friend of hers once applied for a good factory job. The boss called her in and told her apologetically that he knew she could do the work, but that he also knew she was Mrs. Richardson's cook. And the boss, with a friendly laugh, said he couldn't have Mrs. Richardson mad at him for stealing her favorite cook, now could he?

The men I hunt rabbits with each year in Lawson Bottom—Alex and his younger brother Bobby, who is fifty-six, and their friend Carl, who is fifty-five—all were bootleggers in the 1940s. In those days, Lewis Street was much like the corner drug markets that proliferate in American cities today. On weekends, a horde of young black males would mill about waiting for mostly white customers to drive through, roll down their windows, and buy whiskey. Today, Alex, Bobby, and Carl aren't embarrassed that they were bootleggers. They're proud of it.

"A black man couldn't get a good job in those days," says Bobby, a short, round man who absently lifts his blue cap and smooths his hand lightly over a bald head. Bobby, in Toughskins bib overalls and a gray hooded sweatshirt, is working at his barn today, creating a small corral of electric wire to enclose two black steers he plans to fatten for slaughter. Normally, Bobby leaves the castrated males in the cow herd as "markers"—they mount and ride a cow when she's in heat, thus notifying the farmer it's time to mate her with a fertile bull. "Them steers got pistols," Bobby quips, "but they ain't got no bullets." We lift an old Agstar water trough into the barn and Bobby goes to get the hose to fill it. The late autumn afternoon is warm and bright, 51 degrees, and a white cat suns itself against the concrete foundation of the red rackside barn. In odd juxtaposition, the trees in the pasture are naked for the winter while the Kentucky grass still is green and growing. "Nope," Bobby says, picking up the thread again when he returns with the hose, "the best job a black could get was being a janitor, and there weren't many of them,"

Bobby had a respectable job for a while after he dropped out of high school: He was a janitor at Glasgow's hospital, where his mother worked. He earned $100 a month and bolstered his income with light bootlegging. Then one day, Bobby saw the paycheck of a white kid whose job was to scrape gum off the hospital floors. "It was more than mine!" Bobby says, still incredulous. Bobby went to the hospital chief, a white man who was one of his best bootlegging customers, and asked for a raise. "Bobby," the chief said, "they won't let me pay coloreds what I pay whites." So Bobby quit and took up bootlegging full-time. At his peak, between the ages of about sixteen and nineteen, three men sold whiskey for him. Bobby would drive the thirty-two miles to Bowling Green, where liquor could be bought legally, and pay $1.25 for a half-pint, which he sold for $2.50. In his heyday, Bobby sold six cases of half-pints, 288 bottles, a week. After paying his salesmen, that was $216 a week for Bobby, more than $800 a month—compared with $100 at his respectable hospital job. He bought his mother clothes, gifts, and groceries.

"Let me tell you," Bobby says, "you won't find a black in Glasgow who's got anything that somewhere along the line, bootlegging didn't touch their lives. Very few. Because the people workin' weren't paid anything. It was either work and be dirt poor, or risk going to jail and be a bootlegger." Bobby finally did get arrested and went to court. But the Glasgow police chief had broken up the bootleg transaction before Bobby was paid, meaning no illegal sale had taken place. When Bobby's lawyer pointed this out to the all-white jury, the prosecutor was flabbergasted. "I'll never forget it," Bobby says, laughing. "He said, 'I guess we should put the chief of police in jail and turn this nigger loose.'" Bobby was acquitted. And eventually, he—like Alex before him—joined the military and got out of town a hot-step ahead of the law.

In those times, race was everywhere and nowhere. The movies, restaurants, and public bathrooms were segregated, of course, as were the downtown Glasgow water fountains. As boys, Alex and Bobby gleefully rubbed their spit onto the spout of the whites-only fountain. Yet neither Alex nor Bobby can recall a single time anyone in Glasgow treated them rudely because they were black. Race was like a colorless, tasteless, odorless gas in the air. Alex remembers noticing that the football goalposts at his black school were always broken. He didn't question this. He remembers that he was once sent to a white school to pick up his teacher's paycheck and he noticed something amazing: On the tables in the white cafeteria sat entire bowls of fresh apples. Alex didn't think this was unfair, only that it was strange and mysterious. Bobby then tells this story: As he would walk to school, the white kids would ride by in their bus and make faces at him, but he would think nothing of it. "It's like the old joke about the Indian riding a horse with his squaw walking next to him," Bobby explains. "A guy asks the Indian, 'Why are you ridin' and your squaw's walkin'?' The Indian looks up at the man, thinks, and then says, 'She no have 'em horse.'" We both laugh at the punch line.

"Well, it was like that," Bobby says. 'We didn't have a horse."

Yet it's eerie how things no one seemed to notice can live so long, as in the mind of Alex and Bobby's friend and my hunting companion, Carl, who grew up outside Glasgow in a barn-wood shack. These days, Carl is never without at least the stub of a cigar working in the corner of his mouth. He's big as a bear, thick every-where—stomach, chest, neck, legs, arms, even his fingers. Not fat, thick. This morning, he's out checking on his cows, breaking the ice in their water trough with a shovel. He wears insulated cam-ouflage overalls and green rubber boots. He has a deep, bass voice and a head that seems to sit directly atop his massive shoulders. He is gentle and threatening at once. As a boy, there was no black school near Carl, so he didn't start until he was nine. "I'm still awful proud I graduated high school," he says, "considering where I began." Next door was a nice white family who let Carl ride their pony. He took the rides but deeply resented the family. Carl believed then that he resented them so much because they were white. But looking back, he knows that skin color was only a stand-in: As the black kids in Lawson Bottom had resented Berry Lawson's kids because they were rich, Carl resented his white neighbors because they too were rich.

Unlike Alex and Bobby, who got out of town for decades, Carl has lived in Glasgow all his life. He worked at the Texaco station for twelve years—as a "wash boy," scrubbing cars, cleaning the grease pit. He earned $60 a week, far less than his white coworkers. One day, Carl noticed that a white mechanic had worked on a car all morning and gone to lunch still unable to get it started. Carl got it started. The boss was so happy, he bought Carl a Coke. Finally, in 1965 Carl got one of the first area factory jobs that went to a black man. For the first time in his life, at thirty-one, he was paid a white man's wage. He now drives a forklift at another fac-tory and makes good money. He's now got good white friends. Thirty years ago, Carl would have said that was impossible. He marvels when he hears young black and white men at work bantering back and forth with racial digs. Even today, Carl couldn't do that without getting mad. He doesn't know exactly why.

Just the other day he was listening to a couple of young white men bragging about the University of Kentucky basketball team, and Carl felt as if they were pulling an invisible thread in his brain. He thought about the time three decades ago when he happened to sit down fishing next to UK's venerated coach, Adolph Rupp. That year, a local black basketball star was trying to get into Kentucky, which had never had a black player, and Carl asked Rupp if he was going to take him. "He can't pass the academic tests," Rupp said smugly. "Some schools will lower their standards to take him anyway, but not Kentucky."

Then Carl thought about all those years at the Texaco station, how he acted like "a nice colored man" when he sometimes wanted to slug the white men making more money for no more work. And about the day he got that car started and the boss bought him a Coke. *A Coke!* He thought about how they wouldn't let him go to school till he was nine, how far behind he was, how foolish he felt. He thought about the days when banks wouldn't lend a black $500 without a white cosigner, how as a boy he had to stand in the store and wait until all the whites were served, how even his daddy had to wait patiently, like a nice colored man.

And he got hotter and hotter.

"I had to catch myself not to say anything," Carl says. "These are good guys. They're thirty years old. They didn't know Adolph Rupp. But all that brings back through your head everything else that came before. It can eat at you. And you start lookin' for each and every thing. It eats you up. The next thing you know, you're angry and you don't know what you're angry about."

The summer after the last season I played baseball with Pee Wee, after my first year in college and who-knows-what for Pee Wee, I was with a girlfriend driving through Chicago Heights on the way to the Indiana dunes on Lake Michigan. I had what for me was a lot of money in my pocket. We stopped at a Tastee-Freez, and as we stood licking our cones in the sunlight, about a dozen black kids, maybe thirteen, fourteen years old, rode up on their bikes and surrounded us in a shrinking half-circle against the shiny white wall.

"Got any change?"

Then, "Got any folding money?"

The next question seemed inevitable. So as I dug into my pocket, I asked, "Hey, any you guys know Pee Wee?" The boys glanced around at one another.

"You know Pee Wee, man?"

"Oh, yeah, Pee Wee and me, we go way back, man, played ball together."

Before long, we were laughing and swapping Pee Wee stories. Before long, I'd gotten away for small change. I drove carefully. I think I held my breath.

The Kingdom through a different lens . . .

As children, my wife and her two younger brothers saw Glasgow as a foreign land. They were military brats, kids who'd spent half their childhoods in West Germany, France, England, on the West Coast, always in military housing, always attending military schools. Alex can tell some pretty grim tales about his early days in the military. The black soldiers' breakfasts were always cold because they were trucked over from the white kitchen. The only day blacks could use the swimming pool was Wednesday—after which they changed the pool water for the week. He can't help chuckling at the memory. But by the middle 1950s Alex believed that no place in American society gave blacks a better shake. By then, everything in the military was integrated—housing, clubs, jobs, schools.

Into this brave new world came my wife and her brothers. Their playmates were mostly white, and out of, say, twenty kids in a military school classroom, only one, two, maybe three, would be black. In Europe, there were no "Whites Only" signs and no one was turned away at a restaurant door. Keran and her brother Alex Jr. can't recall a time when they were overseas that race seemed to make a difference in their lives. Keran was wild about the Beatles and thought she'd really die if she couldn't marry Paul. Alex Jr.

was always the most popular kid in his class. "I didn't know race was supposed to be a handicap," he says. Howard, the youngest, does remember that when the family went to the Oktoberfest in Munich, people stared awfully hard. He remembers noticing at picnics that children with southern accents seemed not to play with him much. But Howard must rack his brain for these memories.

So when the kids visited Glasgow, it was culture shock. Blacks and whites didn't mingle, and that was odd enough. But the rural poverty was shocking. Two generations out of Lawson Bottom, a generation out of the Kingdom, the kids would sit on the porch of the house Grandma Stella shared with Aunt G since their husbands had died, and look across Back Street at mind-boggling destitution. "It wasn't race," says Howard, who, after flying jets in the Air Force, is now a pilot for UPS. "It was poverty. It was poverty like in Africa." He remembers the nights they would listen to the people across Back Street chasing rats from their bedrooms. "We used to make fun of those people," says Alex Jr. "I just couldn't comprehend them." Of his father's beloved Kingdom, he says: "The whole area around Aunt G's was a craphole. And all the black kids had these strange accents. It was hillbilly to me. I had the sense of not wanting to be associated with them."

My wife and her brothers all went to college. And they all say that, as far as they know, being black has only helped them. My wife always jokes that as a black woman she fills two quota slots as a manager at Cigna Corp. Alex Jr. figures he got shots at the two biggest jobs in his career because he's black. Howard says UPS didn't even answer his job letter until he sent a picture. "Maybe I'm going through life with blinders," he says, shaking his head, "but when I hear people crying, 'Racism, racism,' I say, 'What are you talking about?' I just haven't seen it." Yes, there were occasional racial slurs at the mostly white Mascoutah, Illinois, high school they attended when the family finally moved off base. Yes, they remember family vacations in the 1950s when motels in the States turned them away. Yes, they remember some mean redneck stares. And, yes, they also remember stares from black kids, who seemed angry and resentful of their white friends. "I noticed it, but I didn't let it bother me," Howard says. "I've been stared at

all my life—at the Oktoberfest, in Mascoutah, and years later when
I'd take planes into Iceland. People stare for a minute and then
they come up and talk to you. It hit home very early that through
hard work you can make it too. That wasn't true in my dad's day.
And that's different."

I think of what Bobby had said about his emasculated cattle:
"Them steers got pistols, but they ain't got no bullets." Today
poverty, poor education, and lack of opportunity—the ageless
barriers of class—are formidable obstacles to black achievement.
But the power of racism, though still strong and ugly, is greatly
diminished. For my wife and her brothers—for an entire generation of well-educated young blacks and their children—racism,
like Bobby's steers, is more and more a pistol without bullets. A
slur or a stare, yes, but they're not being turned away because Mrs.
Richardson needs a cook.

I didn't know exactly *what* Keran was when we first met. She's
got rising cheekbones, electrified hair, and a nose that isn't European, but she has no accent except middle American and her skin
is the color of honey. "Maybe," I told a friend, "she's part Fili-
pino." He said, "No, she's black." I didn't think much about it,
and when I first met her parents a month later and saw that she
really was black, I didn't think much about it then either. Keran
was the only black woman I'd ever dated, and I simply told myself that I would not let race matter, that I was beyond it. Besides,
marriage wasn't on my screen in those days.

My mother, it turned out, was more farsighted. When my sister told her I was dating a black woman, I got an anguished late
night call from my mom, asking me, please, to think about what
I was doing, please, think about the children. I told her not to
worry, that I hardly knew the woman, that I wasn't marrying
anybody for a long time.

She said, "But this is how these things start."

My mother the prophet. Five years later, Keran and I were
married. In the years we had dated, strange as it seems, we never
had a problem with race that I knew of. I never heard a slur. I
didn't notice stares. Nobody seemed to care. I was amazed at this

and always figured it had to do with Keran, who didn't wear race as a badge, who talked middle-class talk, and who was light-skinned enough that whites weren't knee-jerk threatened by her.

But I never forgot my mother's phone call, and, about a year before we married, I broke off with Keran. I told myself it was because I wasn't ready to get married, but I knew even then it was also because I feared my parents' reaction. If I were going to marry Keran, I reasoned, I'd better be awfully sure about it. After a few months apart, I was sure.

My parents, who had always taught me to think right about race, freaked out. I'd always been a rebellious kid, and in the '60s— with marijuana, long hair, strange clothes, and radic-lib ideas— my folks saw me purposely rejecting their beliefs. Keran knew better. She joked, "You have to marry a black woman—to prove you're not hopelessly middle class." Indeed, it was my hopelessly middle-class sensibility that attracted her. "I can't marry a jive man," she said. But my folks believed my marriage mocked their values and squandered their sacrifices. "I'm sure Keran is a nice girl from a nice family," my mother said. "This has nothing to do with her." In their minds, as in the minds of so many, race and social class and skin color were hopelessly intertwined.

My parents were dirt poor as children. They struggled all their lives, sacrificed, to keep me in a decent home, decent schools. They struggled to move me up and out. In their view, my marrying across the color line was moving down, not up. I was throwing away all their sacrifices. Who'd hire me? Who'd have me to dinner? What nice neighborhood would take me? We didn't talk for years after my marriage. Then one day, as my mother looked through photos I'd sent—photos of my nice home, my nice yard, my nice kids—she made this telling remark to my sister: "It looks like your brother has built a life for himself." Soon, we were a family again.

Keran's parents had a different reaction: They said not a word about race. Alex asked, "You mean you're marrying that scrawny guy?" They remained true to their lifetime belief that race shouldn't matter, that it should never be an excuse or an explanation, that it should be ignored, pretended away. Their philosophy was simple:

Blacks must act as if they can control their lives, whether or not they can. Otherwise their ambition is sapped and their lives consumed by self-pity. It is the way they have lived their lives, the way they have raised their children.

Alex's advice: Ignore the idiot in the dentist's office. He takes too much energy. He's a jerk, and there are few enough like him today that he can be ignored. Perhaps this was once an illusion, a psychic defense for blacks, but not by the time my wife and her brothers were growing up. And certainly not by the time of my children. I feel like Howard does. Maybe I'm going through life with blinders, but I can't think of a time when I or my wife or our kids have been mistreated because of race. Oh, I know the neighborhood was abuzz when we moved in. Since my revelation in the dentist's chair, I've heard my son's Little League coach talk about the "niggers" and a neighbor joke about the "coons." I hate this. But in the end, these things are pistols without bullets. As it was even in Aunt G's day, a slur without the power to back it up is only a pinprick. My wife and I can work, live where we want, and send our kids to the schools we choose. This is not true for all blacks, but it is true for us, with our power of affluence.

It turns out I'm not the pioneer I thought I was. Because it wasn't me or even my children who first crossed the color line. It was Alex and Celeste, my wife and her brothers and so many other blacks, all of whom ventured into the mainstream white world to face stares and slurs from whites as well as blacks. Thanks to them, not me, life is nearly normal for my children. About that I breathe easier.

But not too easy: The worst barriers are gone, but the confusion about race, class, and color lives on in all of us, as I'm forever reminded.

With my kids, I pull into the McDonald's drive-through. We are in a hurry, and as I come to the squawk box, I see that the car ahead of me has four black people in it. In an instant, my mind makes its unconscious and racist calculation: We'll be sitting here forever while these people decide what to order. I literally shake my head at the awfulness of this thought. I laugh at my own deep prejudice. Then I wait. And wait. And wait. Each of the four people in the car ahead leans out the window and orders individually. The order is changed several times. We sit and sit, and now I am shaking my head again. I know that the buried sentiment that made me predict that these people would be disorganized on the basis of race alone was wrong—bad, not nice, racist. I know there are dozens of other reasons for their behavior, that race was only a convenient stand-in for social class or education or individual stupidity or rudeness. But the prediction was right. So now I chide myself for my racism, then I laugh to myself at my racism's unfortunate predictive power, then I shake my head again, this time at the conundrum that is race in America.

I think of Winston Churchill's line: "A riddle wrapped in a mystery inside an enigma."

That riddle is especially confusing to the young. My four-year-old daughter, for instance, came home from Kinder-Care one day recently and announced that she didn't like the black boys in her class. They were too rough. I'm always fearful of my children's being trapped somewhere between black and white, and I try again and again to make them see that race is only a stand-in for deeper explanations. As we talked, it became clear that Kyle didn't really like *any* of the boys in her class, white or black, which is all I wanted her to understand. In our family, when we talk about how someone looks, my wife and I always ask if the person is tall or short, hefty or thin, dark-haired or light-haired, blue-eyed or brown-eyed, light-skinned or dark-skinned. It was not until my son was in first grade that we saw the impact of this. Matthew came home the first day of school and said there were no black kids in his class. Concerned, I went to his classroom—and found about a dozen black kids.

"What about him?" I asked, nodding toward a black child.

"He's not black," Matthew said, as if I were blind. "He's dark brown."

Yet the seductive power of race as an explanation, as a predictor of behavior, is great. One day, Matthew came home and asked why the dark-skinned kids in his class didn't know as much as the light-skinned kids. As we talked, he realized that he didn't really mean *all* the dark-skinned kids, but a lot of them. What to say? I gave a little history lesson about slavery, about bad schools, about being locked out of good jobs, about how parents with good educations often start their children reading earlier, about how just because a child doesn't read or add well doesn't mean he isn't smart, only that he's behind in reading or adding. Matthew interrupted.

"Dad, Dad!" he said. 'This is *booor*-ing!"

Okay, okay, but sometimes I think, I hope, the message is heard. In psychology, there's a classic experiment in which black kids are asked whether a white or a black doll is prettier. For decades, black children have more often picked the white doll. I once played a game like this with my light-skinned, sandy-haired, hazel-eyed daughter. I laid out five of her dolls—a dark brown Cabbage Patch doll; a pale white cloth doll; a light tan doll from Mexico; a white, blond-haired Barbie doll; and a black friend of Barbie's named Dee-Dee. I asked Kyle to pick the prettiest dolls: In order, she selected the blond Barbie, the black Dee-Dee, the pale white cloth doll, the tan doll from Mexico, and the dark brown Cabbage Patch doll. I asked why.

Barbie? "She has dangly earrings."

The black Dee-Dee? "She has pretty lipstick."

The pale white cloth doll? "She has a diaper."

The tan doll from Mexico? "She has pigtails."

The dark brown Cabbage Patch? "I don't like him because he's bald."

Except that I am going bald, I liked her answers. I know that many blacks don't judge racial progress on whether people are increasingly color-blind and whether blacks and whites mingle together more in society. But I do, and for obvious reasons: My children stand at a doorway to two worlds. I want them to feel comfortable in both, and I want their world—the world between the races—to grow and expand, for the races to melt together, for either-or to disappear. Blacks and whites work together now. We live as neighbors, go to school together, dine together. So much has changed.

My wife's living family encompasses this great arc of race history and psychology, of change and sad similarity: Reid, still stripping tobacco; Aunt G, still proud of her light skin; Nell, still anguished over racism's oldest crime; Carl, still stoically fighting his silent anger; Bobby, still proud that he bootlegged rather than work for next to nothing; Alex and Celeste, still bridging the old world of their childhoods and the new world of their children; my wife and her brothers, learning to live between two worlds long before I came along. Before my journey, I'd known my wife's family and friends for a decade, but rarely had we really talked. After my journey, I will never again think they are just like us, like me.

It's hard not to see the story of my wife's family as an American triumph. So much has changed. What remains, though, is the taboo of men and women and marriage across the color line.

I've often thought one of the reasons blacks haven't melted into the American melting pot is because they've been unable to marry across the line, as have Italians and Irish and all the other once-despised immigrant groups. Blacks haven't been able to marry the boss's daughter and move into the house on the hill, which has had a very real impact on their wealth and opportunity. Remember, Berry Lawson began with the luck of birth and inheritance. But the marriage taboo also exacts a deeper price. It means that the lives of blacks and whites rarely cross in the intimate, human ways that make the burying of differences among people not just a noble social goal, but an emotional necessity. To this day, for instance, Aunt G—chatting from the recliner in her sitting room, with the TV ignored and glowing orange beside her—tells me she will not eat meals with white people. For years, they wouldn't eat with her, and now she will not eat with them.

Surprised, I say, "But you eat with me."

"Oh, that's different," Aunt G says pleasantly. "You're family."

My last visit with Aunt G . . .

The sitting room is a shrine of photographs—her sister, her brothers, daughter, grandchildren, great-grandchildren, nephews, a great-nephew. Every inch of wall is covered. People of all shapes and shades. From here, Aunt G holds court. As a young woman, she moved to Glasgow from Burkesville and married the whitest, richest black man she met. This made sense to her, a woman proud of her light skin and straight hair, a woman accustomed to being relatively well-to-do. She and Mr. Troop, a barber and business-man, had a daughter—beautiful Mackiva, with soft, pearly skin and flowing, wavy hair. Aunt G, who feared she simply couldn't care for a dark-skinned child, was elated.

Her daughter felt differently. 'The kids would call me a half-white, stringy-hair bitch," says Mackiva, who today is fifty-six. Mackiva, who was so light-skinned that when she rode the bus to college in Nashville she sat in the front with the white people, did a 180-degree turn on her mother's outlook. "I decided I'd never marry a bright-skinned man," she says. "My kids would never go through what I went through." And that's what Mackiva did: Her husband, Evans, is handsome and dark-skinned, as are their three grown sons, as are their grandchildren, who are Aunt G's great-grandchildren.

Aunt G turns to me. "Your children are white," she says rather abruptly, using her own either-or standard to describe my tan-skinned children. "So many whites have a horror of black babies. You didn't know what you'd have. How could you have coped if you'd had a black child?"

I can't help but smile. The query brings me full circle, because today Aunt G is babysitting her great-grandchildren, Brittany, age two, and Michael, six months old, who are on the floor before us. They are, in Aunt G's vocabulary, black children. "Aunt G," I say, "you were the woman who was terrified to have black ba-bies. You married a bright man. Then your daughter goes off and marries a dark man and has dark children, who then go off and have these dark grandchildren. Let me ask you, How do you cope?" Aunt G looks startled for a moment, and then she lets out that joyful little cackle that she mutes with a hand put discreetly to her mouth. "I got one as black as July jam and another with hair nappy as a sheep's back," she says, cackling freely now. "And I just love 'em better than anything! I just love 'em!"

And that, really, is the heart of the matter.

# MY DINNER WITH ALI

*Davis Miller*

I'd been waiting for years. When it finally happened, it wasn't what I'd expected; he's been fooling many of us for most of our lives.

For six months, several friends had been trying to connect me with him at his farm in Michigan. When I finally got to see him, it wasn't in Michigan and I didn't have an appointment. I simply drove past his mother's house in Louisville.

It was mid-afternoon on Good Friday, the first of April, two days before Resurrection Day. A block-long white Winnebago with Virginia plates was parked out front. Though he hadn't often been in town lately, I knew it was his vehicle.

I was sure it was him because I know his patterns and his style. Since 1962, when he has traveled unhurried in this country, he has preferred buses or recreational vehicles. And he owns a second farm in Virginia. The connections were obvious. Some people study faults in the earth's crust or the habits of storms or of galaxies, hoping to make some sense of the world and of their own lives. Others meditate on the life and work of one social movement or one man. Since I was ten years old, I have been a Muhammad Ali scholar.

I parked my car behind his Winnebago and grabbed a few old magazines and a special stack of papers I'd been storing under the front seat, waiting for the meeting with Ali I'd been certain would come. Like everyone else, I wondered in what shape I'd find The Champ. I'd heard all about his Parkinson's syndrome and had watched him stumble through the ropes when introduced at recent big fights. But when I thought of Ali, I remembered him as I'd seen him years before, when he was luminous.

I was in my early twenties, hoping to become a world champion kickboxer. And I was fortunate enough to get to spar with him. I later wrote a couple stories about the experience and had copies of those with me today, hoping he'd sign them.

Yes, in those days he had shone. There was an aura of light and confidence around him. He had told the world of his importance: "I am the center of the universe," he had said, and we almost believed him. But recent reports had Ali sounding like a turtle spilled on to his back, limbs pitiably thrashing air.

It was his brother Rahaman who opened the door. He saw the stack of papers and magazines under my arm, smiled an understanding smile, and said, "He's out in the Winnebago. Just knock on the door. He'll be happy to sign those for you."

Rahaman looked pretty much the way I remembered, a little like a black, aging Errol Flynn. There was no indication in his voice or on his face that I would find his brother less than healthy.

I crossed the yard, climbed the couple steps on the side of the Winnebago, and prepared to knock. Ali opened the door before I got the chance. He is, of course, a huge man. His presence filled the doorway. He had to lean under the frame to see me.

I felt no nervousness. Ali's face, in many ways, is as familiar to me as my father's. His skin remained unmarked, his countenance had nearly perfect symmetry. Yet something was different: Ali was no longer the world's prettiest man. This was only partly related to his illness; it was mostly because he was heavier than he needed to be. He remained handsome, but in the way of a youngish granddad who tells stories about how he could have been a movie star, if he'd wanted.

"Come on in," he said and waved me past. His voice had a gurgle to it, as if he needed to clear his throat. He offered a massive hand. His grip was not a grip at all—his touch was gentle, almost feminine. His palm was cool and uncalloused, his fingers were the long, tapered digits of a hypnotist, his knuckles large, slightly swollen and rough. They looked as if he had recently been punching the heavy bag.

He was dressed in white, all white: new leather tennis shoes, cotton socks, custom-tailored linen slacks, short-sleeved safari-style shirt crisp with starch. I told him I thought white was a better color for him than the black he often wore those days.

He motioned for me to sit, but didn't speak. His mouth was tense at the corners; it looked like a kid's who has been forced by a parent or teacher to keep it closed. He slowly lowered himself into a chair beside the window. I took a seat across from him and laid my magazines on the table between us. He immediately picked them up, produced a pen, and began signing. He asked, "What's your name?" without looking up and when I told him, he resumed writing. His eyes were not glazed as I'd read in newspaper accounts, but they looked tired. A wet cough rattled in his throat. His left hand had continuous tremors. In the silence around us, I felt a need to tell him some of the things I'd been wanting to say for decades.

"Champ, you changed my life," I said. It's true. "When I was a kid, I was messed up, couldn't even talk to people."

He raised his eyes from an old healthy image of himself on a magazine cover.

"You made me believe I could do anything," I said.

He was watching me while I talked, not judging, just watching. I picked up a magazine from the stack in front of him. "This is a story I wrote about the ways you've influenced my life."

"What's your name?" he asked again, this time looking right at me. I told him. He nodded. "I'll finish signin' these in a while," he said. He put his pen on the table. "Read me your story."

"You have a good face," he said when I was through. "I like your face."

He'd listened seriously as I'd read, laughing at funny lines and when I'd tried to imitate his voice. He had not been bored. It was more than I could have expected.

"You ever seen any magic?" he asked. "You like magic?"

"Not in years," I said.

He stood and walked to the back of his RV. He moved mechanically. It was my great-grandfather's walk. He motioned for me to follow. There was a sad yet lovely, noble, and intimate quality to his movements.

He did about ten tricks. The one that interested me the most required no props. It was a very simple deception. "Watch my feet," he said. He was standing maybe eight feet away, with his back to me and his arms perpendicular to his sides. Then he seemed to levitate about three inches off the floor. He turned to me and in his thick, slow voice said, "I'm a baadd niggah," and gave me the old easy Ali smile.

I laughed and asked him to do it again; it was a good one. I thought I might like to try it myself, just as twenty years earlier I had stood in front of the mirror in my dad's hallway for hours, pushing my worm of a left arm out at the reflection, wishing mightily that I could replicate Ali's cobra jab. And I had found an old laundry bag, filled it with socks and rags, and hung it from a ceiling beam in the basement. I pushed my left hand into that twenty-pound marshmallow two hundred, three hundred, five hundred times a day, concentrating on speed: dazzling, crackling speed, in pursuit of godly speed—zing, ting, ding went the punches on the bag—and I strove to make the three blows sound as one (like Ali's), strove to make my fists move more quickly than thought, as fast as ionized Minute Rice, and then I'd try to spring up on my toes, as I had watched Ali do: I would try to fly like Ali, bounding away from the bag and to my left.

After the levitation trick, Ali grabbed an empty plastic milk jug from beside a sink. He asked me to examine it. "What if I make this jug rise up from the sink this high and sit there? Will you believe?"

"I'm not much of a believer these days, Champ," I said.

"Watch," he said, pointing at the plastic container, and taking three steps back. I was trying to see both the milk jug and Ali. He waved his hands a couple times in front of his body, said, "Arise, ghost, arise," in a foggy-sounding voice. The plastic container did not move from the counter.

"April Fools'," said Ali. We both chuckled and he walked over and slipped his arm around my shoulders.

He autographed the stories and wrote a note on a page of my book-length manuscript I asked him to take a look at. "To Davis Miller, The Greatest Fan of All Times," he wrote, "From Muhammad Ali, King of Boxing."

I felt my stories were finally complete, now that he'd confirmed their existence. He handed me the magazines and asked me into his mother's house. We left the Winnebago. I unlocked my car and leaned across the front seat, carefully placing the magazines and manuscript on the passenger's side, not wanting to take a chance on damaging them or leaving them behind. Abruptly, there was a chirping, insect-sounding noise in my ear. I jumped back, swatted the air, turned around. It had been Ali's hand. He was standing right behind me, still the practical joker.

"How'd you do that?" I wanted to know. It was a question I'd find myself asking several times that day.

He didn't answer, but raised both fists to shoulder height and motioned me out into the yard. We walked about five paces, I put up my hands, and he tossed a slow jab at me. I blocked and countered with my own. Many fighters and ex-fighters throw punches at each other or at the air or at whatever happens to be around. It's the way we play. Ali must still toss a hundred lefts a day. He and I had both thrown our shots a full half-foot away from the other, but my adrenal gland was pumping at high gear from being around Ali and my jab had come out fast—it had made the air sing. He slid back a half-step and took a serious look at me. A couple kids were riding past on bikes; they recognized Ali and stopped.

"He doesn't understand I'm the greatest boxer of all times," he yelled to the kids. He pulled his watch from his arm, stuck it in his trousers pocket. He'd get down to business now. He danced to his left a little, loosening up his legs. A few minutes before, climbing down the steps of his RV, he'd moved so awkwardly he'd almost lost his balance. I'd wanted to give him a hand, but knew not to. I'd remembered seeing old Joe Louis "escorted" in

that fashion by lesser mortals, and I couldn't do that to Muhammad
Ali. But now that Ali was on his toes and boxing, he was moving
fairly fluidly.

He flung another jab in my direction, a second, a third. He
wasn't one-fifth as fast as he had been in 1975, when I'd sparred
with him, but his eyes were alert, shining like black electric marbles,
and he saw everything and was real relaxed. That's precisely why
old fighters keep making comebacks: We are more alive when
boxing than at almost any other time. The grass around us was
green and was getting high; it would soon need its first cutting. A
bluejay squawked from an oak to the left. Six robins roamed the
yard. I instinctively blocked all three of his blows, then immediately felt guilty about it, like being fourteen years old and knowing for the first time that you can beat your dad at table tennis. I
wished I could've stopped myself from slipping Ali's jabs, but I
couldn't. Reflexive training runs faster and deeper than thought.
I zipped a jab to his nose, one to his body, vaulted a straight right
to his chin, and was dead certain all three would have scored—
and scored clean. A couple cars stopped in front of the house. His
mom's was on a corner lot. Three more were parked on the side.

"Check out the left," a young-sounding voice said from somewhere. The owner of the voice was talking about my jab, not Ali's.

"He's in with the triple greatest of all times," Ali was shouting.
"Gowna let him tire himself out. He'll get tired soon."

I didn't, but pretended to, anyway. "You're right, Champ," I
told him, dropping my hands. "I'm thirty-five. Can't go like I
used to."

I held my right hand to my chest, acting out of breath. I looked
at Ali; his hand was in the exact same position. We were both
smiling, but he was sizing me up a little.

"He got scared," Ali shouted, conclusively. Onlookers laughed
from their bicycles and car windows. Some blew their horns; one
yelled, "Hey, Champ."

"Come on in the house," he said softly in my ear. We walked
toward the door, Ali in the lead, moving woodenly through new
grass, while all around us people rolled up car windows and started
their engines.

★ ★ ★

Ali's family easily accepted me. They were not surprised to have a visitor and handled me with ritualistic charm and grace. Rahaman told me to make myself at home, offered a root beer, went to get it. I took a seat on the sofa beside Ali's mother, Mrs. Odessa Clay. Mrs. Clay was in her early seventies, yet her face had few wrinkles. Short, her hair nearly as orange as a hazy Louisville sunset, she was freckled, fragile-looking, and pretty. Ali's face is shaped much like his mother's. When he was fighting she was quite heavy, but she had lost what looked to be about seventy-five pounds over the past ten years.

Mrs. Clay was watching Oprah Winfrey on TV. Ali had disappeared from the room and I was wondering where he had gone. Rahaman brought the drink, a paper napkin, and a coaster. Mrs. Clay patted me on the hand. "Don't worry," she said. "Ali hasn't left you. I'm sure he's just gone upstairs to say his prayers."

I hadn't realized that my anxiety was showing; Ali's mother had watched him bring home puppies many times during his forty-six years. Mrs. Clay spoke carefully, with a mother's sweet sadness about her. The dignified clip to her voice must once have been affected, but after cometing all over the globe with Ali, it now sounded genuinely British and Virginian in its inflections.

"Have you met Lonnie, Ali's new wife?" she asked. "He's known her since she was a baby. I'm so happy for him. She's my best friend's daughter; we used to all travel to his fights together. She's a smart girl, has a master's degree in business. She's so good to him, doesn't use him. He told me, 'Mom, Lonnie's better to me than all the other three put together.' She treats him so good. He needs somebody to take care of him."

Just then, Ali came back to the room, carrying himself high and with stately dignity, though his footing was unsteady. He fell deep into a chair on the other side of the room.

"You tired, baby?" Mrs. Clay asked.

"Tired, I'm always tired," he said, then rubbed his face a couple times and closed his eyes.

He must have felt me watching or was simply conscious of someone other than family being in the room. His eyes weren't closed ten seconds before he shook himself awake, balled his hands into fists, and started making typical Ali faces and noises at me—grimacing, growling, other playful cartoon kid stuff. After a few seconds he asked, "Y-y-you okay?" He was so difficult to understand that I didn't so much hear him as I conjectured what he must have been saying. "Y-y-you need anything? They takin' care of you?" I assured him I was fine.

He made a loud clucking noise by pressing his tongue against the roof of his mouth and popping it forward. Rahaman came quickly from the kitchen. Ali motioned him close and whispered in his ear. Rahaman went back to the kitchen. Ali turned to me. "Come sit beside me," he said, patting a bar stool to his right. He waited for me to take my place then said, "You had any dinner? Sit and eat with me."

"Can I use the phone? I need to call home and let my wife know."

"You got kids?" he asked. I told him I had two. He asked how old. I told him the ages.

"They know me?" he asked.

"Even the two-year-old. He throws punches at the TV whenever I play your fights."

He nodded, satisfied. "Bring 'em over Sunday," he said, matter-of-factly. "I'll do my magic for 'em. Here's my mother's number. Be sure to phone first."

I called Lyn and told her where I was and what I was doing. She didn't seem surprised. She asked me to pick up a gallon of milk on the way home. I knew she was excited for me but we had a lot of history, some of it rough, and she wouldn't show emotion in her voice simply because I was hanging out with my childhood idol. In September 1977, when Lyn and I were in college, we skipped class, took most of the money from our bank accounts, drove from North Carolina all the way to New York, and attended the Ali–Earnie Shavers bout at Madison Square Garden. For the rest of the year, we had to live off what little money I was able to make posing for anatomy drawings for art students and getting 5 cents each for soda bottles we picked up beside highways on Saturday and Sunday afternoons. But I bet she'd say it was worth it to have seen Ali in what we knew would be one of his last fights.

Now, Rahaman brought two large bowls of chili and two enormous slices of white bread from the kitchen. Ali and I sat at our chairs and ate. He put his face down close to the bowl and the food was gone. Three minutes tops. As I continued to eat, he spoke easily to me.

"Do you know how many people in the world would like to have the opportunity you're getting, how many would like to come into my house and spend the day with me?" he said. "Haven't fought in seven years and still get over four hundred letters a week."

I asked how people got his address.

"I don't know," he answered. "Sometimes they come addressed 'Muhammad Ali, Los Angeles, California, USA.' Don't have a house in L.A. no more, but the letters still get to me.

"I want to get me a place, a coffee shop, where I can give away free coffee and doughnuts and people can just sit around and talk, people of all races, and I can go and talk to people. Have some of my old robes and trunks and gloves around, show old fight films, call it 'Ali's Place.'"

"I'd call it 'Ali's,'" I said, not believing there would or ever could be such a place but enjoying sharing his dream with him. "Just 'Ali's,' that's enough. People would know what it was."

"'Ali's'?" he repeated, and his eyes focused inward, visualizing the dream.

"Do you have copies of your fights?" I asked. He shook his head no. "Well, look," I said, "why don't I go to a video place and see if I can rent some and we can watch them tonight. Would you like that? You want to ride with me?"

"I'll drive," he said.

There was a rubber monster mask in the Winnebago and I wore it on my hand on the way to the video shop, pressing it against the window at stoplights. A couple times people in cars saw the mask, then recognized Ali. Ali wears glasses when he reads and when he drives. When he saw someone looking at him, he carefully removed his glasses, placed them in his lap, made his hands into fists, and put them beside his head.

Ali was the worst driver I'd ever ridden with—other than my alcoholic grandfather near the end of his life. He careened from lane to lane, sometimes riding down the middle of the highway, and he regularly switched lanes without looking or giving turn signals. I balled my fists in my lap and pretended to be relaxed. A group of teenage boys became infuriated when he pulled in front of their old beat-up Firebird and cut them off. Three of them leaned out the windows, shooting him the finger. Ali shot it back.

At the movie store, we rented a tape of his fights and interviews called *Ali: Skill, Brains and Guts,* produced and directed by Jimmy Jacobs, the handball champion, fight historian, and Mike Tyson's comanager. Jacobs had recently died of a degenerative illness. Ali hadn't known of Jacobs' death until I told him. "He was a good man," Ali said. His voice had that same quality that an older person's takes on who daily reads obituaries.

I stopped by my car again on the way into Mrs. Clay's house. There was one more picture I hoped Ali would sign, but earlier I'd felt I might be imposing on him. It was a classic head-shot in a beautiful out-of-print biography by Wilfrid Sheed that featured hundreds of wonderfully reproduced color plates. I grabbed the book from the car and followed Ali into the house.

When we were seated, I handed him the book and he signed the picture on the title page. I was about to ask if he'd mind autographing the photo I especially wanted, but he turned to page two, signed that picture, then the next page and the next. He continued to sign for probably forty-five minutes, writing notes about opponents, wives, parents, Elijah Muhammad, Howard Cosell, then passed the book to his mother and brother to sign a family portrait. Ali autographed nearly every photo in the book, pointing out special comments as he signed.

"Never done this before," he said. "Usually sign one or two."

He closed the book, looked at me dead level, and held it out at arm's length with both hands. "I'm givin' you somethin' very valuable," he said, handing me the biography as if deeding me the book of life.

I stared at the book in my open palms and felt that I should say something, that I should thank him in some way. I carefully placed it on a table, shook my head slightly, and cleared my throat, but found no words.

Excusing myself to the bathroom, I locked the door behind me. A pair of Ali's huge black dress shoes was beside the toilet. The toe of one had been crushed, the other was lying on its side. When I unlocked the door to leave, it wouldn't budge. I couldn't even turn the handle. I knocked, then again. There was laughter from the other room. I yanked fairly hard on the door a couple times. Nothing.

Finally it easily opened. I caught a glimpse of Ali bounding into a side room to the right, laughing and high-stepping like some oversized, out-of-shape, Nubian leprechaun. I peeked around the corner into the room. He was standing with his back flat against the wall. He saw me, jumped from the room, and began tickling me. Next thing I knew, he had me on the floor, balled-up in a fetal position, tears flowing down both sides of my face, laughing. Then he stopped tickling and I climbed to my feet.

Everybody kept laughing. Mrs. Clay's face was round and wide with laughter. She looked like the mom of a leprechaun. "What'd you think happened to the door?" Rahaman asked. I told him I figured it was Ali. "Then why you turnin' red?" he wanted to know.

"It's not every day," I said, "that I go to Muhammad Ali's, he locks me in the bathroom, then tickles me into submission." Everyone laughed again.

Suddenly I recognized the obvious, that all day I'd been acting like a teenage admirer again. And that Muhammad Ali had not lost perhaps his most significant talent—the ability to transport people past thoughts and words to a world of feeling and play. Being around Ali, or watching him perform on TV, has always made me feel genuinely childlike. I looked at his family: They were beaming. Ali still flipped their switches, too.

We finally slipped the Ali tape into the VCR. Rahaman brought everyone another root beer and we settled back to watch, Rahaman to my left, Ali beside me on the right, Mrs. Clay beside Ali. The family's reactions to the tape were not dissimilar to those you or I would have looking at old home movies or high school annuals. Everyone sighed and their mouths arced at tender angles. "Oh, look at Bundini," Mrs. Clay said and, "Hey, there's Otis," Rahaman offered. Whenever there was film of Ali reciting verse, we'd all recite with him. "Those were the days," Rahaman said several times, to which Mrs. Clay wistfully responded, "Yes, yes, they were." After a half an hour or so, she left the room. Rahaman continued to watch the tape with us for a while but then he left, too.

Then: It was just Ali and me. On the TV, it was 1963 and he was framed on the left by Jim Jacobs and on the right by Drew "Bundini" Brown. "They both dead now," he said, acute aware-ness of his own mortality in his tone.

For a time he continued to smile at the old Ali on the screen, but eventually he lost interest in peering at distant mountains of his youth. "Did my mom go upstairs? Do you know?" he asked.

"Yeah, I think she's probably asleep."

He nodded, stood, and left the room. When he came back, he was moving heavily. His shoulder hit the frame of the doorway to the kitchen. He went in and brought out two fistfuls of cook-ies. Crumbs were all over his mouth. He sat beside me on the sofa. Our knees were touching. Usually when a man gets this close I pull away. He offered me a couple cookies. When he was through eating, he yawned a giant's yawn, closed his eyes, and seemed to go dead asleep.

"Champ, you want me to leave?" I said. "Am I keeping you up?"

He slowly opened his eyes and was back to our side of the Great Mystery. The pores on his face suddenly looked huge, his coun-tenance elongated, distorted, like someone's in an El Greco. He rubbed his face the way I rub mine when I haven't shaved in a week.

"No, stay," he said. His voice was very gentle.

"You'd let me know if I was staying too late?"

"I go to bed at eleven," he said.

With the volume turned this low on the TV, you could hear the videotape's steady whir. "Can I ask a serious question?" I said. He nodded okay.

"You're still a great man, Champ, I see that. But a lot of people think your mind is fried. Does that bother you?"

He didn't hesitate before answering. "No, there are ignorant people everywhere," he said. "Even educated people can be ignorant."

"Does it bother you that you're a great man not being allowed to be great?"

"Wh-wh-whatcha mean, 'not allowed to be great'?" he said, his voice barely finding its way from his body.

"I mean . . . let me think about what I mean. . . . I mean the things you seem to care most about, the things the rest of us think of as being Muhammad Ali, those are exactly the things that have been taken from you. It just doesn't seem fair."

"You don't question God," he said.

"Okay, I respect that, but . . . Aw, man, I don't have any business talking to you about this."

"No, no, go on," he said.

"It just bothers me," I said. I was thinking about the obvious ironies, thinking about Ali's continuing to invent, and be invented by, his own mythology. About how he used to talk more easily, maybe better, than anybody else in the world; how he still seems to think with speed and dazzle, but it takes serious effort for him to communicate even with people close to him. About how he may have been the world's best athlete—when walking, he had the grace of a cat turning a corner; now, at night, he stumbles around the house. About how it's his left hand, the most visible phenomenon of his boxing greatness, the hand that dominated more than 150 sanctioned fights and countless sparring sessions, it's his left hand, not the right, that shakes almost continuously. And I was thinking how his major source of pride, his "prettiness," remains more or less intact. If Ali lost thirty pounds, he would still look classically Greek. Despite not expecting to encounter the miraculous any more than any other agnostic, I was sort of spooked by the seeming precision with which things have been excised from Ali's life.

"I know why this has happened," Ali said. "God is showing me, and showing you"—he pointed his trembling index finger at me and widened his eyes—"that I'm just a man, just like everybody else."

We sat a long quiet time then, and watched Ali's flickering image on the television screen. It was now 1971 and there was footage of him training for the first Joe Frazier fight. Our Most Public Figure was then the World's Most Beautiful Man and the Greatest Athlete of All Time, his tight copper-colored skin glowing under the fluorescents, secret rhythms springing in loose firmness from his fingertips.

"Champ, I think it's time for me to go," I said and made an effort to stand.

"No, stay. You my man," he says and pats my leg. I take his accolade as among the greatest compliments of my life.

"I'll tell you a secret," he says, and leans close. "I'm gowna make a comeback."

"What?" I think he's joking, hope he is, but something in the way he's speaking makes me uncertain. "You're not serious."

And suddenly there is musk in his voice. "I'm gowna make a comeback," he repeats louder, more firmly.

"Are you serious?"

"The timing is perfect. They'd think it was a miracle, wouldn't they?" He's speaking in a distinct, familiar voice; he's easy to understand. It's almost the voice I remember from when I first met him in 1975, the one that seemed to come roiling up from down in his belly. In short, Ali sounds like Ali.

"Wouldn't they?" he asks again.

"It would be a miracle," I say.

"Nobody'll take me serious. But then I'll get my weight down to two-fifteen and have an exhibition at Yankee Stadium or someplace. Then they'll believe. I'll fight for the title. It'll be bigger than the Resurrection." He stands and walks to the center of the room.

"It'd be good for you to get your weight down," I say.

"Watch this," he says and dances to his left. He's watching himself in the mirror above the TV. His clean white shoes bound smoothly around the room; I marvel at how easily he moves. His white clothing accentuates his movements in the dark room. The white appears to make him glow. He starts throwing punches, not the kind he'd tossed at me earlier, but now really letting them zing. I'd thought that what he'd thrown in the yard was indicative of what he had left. But what he'd done was allow me to play; he'd wanted me to enjoy myself.

"Look at the TV. That's 1971 and I'm just as fast now." It's true, the old man can still do it. He can still make fire appear in the air. One second, two seconds—ten punches flash in the night. He looks faster standing in front of me than do the ghostlike Ali images on the screen. God, I wish I had a video camera to tape this. Nobody would believe me.

"And I'll be even faster when I get my weight down."

"You know more now, too," I find myself admitting. Jesus, what am I saying? And why am I saying this?

"Do you believe?" he asks.

"Well . . . ," I say. The Parkinson's is affecting his sanity. Look at the gray shining in his hair.

And Ali throws another three dozen blows at the gods of mortality—he springs a triple hook off of a jab, drops straight right leads in multiples, explodes into a blur of uppercuts, and the air pops, and his fists and feet whir. This is his best work. His highest art. When Ali was fighting, he typically held back a little; this is the stuff he seldom chose, or had, to use against opponents.

"Do you believe?" he asks, breathing hard, but not much harder than I would if I'd thrown the number of punches he's just thrown.

"They wouldn't let you, even if you could do it," I'm thinking. "There's so much concern everywhere for your health. Everybody thinks they see old Mr. Thanatos calling you."

"Do you believe?" he asks again.

"I believe," I hear myself say.

He stops dancing and points a magician's finger at me. Then I get the look, the smile, that has closed one hundred thousand interviews. "April Fools'," he says and sits down hard beside me again.

We sit in silence for several minutes. I look at my watch. It's eleven-eighteen. I hadn't realized it was that late. I'd told Lyn I'd be in by eight.

"Champ, I better go home. I have a wife and kids waiting."

"Okay," he says almost inaudibly and yawns the sort of long uncovered yawn people usually do among family.

He's bone-tired, I'm tired, too, but I want to leave him by saying something that will mean something to him, something that will set me apart from the two billion other people he's met, that will imprint me indelibly in his memory and will make the kind of impact on his life he has made on mine. I want to say the words that will cure his Parkinson's.

Instead I say, "We'll see you Easter, Champ."

He coughs and gives me his hand. "Be cool and look out for the ladies." His words are so volumeless and full of fluid that I don't realize what he's said until I'm halfway out the door.

I don't recall picking up the book he signed, but I must have; it's sitting beside my typewriter now. I can't remember walking across his mom's yard and don't remember starting the car.

I didn't forget Lyn's gallon of milk. The doors to the grocery store whooshed closed behind me. For this time of night, there were quite a few customers in the store. They seemed to move more as floating shadows than as people. An old feeling came across me that I immediately recognized. The sensation was much like going out into the day-to-day world shortly after making love for the first-ever time. It was that same sense of having landed in a lesser reality. And of having a secret that the rest of the world can't see. I'd have to wake Lyn and share the memory of this feeling with her.

I reached to grab a jug of milk and caught a reflection of myself in the chrome at the dairy counter. There was a half-smile on my face and I hadn't realized it.

# RESURRECTING THE CHAMP

*J. R. Moehringer*

## 1.

I'm sitting in a hotel room in Columbus, Ohio, waiting for a call from a man who doesn't trust me, hoping he'll have answers about a man I don't trust, which may clear the name of a man no one gives a damn about. To distract myself from this uneasy vigil—and from the phone that never rings, and from the icy rain that never stops pelting the window—I light a cigar and open a forty-year-old newspaper. "Greatest puncher they ever seen," the paper says in praise of Bob Satterfield, a ferocious fighter of the 1940s and 1950s. "The man of hope—and the man who crushed hope like a cookie in his fist." Once again, I'm reminded of Satterfield's sorry luck, which dogged him throughout his life, as I'm dogging him now. I've searched high and low for Satterfield. I've searched the sour-smelling homeless shelters of Santa Ana. I've searched the ancient and venerable boxing gyms of Chicago. I've searched the eerily clear memory of one New York City fighter who touched Satterfield's push-button chin in 1946 and never forgot the panic on Satterfield's face as he fell. I've searched cemeteries, morgues, churches, museums, skims, jails, courts, libraries, police blotters, scrapbooks, phone books, and record books. Now I'm searching this dreary, sleet-bound Midwestern city, where all the streets look like melting Edward Hopper paintings and the sky like a storm-whipped sea. Maybe it's fatigue, maybe it's caffeine, maybe it's the fog rolling in behind the rain, but I feel as though Satterfield has become my own 180-pound Moby Dick. Like Ahab's obsession, he casts a harsh light on his pursuer. Stalking him from town to town and decade to decade, I've learned almost everything there is to know about him, along with valuable lessons about boxing, courage, and the eternal tension between fathers and sons. But I've learned more than I bargained for about myself, and for that I owe him a debt. I can't repay the debt unless the phone rings.

## 2.

We met because a coworker got the urge to clean. It was early January 1996. The cop reporter who sits near me at the Orange County edition of the *Times* was straightening her desk when she came across an old tip, something about a once-famous boxer sleeping on park benches in Santa Ana. Passing the tip along, she deflected my thank-you with an off-the-cuff caveat, "He might be dead."

The tipster had no trouble recalling the boxer when I phoned. "Yeah, Bob Satterfield," he said. "A contender from the 1950s. I used to watch him when I watched the fights on TV." Forty years later, though, Satterfield wasn't contending anymore, except with cops. When last seen, the old boxer was wandering the streets, swilling whiskey and calling himself Champ. "Just a guy that lived too long," the tipster said, though he feared this compassion might be outdated. There was a better-than-ever chance, he figured, that Satterfield was dead.

If Satterfield was alive, finding him would require a slow tour of Santa Ana's seediest precincts. I began with one of the city's largest men's shelters. Several promising candidates lingered inside the shelter and out, but none matched my sketchy notion of an elderly black man with a boxer's sturdy body. From there I drove to 1st Street, a wide boulevard of taco stands and bus stops that serves as a promenade for homeless men. Again, nothing. Next

I cruised the alleys and side streets of nearby McFadden Avenue, where gutters still glistened with tinsel from discarded Christmas trees. On a particularly lively corner I parked the car and walked, stopping passersby and asking where I might find the fighter from the 1950s, the one who called himself Champ, the one who gave the cops all they could handle. No one knew, no one cared, and I was ready to knock off when I heard someone cry out, "Hiya, Champ!"

Wheeling around, I saw an elderly black man pushing a grocery cart full of junk down the middle of the street. Rancid clothes, vacant stare, sooty face, he looked like every other homeless man in America. Then I noticed his hands, the largest hands I'd ever seen, each one so heavy and unwieldy that he held it at his side like a bowling ball. Hands such as these were not just unusual, they were natural phenomena. Looking closer, however, I saw that they complemented the meaty plumpness of his shoulders and the brick-wall thickness of his chest, exceptional attributes in a man who couldn't be getting three squares a day. To maintain such a build on table scraps and handouts, he must have been immense back when.

More than his physique, what distinguished him was a faint suggestion of style. Despite the cast-off clothes, despite the caked-on dirt, there was a vague sense that he clung to some vestigial pride in his appearance. Under his grimy ski parka he wore an almost professorial hound's-tooth vest. Atop his crown of graying hair was a rakish brown hat with a pigeon feather tucked jauntily in its brim.

His skin was a rich cigar color and smooth for an ex-boxer's, except for one bright scar between his eyebrows that resembled a character in the Chinese alphabet. Beneath a craggy five-o'clock shadow, his face was pleasant: Dark eyes and high cheekbones sat astride a strong, well-formed nose, and each feature followed the lead of his firm, squared-off chin. He was someone's heartthrob once. His teeth, however, were long gone, save for some stubborn spikes along the mandible.

I smiled and strolled toward him.

"Hey, Champ," I said.

"Heyyy, Champ," he said, looking up and smiling as though we were old friends. I half expected him to hug me.

"You're Bob Satterfield, aren't you?" I said.

"Battlin' Bob Satterfield!" he said, delighted at being recognized. "I'm the Champ, I fought 'em all, Ezzard Charles, Floyd Patterson—"

I told him I was a reporter from the *Los Angeles Times,* that I wanted to write a story about his life.

"How old are you?" I asked.

"I count my age as sixty-six," he said. "But *The Ring Record Book,* they say seventy-two."

"Did you ever fight for the title?"

"They just didn't give me the break to fight for the title," he said woefully. "If they'd given me the break, I believe I'd be the champ."

"Why didn't they give you the break?"

"You got to be in the right clique," he said, "to get the right fight at the right time."

His voice was weak and raspy, no more than a child's whisper, his words filled with the blurred vowels and squishy consonants of someone rendered senseless any number of times by liquor and fists. He stuttered slightly, humming his "m," gargling his "l," tripping over his longer sentences. By contrast, his eyes and memories were clear. When I asked about his biggest fights, he rattled them off one by one, naming every opponent, every date, every arena. He groaned at the memory of all those beatings, but it was a proud noise, to let me know he'd held his own with giants. He'd even broken the nose of Rocky Marciano, the only undefeated heavyweight champion in history. "He was strooong, I want to tell you," Champ said, chuckling immodestly.

It happened during a sparring session, Champ said, demonstrating how he moved in close, slipping an uppercut under Marciano's left. Marciano shivered, staggered back, and Champ pressed his advantage with another uppercut. Then another. And another. Blood flowed.

"I busted his nose!" Champ shouted, staring at the sidewalk where Marciano lay, forever vanquished. "They rushed in and called off the fight and took Rock away!"

Now he was off to get some free chow at a nearby community center. "Would you care for some?" he asked, and I couldn't decide which was more touching, his largesse or his mannerly diction.

## 3.

"I was born Tommy Harrison," he said, twirling a chicken leg in his toothless mouth. "That's what you call my legal name. But I fought as Bob Satterfield." His handlers, he explained, didn't want him confused with another fighter, Tommy "Hurricane" Jackson, so they gave him an alias. I asked how they chose Bob Satterfield and he shrugged.

As a boy in and around Chicago, he built his shoulders by lifting ice blocks, a job that paid pennies at first but huge dividends years later in the ring. At fifteen, he ran away from home, fleeing a father who routinely whipped him. For months he rode the rails as a hobo, then joined the Army. Too young to enlist, he pretended to be his older brother, George, paying a prostitute to pose as his mother at the induction center.

He learned to box in the Army as a way of eating better and avoiding strenuous duty. Faced with older and tougher opponents, he developed a slithery, punch-and-move style, which must have impressed Marciano, who was collecting talented young fighters to help him prepare for a title shot against Jersey Joe Walcott. Upon his discharge, Champ became chief sparring partner to the man who would soon become the Zeus of modern boxing. Flicking his big fists in the air, each one glimmering with chicken grease, Champ again re-created the sequence of punches that led to Marciano's broken nose, and we laughed about the blood, all that blood.

When he left Marciano's camp and struck out on his own, Champ won a few fights, and suddenly the world treated him like a spoiled prince. Women succumbed, celebrities vied to sit at his side. The mountaintop was within view. "I never really dreamed of being champ," he said, "but as I would go through life, I would think, if I ever get a chance at the title, I'm going to win that fight!"

Instead, he lost. It was February 1953. Ezzard Charles, the formidable ex-champion, was trying to mount a comeback. Champ was trying to become the nation's top-ranked contender. They met in Detroit before a fair-size crowd, and Champ proved himself game in the early going. But after eight rounds, his eye swollen shut and his mouth spurting blood, he crumbled under Charles's superior boxing skills. The fateful punch was a slow-motion memory four decades later. Its force was so great that Champ bit clean through his mouthpiece. At the bell, he managed to reach his corner. But when the ninth started, he couldn't stand.

Nothing would ever be the same. A procession of bums and semi-bums made him look silly. Floyd Patterson dismantled him in one round. One day he was invincible, the next he was retired.

As with so many fighters, he'd saved nothing. He got $34,000 for the Charles fight, a handsome sum for the 1950s, but he frittered it on good times and "tutti-frutti" Cadillacs. With no money and few prospects, he drifted to California, where he met a woman, raised a family, and hoped for the best. The worst came instead. He broke his ankle on a construction job and didn't rest long enough for it to heal. The injury kept him from working steadily. Then, the punch he never saw coming. His son was killed.

"My son," Champ said, his voice darkening. "He was my heart."

"Little Champ" fell in with the wrong people. An angry teenager, he got on somebody's bad side, and one night he walked into an ambush. "My heart felt sad and broke," Champ said. "But I figured this happened because he was so hotheaded."

Racked with pain, Champ left the boy's mother, who still lived in the house they once shared, not far from where we sat. "Sometimes I go see her," he said. "It's kind of hard, but somehow I make it."

Park benches were his beds, though sometimes he slept at the shelter and sometimes in the backseat of a periwinkle and navy-blue Cadillac he bought with his last bit of money. He missed the good life but not the riches, the fame, or the women. He missed knowing that he was the boss, his body the servant. "The hard work," he whispered. "Sparring with the bags, skipping rope.

Every night after a workout we'd go for a big steak and a half a can of beer. Aaah."

Finishing his lunch, Champ wrapped the leftovers in a napkin and carefully stowed them in a secret compartment of his grocery cart. We shook hands, mine like an infant's in his. When we unclasped, he looked at the five-dollar bill I'd slipped him.

"Heyyy," he said soulfully. "Thanks, amigo. All right, thank you."

My car was down the block. When I reached it, I turned to look over my shoulder. Champ was still waving his massive right hand, still groping for words. "Thank you, Champ!" he called. "All right? Thank you!"

### 4.

Like Melville's ocean, or Twain's Mississippi, boxing calls to a young man. Its victims are not only those who forfeit their wits and dive into the ring. The sport seduces writers, too, dragging them down with its powerful undertow of testosterone. Many die a hideous literary death, drowning in their own hyperbole. Only a few—Ernest Hemingway, Jimmy Cannon, A. J. Liebling—cross to safety. Awash in all that blood, they become more buoyant.

For most Americans, however, boxing makes no sense. The sport that once defined the nation now seems hopelessly archaic, like jousting or pistols at six paces. The uninitiated, the cultivated, the educated don't accept that boxing has existed since pre-Hellenic Greece, and possibly since the time of the pharaohs, because it concedes one musky truth about masculinity: Hitting a man is sometimes the most satisfying response to *being* a man. Disturbing, maybe, but there it is.

Just the sight of two fighters belting each other around the ring triggers a soothing response, a womblike reassurance that everything is less complicated than we've been led to believe. From brutality, clarity. As with the first taste of cold beer on a warm day, the first kiss of love in the dark, the first meaningful victory over an evenly matched foe, the brain's simplest part is appeased. Colors become brighter, shapes grow deeper, the world slides into smoother focus. And focus was what I craved the day I went searching for Champ. Focus was what made a cop reporter's moth-eaten tip look to me like the Hope diamond. Focus was what I feared I'd lost on the job.

As a newspaper writer, you spend much of your time walking up dirty steps to talk to dirty people about dirty things. Then, once in a great while, you meet an antidote to all that dirt. Champ wasn't the cleanest of men—he may have been the dirtiest man I ever met—but he was pure of heart. He wasn't the first homeless heavyweight either, not by a long shot. Another boxer lands on Skid Row every day, bug-eyed and scrambled. But none has a résumé to compare with Champ's, or a memory. He offered a return to the unalloyed joy of daily journalism, not to mention the winning ticket in the Literary Lottery. He was that rarest of rare birds, a people-watcher's version of the condor: *Pugilisticum luciditas*. He was noble. He was innocent. He was all mine.

I phoned boxing experts throughout the nation. To my astonishment, they not only remembered Champ, they worshiped him. "Hardest hitter who ever lived." "Dynamite puncher." "One of the greatest punchers of all time." Boxing people love to exaggerate, but there was a persuasive sameness to their praise. Bob Satterfield was a beast who slouched toward every opponent with murder in his eye. He could have, should have, would have been champion, except for one tiny problem. He couldn't take a punch.

"He was a bomber," said boxing historian Burt Sugar. "But he had a chin. If he didn't take you out with the first punch, he was out with the second."

Every fighter, being human, has one glaring weakness. For some, it's a faint heart. For others, a lack of discipline. Satterfield's shortcoming was more comic, therefore more melodramatic. Nobody dished it out better, but few were less able to take it. He knocked out seven of his first twelve opponents in the first round, a terrifying boxing blitzkrieg. But over the course of his twelve-year professional career he suffered many first-round knockouts himself. The skinny on Satterfield spliced together a common male fantasy with the most common male fear: Loaded with raw talent, he was doomed to fail because of one factory-installed flaw.

Rob Mainwaring, a researcher at boxing's publication of record, *The Ring* magazine, faxed me a fat Satterfield file, rife with vivid accounts of his fragility and prowess. Three times, Satterfield destroyed all comers and put himself in line for a title shot. But each time, before the big fight could be set, Satterfield fell at the feet of some nobody. In May 1954, for instance, Satterfield tangled with an outsized Cuban fighter named Julio Mederos, banging him with five fast blows in the second round. When Mederos came to, he told a translator: "Nobody ever hit me that hard before. I didn't know any man could hit that hard." Satterfield appeared unstoppable. Six months later, however, he was stopped by an also-ran named Marty Marshall, who found Satterfield's flukish chin before some fans could find their seats.

Viewed as a literary artifact, the Satterfield file was a lovely sampler of overwrought prose. "The Chicago sleep-inducer," one fight writer called him. "Embalming fluid in either hand," said another, Then, in the next breath, came the qualifiers: "Boxing's Humpty-Dumpty." "A chin of Waterford." "Chill-or-be-chilled." It was a prankish God who connected that dainty jaw and that sledgehammer arm to one man's body, and it was the same almighty jokester who put those Hemingway wannabes in charge of chronicling his rise and fall.

Mainwaring faxed me several photos of Satterfield and one of a wife named Iona, whom he divorced in 1952. The library at the *Times,* meanwhile, unearthed still more Satterfield clippings, including a brief 1994 profile by *Orange County Register* columnist Bill Johnson. ("Bob Satterfield, one of the top six heavyweight fighters in the world from 1950 to 1956, today is homeless, living in old, abandoned houses in Santa Ana.") From Chicago newspapers, the library culled glowing mentions of Satterfield, including one describing his nightmarish blood bath with middleweight Jake LaMotta, the fighter portrayed by Robert De Niro in Martin Scorsese's 1980 *Raging Bull.* Midway through the film, Satterfield's name fills the screen—then, as the name dissolves, LaMotta–De Niro smashes him in the face.

## 5.

"Mr. LaMotta," I said. "I'm writing a story about an old opponent of yours, Bob Satterfield."

"Hold on," he said. "I'm eating a meatball."

I'd phoned the former champion in Manhattan, where he was busy launching his new spaghetti sauce company, LaMotta's Tomatta. His voice was De Niro's from the film—nasal, pugnacious, phlegm-filled, a cross between Don Corleone and Donald Duck. At last he swallowed and said, "Bob Satterfield was one of the hardest punchers who ever lived."

Reluctantly, I told LaMotta the bad news. Satterfield was sleeping on park benches in Santa Ana.

"You sure it's him?" he said. "I heard he was dead."

"No," I assured him, "I just talked to him yesterday."

"Awww," he said, "that's a shame. He put three bumps on my head before I knocked him out. Besides Bob Satterfield, the only ones who ever hurt me were my ex-wives."

LaMotta began to reminisce about his old nemesis, a man so dangerous that no one dared spar with him. "He hit me his best punch," he said wistfully. "He hit me with plenty of lefts. But I was coming into him. He hit me with a right hand to the top of the head. I thought I'd fall down. Then he did it again. He did it three times, and when nothing happened he sort of gave up. I knocked him on his face. Flat on his face."

LaMotta asked me to say hello to Satterfield, and I promised that I would. "There but for the grace of God go I," he said. "God dealt me a different hand."

I visited Champ that day to deliver LaMotta's best wishes. I visited him many times in the days ahead, always with some specific purpose in mind. Flesh out the details of his life. Ask a few more questions. See how he was faring. Each time the drill was the same. I'd give him five dollars and he'd give me a big tumble, making such a fuss over me that I'd turn red.

"A boxer, like a writer, must stand alone," Liebling wrote, inadvertently explaining the kinship between Champ and me. To my mind, anyone who flattened Rocky Marciano and put three bumps on Jake LaMotta's melon ranked between astronaut and Lakota warrior on the delicately calibrated scale of bad asses, and thus deserved at least a Sunday profile. To Champ's mind, anyone willing to listen to forty-year-old boxing stories could only be a bored writer or a benevolent Martian. Still, there was something more basic about our connection. As a man, I couldn't get enough of his hyper-virile aura. As a homeless man, he couldn't get enough of my patient silence. Between his prattling and my scribbling, we became something like fast friends.

Our mutual admiration caused me to sputter with indignation when my editors asked what hard evidence I had that Champ was Satterfield. What more hard evidence do you need, I asked, besides Champ's being the man in these old newspaper photos— allowing for forty years of high living and several hundred quarts of cheap whiskey? Better yet, how about Champ's being able to name every opponent, and the dates on which he fought them— allowing for an old man's occasional memory lapses?

If the evidence of our senses won't suffice, I continued, let's use *common* sense: Champ is telling the truth because he has no reason to lie. For being Bob Satterfield, he gets no money, no glory, no extra chicken legs at senior centers and soup kitchens. Pretending to be a fighter forgotten by all but a few boxing experts? Pretending in such convincing fashion? He'd have to be crazy. Or brilliant. And I could say with some confidence that he was neither. Even so, the editors said, get something harder.

## 6.

Champ's old house in Santa Ana sat along a bleak cul-de-sac, its yard bursting with cowlick-shaped weeds, its walls shedding great slices of paint. It looked like a guard shack at the border crossing of some desolate and impoverished nation.

An unhappy young woman scowled when I asked to see Champ's ex-girlfriend. "Wait here," she said.

Minutes later, she returned with a message: Go away. Champ's
things have been burned, and no one has any interest in talking to
you.

Next I tried the Orange County courthouse, hoping arrest
records would authenticate Champ. Sure enough, plenty of data
existed in the courthouse ledger. Finding various minor offenses
under Thomas Harrison, alias Bob Satterfield, I rejoiced. Here was
proof, stamped with the official seal of California, that Champ was
Satterfield. A scoundrel, yes, but a truthful one.

Then I saw something bad. Two felony arrests, one in 1969,
one in 1975. Champ had been candid about his misdemeanors,
but he had never mentioned these more serious offenses. "Oh,
God," I said, scanning the arrest warrant: "Thomas Harrison, also
known as Bob Satterfield . . . lewd and lascivious act upon and
with the body . . . child under the age of 14 years." Champ molesting his girlfriend's ten-year-old daughter. Champ punching the
little girl's aunt in the mouth.

"Did you know [Champ] to be a professional prizefighter?" a
prosecutor asked the aunt during a hearing.

"Yes," she said.

"Did you know that he was once a contender for the heavyweight boxing championship of the world?"

Before she could answer, Champ's lawyer raised an objection,
which the judge sustained.

Champ pleaded guilty to assaulting the aunt—for which he
received probation—and the molestation charge was dropped.

Then, six years later, it happened again. Same girlfriend, different daughter.

"Thomas Harrison, also known as Tommy Satterfield, also
known as Bobby Satterfield . . . lewd and lascivious act."

Again, Champ avowed his innocence, but a jury found him guilty.
In May 1976, Champ wrote the judge from jail, begging for a sec-
ond chance. He signed the letter, "Yours truly, Thomas Harrison.
Also Known as Bob Satterfield, Ex-Boxer, 5th in the World."

"This is how it happens," I thought. "This is how a newspaper
writer learns to hate the world." I could feel the cynicism setting

inside me like concrete. My reprieve from the dirtiness of every-day journalism had turned into a reaffirmation of everything I loathed and feared. My noble warrior, my male idol, my friend, was a walking, talking horror show, a homeless Humbert Humbert.

7.

He greeted me with his typical good cheer, doffing his hat.

"Hey, Champ, whaddya say!?" he cried. "Long time no see, amigo."

"Hey, Champ," I said, glum. "Let's sit down here and have a talk."

I led him over to some bleachers in a nearby baseball field. We passed the afternoon talking about all the major characters of his life—Marciano, Charles, Little Champ. Abruptly, I mentioned the ex-girlfriend.

"Now that I'm on the outside looking in," he mumbled, "I see she wasn't a hundred percent in my corner."

"Because she accused you of doing those awful things to her baby?"

He lifted his head, startled. He was spent, punch-drunk, perma-nently hung over, but he knew what I was saying. "They just took her word for it," he said of the jury. "The only regret I have in life is that case she made against me with the baby." Only a monster would hurt a child, Champ said. He begged his ex-girlfriend to recant those false accusations, which he blamed on her paranoia and jeal-ousy. And she did recant, he said, but not to the judge.

More than this he didn't want to say. He wanted to talk about Chicago, sweet home, and all the other way-off places where he knew folks. How he yearned for friendly faces, especially his sis-ter, Lily, with whom he'd left his scrapbook and other papers for safekeeping. He told me her address in Columbus, Ohio, and her phone number. He wanted to see her before he died. See any-one. "Get me some money and head on down the road," he said, eyes lowered, half to himself.

A cold winter night was minutes off, and Champ needed to find a bed, fast. This posed a problem, since taking leave of Champ was never fast. It was hard for him to overcome the inertia that crept into his bones while he sat, harder still to break away from anyone willing to listen. Watching him get his grocery cart going was like seeing an ocean liner off at the dock. The first movement was imperceptible. "See you later, Champ," I said, hurrying him along, shaking that catcher's mitt of a hand. Then I accidentally looked into his eyes, and I couldn't help myself. I believed him.

Maybe it was faith born of guilt. Maybe it was my way of atoning. After all, I was the latest in a long line of people—managers, promoters, opponents—who wanted something from Champ. I wanted his aura, I wanted his story, I wanted his friendship. As partial restitution, the least I could give him was the benefit of the doubt.

Also, he was right. Only a monster would commit the crimes described in those court files, and I didn't see any monster before me. Just a toothless boxer with a glass chin and a pigeon feather in his hat. Shaking his hand, I heard myself say, "Go get warm, Champ," and I watched myself slip him another five-dollar bill.

## 8.

LaMotta would not let up. He refused to let me write. Each time I tried, he swatted me around my subconscious. "Besides Bob Satterfield," he'd said, "the only ones who ever hurt me were my ex-wives." Men seldom speak of other men with such deference, such reverence, particularly men like LaMotta. One of the brashest fighters ever, he discussed Satterfield with all the bluster of a curtsy. "You sure it's him?" he'd asked, distressed. "I heard he was dead."

You sure it's him? The courts were sure, the cops were sure, the editors were pretty sure. But I was getting ready to tell several million people that Bob Satterfield was a homeless wreck and a convicted child molester. Was I sure?

I phoned more boxing experts and historians, promoters and managers, libraries and clubs, referees and retired fighters, and that's when I found Ernie Terrell, former heavyweight champion. I reached him in Chicago at the South Side offices of his janitorial business.

"You remember Bob Satterfield?" I asked.

"One of the hardest punchers who ever lived," he said.

I've been hanging out with Satterfield, I said, and I need someone who can vouch for his identity. A long silence followed. A tingly silence, a harrowing silence, the kind of silence that precedes the bloodcurdling scream in a horror film. "Bob Satterfield is dead," Terrell said.

"No he's not," I said, laughing. "I just talked to him."

"You talked to Bob Satterfield."

"Yes. He sleeps in a park not ten minutes from here."

"Bob Satterfield?" he said. "Bob Satterfield the fighter? Bob Satterfield's dead."

Now it was my turn to be silent. When I felt the saliva returning to my mouth, I asked Terrell what made him so sure.

"Did you go to his funeral?" I asked.

He admitted that he had not.

"Do you have a copy of his obituary?"

Again, no.

"Then how do you know he's dead?" I asked.

Suddenly, he seemed less sure.

"Hold on," he said. "We're going to get to the bottom of this."

He opened a third phone line and began conference-calling veteran corner men and trainers on the South Side. The voices that joined us on the line were disjointed and indistinct, as though recorded on scratchy vinyl records. Rather than a conference call, we were conducting a séance, summoning the spirits of boxing's past. He dialed a gym where the phone rang and rang. When someone finally answered, Terrell asked to speak with D.D. The phone went dead for what seemed a week. In the background, I heard speed bags being thrummed and ropes being skipped, a sound like cicadas on a summer day. At last, a scruffy and querulous voice came on the line, more blues man than corner man.

"Who's this?"

"It's Ernie."

"Ernie?"

"Ernie."

"Ernie?"

"Ernie!"

"Yeah, Ernie, yeah."

"I got a guy here on the other line from the *Los Angeles Times,* in California, says he's writing a story about Bob Satterfield. You remember Bob Satterfield."

"Suuure."

"Says he just talked to Satterfield and Satterfield's sleeping in a park out there in Santa Ana."

"Bob Satterfield's dead."

"No," I said.

I told them about Champ's encyclopedic knowledge of his career. I told them about Champ's well-documented reputation among cops, judges, and reporters. I told them about Champ's face matching old Satterfield photos.

"Then I will come out there and shoot that dude," D.D. said. "Because Bob Satterfield is *dead.*"

Ten minutes later I was in Santa Ana, where I found Champ sweeping someone's sidewalk for the price of a whiskey bottle. It was a hot spring day, and he looked spent from the hard work.

"Look," I said, "a lot of people say you're dead."

"I'm the one," he said, bouncing on his feet, shadowboxing playfully with me. "Battlin' Bob Satterfield. I fought 'em all. Ezzard Charles, Rocky Marciano—"

"Don't you have any identification?" I said, exasperated. "A birth certificate? A union card? A Social Security card?"

He patted his pockets, nothing. We'd been through this.

"In that case," I said, "I'm going to have to give you a test."

Far from offended, he couldn't wait. Leaning into me, he cocked his head to one side and closed his eyes, to aid concentration.

"Who was Jack Kearns?" I asked, knowing that "Doc" Kearns, who managed Jack Dempsey in the 1920s, briefly managed Satterfield's early career.

"Jack Kearns," Champ said. "He was the first manager I ever had."

"All right," I said. "Who's this?"

I held before his nose a forty-five-year-old wire photo of Iona Satterfield. Champ touched her face gingerly and said, "That's Iona. That's the only woman I ever loved."

## 9.

Asked to explain myself, I usually start with my father, who disappeared when I was seven months old, walked away from his only son the way some people leave a party that's grown dull. At precisely the moment I learned to crawl, he ran. An unfair head start, I always felt.

As a boy, I could repress all stirrings of curiosity about him, because I knew what he sounded like, and this seemed sufficient. A well-known radio man in New York City, he often came floating out of my grandmother's olive-drab General Electric clock-radio, cracking jokes and doing bits, until an adult passing through the room would lunge for the dial. It was thought that The Voice upset me. No one realized that The Voice nourished me. My father was invisible, therefore mythic. He was whatever I wanted him to be, and his rumbling baritone inspired mental pictures of every male archetype, from Jesus to Joe Namath to Baloo the bear in *The Jungle Book.*

Over time, I grew impatient with the mystery surrounding him, the not knowing, particularly when he changed his name and vanished altogether. (Seeing fatherhood and child support as a maximum-security prison, he took a fugitive's pains to cover his tracks once he escaped.) As his absence came to feel more like a constant presence, I spent long hours puzzling about the potential intersections between his identity and mine. My predecessor in the generational parade, my accursed precursor, was a voice. It unnerved me. It unmanned me. One day, shortly before my seventeenth birthday, I made what felt like a conscious decision to find him. At least, that's what I thought until I met Champ, who forced me to see that no such conscious decision ever took place, that I'd been trying to find my father all my life, that every man is trying to find his father.

True, a love of boxing and a budding disenchantment with daily journalism sparked my original interest in Champ. Then a genuine fondness made me befriend him. But what made me study him like an insect under a microscope was my inescapable fascination with anyone who disappears, dissolves his identity, walks away from fame and family. When pushed to deconstruct my relationship with Champ, I saw that we were trading more than fivers and fellowship. Champ was using me as a surrogate for his dead son, and I was using him as a stand-in for my own deep-voiced demon, whom I met after a brief, furious search.

We sat in an airport coffee shop and talked like strangers. Strangers who had the same nose and chin. I remember random things. I remember that he was the first man I ever made nervous. I remember that he wore a black leather coat, ordered eggs Benedict, and flirted relentlessly with a waitress, asking like some fussy lord if the chef made his own Hollandaise sauce. I remember that he was portly and jovial, with wild eyebrows that forked straight out from his head. I remember laughing at his stories, laughing against my will because he could be painfully funny. I remember breathing in his peppery scent, a uniquely male cocktail of rubbing alcohol, hair spray, and Marlboro 100s. I remember the hug when we parted, the first time I ever hugged another man.

But what we said to each other over the hours we sat together, I don't know. The meeting was so emotionally high-watt that it shorted my memory circuits. My only other impression of that night is one of all-pervasive awe. My father, my mythic father, had boozed away his future and parlayed his considerable talents into a pile of unpaid bills. I saw none of that. If losing him was a hardship, losing my mythic idea of him would have been torture. So I chose to see him as a fallen god, an illusion he fostered with a few white lies. I loved him in the desperate way you love someone when you need to.

Now, months after meeting Champ, I asked myself if I wasn't viewing this poor homeless man through the same hopeful myopia. If so, why? The answer dawned one day while I was reading *Moby-Dick,* the bible of obsession, which provides a special sort of reading pleasure when you substitute the word "father" for "whale": "It is a thing most sorrowful, nay shocking, to expose the fall of valor in the soul. . . . That immaculate manliness we feel within ourselves . . . bleeds with keenest anguish at the undraped spectacle of a valor-ruined man."

When the valor-ruined man is your father, the anguish quadruples and the manliness hemorrhages. Sometimes the anguish reaches such a crescendo that you simply disobey your eyes. Anything to stanch the bleeding.

Because he recalled the specter of my father and his equally enigmatic cop-out, Champ might have revived that early talent I showed for self-deception. He also either benefited or suffered from the trinity of habits that constitutes my father's legacy. An obsession with questions of identity. A tendency to overestimate men. And an inability to leave the past alone.

## 10.

Not every homeless man can look nonchalant speaking into a cellular phone, but Champ acclimated himself to the technology, even if he did aim the phone at that part of the heavens where he imagined Ohio to be. He told his sister he was fine, getting by, and urged her to cooperate. "Please," he said, handing me the phone, "let this man look at my scrapbook."

Establishing Champ's credibility was one thing. Establishing mine with his sister was another. Lily couldn't imagine what I wanted from her poor brother, and I couldn't blame her. I tried to explain that Champ merited a newspaper story because he'd contended for the title.

"You remember your brother fighting," I said, "as Bob Satterfield?"

"Yes," she said casually.

"And you have a scrapbook with clippings and photos?"

"I've had that scrapbook for years."

I asked her to mail me the book, but she refused. She wasn't about to ship a family heirloom to someone she'd never met. Again, I couldn't blame her.

It was then that I heard from a former boxing writer. He'd been watching TV recently when he hit on something called the Classic Sports Network, which was airing a prehistoric episode of Rocky Marciano's TV show, wherein Marciano analyzed a 1951 bout at Madison Square Garden between Rex Layne and Bob Satterfield.

When the tape arrived the next morning, I cradled it like a newborn to the nearest VCR. There was Marciano, pudgy and past his prime, a real-life version of Fred Flintstone. Beside him sat his guest, comic Jimmy Durante. After several excruciating minutes of idle chitchat, Marciano turned to Durante and said, "I want to show you the Bob Satterfield–Rex Layne fight."

Durante's eyes widened.

"Satterfield?" he said.

"You remember him?" Marciano asked.

"So help me," Durante said, "he's my favorite. A great, great fighter. I thought he'd be a champion."

"He had the punch, Jim," Marciano said, shaking his head.

The screen went dark. A ring appeared. In the foreground stood a man in a hooded robe, his back to the camera. On either side of him stood corner men in cardigan sweaters, "SATTERFIELD" emblazoned across their backs. Doffing his robe, the fighter started forward, his torso atremble with muscles. Slowly he turned toward the camera, and I saw that he was not Champ. The resemblance was strong, as the resemblance between Champ and old photos of Satterfield had been strong. But they were different men.

My stomach tightened as the "real" Satterfield threw a walloping right. Layne dropped to one knee and shook his head, not knowing what hit him. I knew exactly how he felt.

Champ a fake. Somehow I felt less betrayed when I thought he was a child molester. It made me sick. It made no sense. He knew too much about Satterfield. He knew the record. He knew Doc Kearns. He recognized Iona. Plus, he was built like a fighter —that body, those hands. "Yes," I thought, "he's built like a fighter."

I phoned *The Ring* and asked Mainwaring to check his records for a heavyweight named Tommy Harrison. Minutes later, he faxed me the file. There, at long last, was Champ. This time, no allowance needed to be made for the passage of years and the corrosive effects of whiskey. That body, those hands.

Besides his name, it seemed, Champ was frequently telling the truth. Not only did he break Marciano's nose, the injury postponed a storied rematch with Walcott. Like Satterfield, he *had* been a highly touted contender, a guy within striking distance of the championship. Like Satterfield, he *had* fought Ezzard Charles. In fact, Harrison and Satterfield had fought many of the same men.

Opponents weren't the only thing they had in common. Both were Army veterans. Both were right-handers. Both were built like light-heavyweights. Both were anxious to break into the heavyweight division. Both were clobbered when they tried. Both retired in the mid-1950s. Both were born in November; their birthdays were one day apart.

"He's fast," Marciano said of Harrison in one clipping. "Has a great ring future. In a year or so, if I'm still champ, I expect trouble from him."

The file proved that Champ was a fraud, or delusional, or something in between. But it couldn't explain his motives, nor account for his corroborative sister. In fact, it raised more questions than it answered, including the most pressing question of all: If Champ wasn't Satterfield, who was?

Ernie Terrell said Satterfield was dead. But I couldn't find an obituary—not even in Chicago. How did a fighter of Satterfield's stature not rate a death notice in his native city?

Phone directories in scores of area codes listed hundreds of Satterfields, too many to dial. A search of databases throughout the Midwest found one Illinois death certificate in the name of Robert Satterfield, a truck driver buried in Restvale Cemetery, Worth, Illinois. Under next of kin, a son on the South Side of Chicago.

"Robert Satterfield Junior?" I asked when the son answered the phone.

"Yes?"

"I'm writing a story about Bob Satterfield, the heavyweight of the 1950s, and I was wondering if you might be any—"

"That's my father," he said proudly.

## 11.

The neighborhood was dodgy, some houses well-kept and others falling down. Few addresses were visible and some street signs were gone, so I drove in circles, getting lost twice, doubling back, and that's when I saw him. Bob Satterfield. In the flesh.

After staring at old newspaper photos and studying the tape of his fight with Rex Layne, I'd committed Satterfield's face to memory—never realizing he might have bequeathed that face to his son. Seeing Satterfield Jr. outside his house, the resemblance fooled me like a mirage, and I did what anyone in my shoes would have done: I backed straight into his neighbor's truck.

The first time I ever laid eyes on Bob Satterfield, therefore, he flinched, as though bracing for a punch.

After making sure I'd left no visible dent, we shook hands and went inside his brick house, the nicest on the block. The living room was neat and intensely bright, morning sunlight practically shattering the glass windows. He introduced me to his wife, Elaine, who took my hand somewhat timidly. Together, they waved me toward the couch, then sat far away, grimacing.

They were visibly afraid of me, but they did everything possible to make me feel welcome. She was all smiles and bottled-up energy; he was old-school polite, verging on courtly. He'd just finished a double shift at O'Hare, where he loaded cargo for a living, and he actually apologized for his exhaustion. I looked into his basset-hound eyes and cringed, knowing I'd soon add to his burdens.

I started by acknowledging their apprehension. As far as they knew, I'd come all the way from California to ask questions about a fighter few people remembered. It seemed suspicious.

"But the first time I heard the name Bob Satterfield," I said, "was when I met this man."

I dealt them several photos of Champ, like gruesome playing cards, then court papers and clippings describing Champ as Satterfield. Another profile had recently appeared in a college newspaper, and I laid this atop the pile. Lastly, I outlined Champ's criminal past. They looked at each other gravely.

"I hate this man," Elaine blurted.

Satterfield Jr. lit a cigarette and gazed at Champ. He murmured something about a resemblance, then walked to a sideboard, from which he pulled a crumbling scrapbook. Returning to his chair, he balanced the book on one knee and began assembling photos, clippings, documents, anything to help me recognize that Champ's impersonation was no victimless crime.

While I scrutinized the scrapbook, Satterfield Jr. talked about his father's life. He told me about his father's close friends, Miles Davis and Muhammad Ali, who met his first wife through Satterfield. He told me about his father's triumphs in the ring and the difficult decision to retire. (After suffering a detached retina in 1958, Satterfield fled to Paris and studied painting.) He told me about his father's ancestry, back, back, back, and I understood the desperation seeping into his voice, a desperation that made him stammer badly. He'd opened his door to a total stranger who repaid the hospitality by declaring that countless other strangers believed his beloved father was a "valor-ruined man." I'd walked up clean steps to talk to clean people and made them feel dirty.

Lastly, Satterfield Jr. produced his father's birth certificate, plus a 1977 obituary from a now-defunct Chicago newspaper. To these precious items he added a photo of his parents strolling arm in arm, kissing. When I told Satterfield Jr. about Champ pointing to Iona and calling her "the only woman I ever loved," I thought he might eat the coffee table.

"That somebody would intrude on his memory like this," Elaine said. "My father-in-law was a man. He was a man's man, nothing like the men of today. He was a prideful man. He continued to work up until his operation for cancer. If a person knows he's dying, and he still gets up to go to work, that says a lot about him as a man, and if he knew some homeless man sleeping on a park bench was impersonating him—"

She stopped herself and went to the window, struggling to keep her composure. Satterfield Jr. now began phoning family.

"I'm sitting here with a reporter from the *Los Angeles Times*," he shouted into the phone, "and he says there's a man in California who's telling everybody he's Bob Satterfield the fighter. He's homeless and he has a very bad record, and he's been molesting children and he's using Pop's name. Yeah. Uh huh, Now, now, don't cry. . . ."

## 12.

An old boxing hand once said, "You never learn anything until you're tired," and by that criterion I'm capable of learning plenty right now. After the overnight flight, after the cab ride through the rainy dawn to this downtown Columbus hotel, I'm tired enough to understand why Champ's sister doesn't trust me, and why she's turned me over to Champ's nephew, Gregory Harrison, who trusts me even less. I left word for him two hours ago saying I'd arrived, but he seems like a guy who'd rather give me a stiff beating than a straight answer, so the chance of seeing Champ's scrapbook seems remote.

Above all, I'm tired enough to understand that Champ isn't Satterfield, never was Satterfield, never will be, no matter how hard I try. But I'm also tired enough to understand why he pretended to be Satterfield. He became Satterfield because he didn't like being Tommy Harrison.

It was Satterfield Jr. who made me appreciate how ripe his father was for imitation. Fast, stylish, pretty, Satterfield was Champ's superior in every way. He was the ballyhooed one, the better one. Yes, he had the famously weak chin. But he led with it, time after time, meaning he had one hellacious heart. Champ must have studied Satterfield from afar, longingly, as I did. He must have gone to school on Satterfield, devouring facts about his life, as I did. He must have viewed Satterfield as a model, an ideal, as I also did. One day, Champ must have spied Satterfield across a musty gym, perhaps with Doc Kearns, or a smoky nightclub, where Iona was the prettiest girl in the joint, and said, "Ah, to be him." From there, it was a short, dizzy trip to "I *am* him."

As a man, you need someone to instruct you in the masculine verities. Your father is your first choice, but when he drops out, you search for someone else. If you're careless, the search creeps into your psyche and everyone becomes a candidate, from homeless men to dead boxers. If you're careless and unlucky, the search devours you. That doppelganger eats you up.

"One of the primary things boxing is about is lying," Joyce Carol Oates writes in *On Boxing*. "It's about systematically cultivating a double personality: the self in society, the self in the ring."

What Champ did, I think, was sprout a third self, a combination of the two, which may be what Champ has been trying to tell me all along.

After Chicago, I wanted to scold him about the people his lies were hurting. But when I found him wearing a ten-gallon cowboy hat and a polo shirt with toothbrushes stuffed in the breast pocket, my anger drained away.

"Champ," I said, "when you pretended to be Bob Satterfield, weren't you afraid the other Bob Satterfield would find out?"

Without hesitating, he put a hand to his chin and said, "I always figured the other Bob Satterfield knew about me. As long as everyone got paid, I didn't think the other Bob Satterfield would mind."

"What?"

"This is just you and me talking," he said. "But my manager, George Parnassus, he told me like this here: 'If you go to fight in Sioux City, Iowa, and you say you is Bob Satterfield, then you get a big crowd, see? But if you say you is Tommy Harrison, and like that, you only get a medium-size crowd.'"

Champ's manager had been dead twenty years. But his son, Msgr. George Parnassus, was pastor of St. Victor's Roman Catholic Church in West Hollywood. I phoned Parnassus and told him about Champ, then asked if his father might have staged bogus fights in the 1950s. Before TV came along, I ventured, most fighters were faceless names in the dark, so it might have been easy, and it might have been highly profitable, to promote lookalike fighters in out-of-the-way places. Say, Sioux City.

"Why do you say Sioux City?" he demanded.

"Because Champ said Sioux City."

"My father moved to Sioux City in the 1950s and staged fights there for a number of years."

Which is why I'm in Columbus this morning. I owed it to Champ to take one last stab at the truth. I owed it to myself. More than anyone, I owed it to Satterfield, whose absence I've come to feel like a constant presence.

"I've had a lot of disappointments," Satterfield told a reporter in 1958, sitting in a hospital with his detached retina. "I don't remember all the disappointments I've had." Maybe, forty years later, he's still disappointed. Maybe he knows someone swiped the only shiny prize he ever had—his good name—and he can't rest until he gets it back. All this time, I've been casting Satterfield as Moby Dick, myself as Ahab. Now I'm wondering if Satterfield is the real Ahab, and Champ the whale. Which makes me the harpoon.

The phone rings.

"I'm downstairs."

## 13.

Champ's nephew is sitting in the middle of the lobby, unaware or pretending to be unaware that people are staring. It's not that he looks out of place, with his floor-length black leather overcoat and gold-rimmed sunglasses. It's that he looks famous. He also looks like a younger, fitter, toothier version of Champ.

He shakes my hand tentatively and we duck into the hotel restaurant. The place is closed, but a waiter says we're welcome to have coffee. We sit by a rain-streaked window. I thank him for meeting me, but he whips off his sunglasses and stares.

"I'm not here for you," he says. "I'm here for my uncle Tommy. And before I tell you anything you need to know, I need to know from you why you would get on a plane and fly all night, come all the way from California, to Columbus, Ohio, to write a story about *my uncle?*"

I try explaining my complicated relationship with his uncle, but the subject makes me more mumbly than Champ. Interrupting, he says softly: "Uncle Tommy was the father I should have had."

He tells me about the only time he met his uncle, a meeting so charged that it defined his life, and I wonder if he notices the strange look on my face.

"My uncle Tommy was like the Last Action Hero," he says. "I wanted to be just like him."

"You were a boxer," I say.

"I was a sparring partner of Buster Douglas," he says, sitting straighter.

His nickname was Capital City Lip, but everyone nowadays calls him Lip. With the waiters watching, he throws his right, jabs his left, bobs away from an invisible opponent, taking me through several hard-won fights, and I'm reminded of the many times his uncle broke Marciano's nose for my enjoyment.

"When you hit a guy," he says dreamily, "when you hit him in the body, you demean his manner, you know? You sap his strength, you impose your will on him. I was in the tippy-top physical shape of my life! No one could beat me! I was *good*!"

"What happened?"

He purses his lips. His story is Champ's story, Satterfield's story, every fighter's story. One day, there was someone he just couldn't beat.

"Now I race drag bikes," he says.

"Drag bikes? Why?"

"Because someday I want to be world champion of something."

His father got him interested, he says, mentioning the man in a curious way. "My father walks down the street, people part ways," he says. "Big George, that's what everyone in Columbus calls my father. He was a boxer, too, although he didn't go as far as Uncle Tommy."

Feeling an opening, I try to tell Lip about my father. He seems confused at first, then instantly empathetic. He understands the link between boxing and growing up fatherless. Maybe only a boxer can fathom that kind of fear.

"Have you ever heard the name Bob Satterfield?" I ask.

"Yes, I have heard that name."

As a boy, Lip often heard that Uncle Tommy fought as Bob Satterfield, but he never knew why.

He promises to bring me Champ's scrapbook tomorrow, then take me to meet his father. I walk him outside to his Jeep, which is double-parked in a tow zone, hazard lights flashing, just as he left it three hours ago.

## 14.

White shirt, white pants, white shoes, Lip comes for me the next morning looking like an angel of the streets. As we zoom away from the hotel, I scan the backseat, floor, dashboard. No scrapbook. The angel shakes his head.

"Aunt Lily just doesn't trust you," he says. "I was over there all morning, but she won't let that book out of her house."

I groan.

"I looked through the book myself, though," he says, lighting a cigarette, "and I don't think it has what you want. This Bob Satterfield, the book has lots of newspaper articles about his career, and there's a picture of him with my uncle—"

I wince.

"—and an article saying Satterfield and my uncle Tommy were scheduled to fight."

Disconsolate, I stare at the bullet hole in the windshield.

We drive to Lip's father's house, where a candy-apple red Cadillac the size of a fire engine sits outside, license plate "BIG GEO." Lip takes a deep breath, then knocks. Whole minutes crawl by before the door flies open and Champ's brother appears. He looks nothing like Champ, mainly because of old burn scars across his face. But wrapped in a baby-blue bathrobe and glowering hard, he does look like an old boxer. He turns and disappears inside the house. Meekly, we follow.

Off to the left is a small room crammed with trophies and boxing memorabilia. To the right seems to be the living room, though it's impossible to tell because all the lights are off. Big George keeps moving until he reaches a high-backed chair. Despite the oceanic darkness of the place, he remains clearly visible, as if lit from within by his own anger. I can see why he's such a force in Lip's life. He scares the wits out of me.

Rubbing his palms together, Lip tells his father I'm writing a story about Uncle Tommy.

"Hmph," Big George scoffs. "Tommy. He's a stranger to me. He's my brother and I love him, but he's a stranger."

"Have you ever heard the name Bob Satterfield?" I ask.

"Bob Satterfield," Big George says, "was one of the hardest punchers of all time—"

He coughs, a horrifying cough, then adds:

"—but he couldn't take a punch."

"Do you remember Tommy ever fighting as Bob Satterfield?" I ask.

"Tommy never fought as nobody else."

He stands and goes to a sideboard, where he rifles through a stack of papers and bills. "Here," he says, yanking loose a yellowed newspaper account of the night in 1953 when Champ's life began its downward spiral.

"Tommy wasn't ready for Ezzard Charles," Big George says with sudden tenderness while Lip and I read over his shoulder. "They rushed him."

The three of us stand together, silently, as though saying a prayer for Champ. Then, without warning, Lip breaks the mood, mentioning a beef he's having with Big George. They start to argue, and I see that Lip brought me here for more than an interview. He's hoping I can play referee. As with Champ, I was too busy using him to notice that he was using me.

Father and son argue for five minutes, each landing heavy verbal blows. Then Big George makes it plain that these will be the final words spoken on the subject.

"The Bible say this," he bellows. "Honor your parents! Honor your mother and father! Regardless what they say, what they do, all mothers and dads love their children! All of them!"

"He's lying to you," Lip says when we get in the car.

I look at him, startled.

"About what?"

"He knows all about Satterfield."

We drive to a beloved old gym that former champion Buster Douglas helped rebuild after knocking down Mike Tyson. Inside, we find Douglas's father, Bill, training a young featherweight. When Lip tells Douglas that I'm writing about his uncle, "a former heavyweight con-TEN-der," Douglas nods his head several times, and I feel Lip's self-worth balloon with each nod.

We watch the featherweight work the heavy bag, a black, water-filled sack that hangs from the ceiling. Each time he snaps a hard right, the bag swings like a man in a noose. His name is Andre Cray, and he's twenty-five. Rawboned and scowling, with a flat head and rubbery limbs, he looks like an angry Gumby. When his workout ends, we ask him why he chose boxing as a trade.

"To me it's like an art," he says quietly, unwinding the padded white tape from his fists.

But this isn't the real reason, he admits. Growing up without money, without a father, boxing was the only straight path to manhood. Many of his friends chose the crooked path, a choice they didn't always live to regret. Those who prospered in the crack trade often gave Cray money and begged him not to follow their lead. Some even bought him gloves and shoes, to make sure the streets didn't claim another boxer.

He remembers those early patrons, uses their fate as inspiration. His future is bright, he figures, if he can just protect his chin and not lose heart. In nineteen fights, he's scored seventeen wins. When he loses, he says, the anguish is more than he can stand.

"You have family?" Lip asks.

"Yeah," Cray says. "I have a son. He'll be one on Tuesday."

"What's his name?"

"Andre Cray *Junior.*"

"I imagine he inspires you a lot."

"Yeah," Cray says, looking down at his oversize hands.

Lip nods, solemn. Douglas nods. I nod.

## 15.

Like a favorite movie, the one-reel *Satterfield Versus Layne* says something different every time I watch, each punch a line of multilayered dialogue. After several hundred viewings, the core theme emerges. It's about pressing forward, I think. Ignoring your pain. Standing.

"Satterfield is out of this world," Marciano says in his narrative voice-over. "He's one of the hardest hitters I've ever seen."

Satterfield lives up to his reputation in the very first minute, greeting Layne with a vicious second-clefter on the point of the chin. Kneeling, Layne takes the count, then staggers upright and hugs Satterfield until the bell.

Satterfield, in white trunks, with a pencil-thin mustache and muscles upon muscles, is a joy to look at. Decades before Nautilus, his biceps look like triple-scoop ice cream cones. By contrast, Layne looks like a soda jerk who's wandered mistakenly into the ring. Over the first three rounds he does little more than push his black trunks and flabby belly back and forth while offering his square head as a stationary target.

Still, Layne seems the luckier man. In the sixth, Satterfield puts every one of his 180 pounds behind a right hook. He brings the fist from behind his back like a bouquet of flowers, but Layne weaves, avoiding the punch by half an inch. "Just missed!" Marciano shouts. "That would have done it!"

Had that punch landed, everything would be different. Layne would be stretched out on the canvas, Satterfield would be looking forward to the title shot he craves. Instead, the eighth begins, and Satterfield's wondering what more he can do. It's LaMotta all over again. No matter what you do, the other guy keeps coming— obdurate, snarling, fresh.

Far ahead on points, Satterfield can still win a decision, as long as he protects himself, covers up, plays it safe. He does just the opposite, charging forward, chin high, the only way he knows. In the kind of punch-for-punch exchange that went out with fedoras, Satterfield and Layne stand one inch apart, winging at each other from all directions, Satterfield trying frantically to turn out Layne's dim bulb—until Layne lands a right hook on the magic chin.

"I don't think [he] can get up," Marciano says as Satterfield lies on his back, blinking at the house lights. "But look at this guy try."

Boxing's Humpty-Dumpty. The book on Satterfield proves true. Or does it? Always, this is the moment I hit the pause button and talk to Satterfield while he tries to tap some hidden wellspring of strength. Somehow, he taps it every time, a display of pure grit that never fails to make my heart beat faster.

"He's hurt bad," Marciano says, as Satterfield stands and signals the referee that he's ready for another dose. Dutifully, Layne steps forward and sends a crashing left into Satterfield's head. Then a right. And another right. Finally, the referee rushes forward and removes Satterfield's mouthpiece. Corner men leap into the ring. Photographers with flashes the size of satellite dishes shoot the covers of tomorrow's sports pages. Amid all the commotion, Layne takes a mincing step forward and does something shocking.

It's hard to believe, in an age of end-zone dances and home-run trots, that boxers in a bygone era often hugged after their meanest fights. (Some actually kissed.) But Layne gives that postfight tenderness a new twist. As Satterfield sags against the ropes, dead-eyed, Layne reaches out to touch him ever so lightly on the cheek.

It's a haunting gesture, so intimate and unexpected that it begs imitation. Like Layne—like Champ—I want to reach out to Satterfield, to show my admiration. I want to tell him how glad I am to make his acquaintance, how grateful I am for the free instruction. More than all that, I suppose, I just want to thank him for the fight.

One day, after watching his greatest defeat, I visit his impostor.

"Heyyy," Champ says, beaming, waving hello. "What do you know about that? Hey, your picture ran through my mind many times, and then I'd say, well, my friend, he give me up."

He's wearing a white karate uniform, mismatched sneakers, and a shirt from the Orange County Jail. Clouds of flies swarm around his head and grocery cart this warm November afternoon, Champ's sixty-seventh birthday. Tomorrow would have been Satterfield's seventy-third.

There are many things about Champ that I don't know, things I'll probably never know. He either got money to be Satterfield, then forgot to drop the con, or wished he were Satterfield, then let the wish consume him. Not knowing doesn't bother me as I feared it would. Not getting his scrapbook doesn't torment me as I thought it might. Every man is a mystery, because manhood itself is so mysterious; that's what Champ taught me. Maturity means knowing when to solve another man's mystery, and when to respect it.

"Been traveling," I tell him. "And guess where I went?"

He cocks his head.

"Columbus. And guess who I saw? Your nephew, Gregory."

"That's my brother's son!"

"Yep. And guess who else I met. Big George."

He pulls a sour face, like his brother's, and we both laugh.

We talk about George, Lily, and Lip, and Champ grows heavy with nostalgia. He recalls his childhood, particularly his stern father, who hit him so hard one day that he flayed the muscle along Champ's left bicep. Champ rolls up his sleeve to show me the mark, but I look away.

To cheer him up, to cheer us both up, I ask Champ to tell me once more about busting Marciano's nose.

"Marciano and I were putting on an exhibition that day," he says, crouching. "We were going good. But he had that long overhand right, and every time I seen it coming, I'd duck it. And I'd come up, and I'd keep hitting him on the tip of his nose."

He touches my nose with a gentle uppercut, flies trailing in the wake of his fist.

"On the tip, on the tip, I kept hitting," he says. "Finally, his nose started bleeding, and they stopped the fight."

Smiling now, more focused than I've ever seen him, Champ says he needs my advice. He's been reviewing his life lately, wondering what next. Times are hard, he says, and maybe he should head on down the road, polish up the Cadillac and return to Columbus, though he fears the cold and what it does to an old boxer's bones.

"What do you think?" he says.

"I think you should go be with people who love you and care about you," I say.

"Yeah, that's true, that's true."

We watch the cars whizzing by, jets roaring overhead, strangers walking past.

"Well, Champ," I say, slipping him five dollars. "I've got to get going."

"Yeah, yeah," he says, stopping me. "Now, listen."

He rests one of his heavy hands on my shoulder, a gesture that makes me swallow hard and blink for some reason. I look into his eyes, and from his uncommonly serious expression, I know he's getting ready to say something important.

"I know you a long time," he says warmly, flashing that toothless smile, groping for the words. "Tell me your name again."

# HER BLUE HAVEN

## Bill Plaschke

*B*ill *Plaschke predicted doom for the Dodgers in 2001. . . . Plaschke
criticized. . . . Plaschke forgot. . . . Plaschke compared unfairly. . . .
The Dodgers need encouragement, not negativity. . . .*

That was part of a 1,200-word screed e-mailed to me last December, a holiday package filled with colorful rips. It was not much different from other nasty letters I receive, with two exceptions. This note contained more details than the usual "You're an idiot." It included on-base percentages and catchers' defensive statistics. It was written by someone who knew the Dodgers as well as I thought I did.

And this note was signed. The writer's name was Sarah Morris. She typed it at the bottom.

Most people hide behind tough words out of embarrassment or fear, but Sarah Morris was different. She had not only challenged me to a fight, but had done so with no strings or shadows.

I thought it was cute. I wrote her back. I told her I was impressed and ready for battle.

Little did I know that this would be the start of a most unusual relationship, which eight months later is being recounted from a most unusual place. I am writing this from the floor, Sarah Morris having knocked me flat with a punch I never saw coming.

*May I ask you a question? For two years I have been running my own Web site about the Dodgers. I write game reports and editorials. How did you become a baseball editorialist? That is my deam.*

This was Sarah's second e-mail, and it figured. Every time I smile at someone, they ask me for a job.

Her own Web site? That also figured. Everybody has a Web site. The Dodgers guess there are more than two dozen Web sites devoted to kissing the almighty blue.

So my expert wasn't really an expert, but rather a computer nerd looking for work. I didn't need any more pen pals with agendas.

But about that last line. I chewed my lower lip about it. The part about "my deam."

Maybe Sarah Morris was just a lousy typist. But maybe she was truly searching for something, yet was only one letter from finding it. Aren't all of us sometimes like that?

It was worth one more response. I wrote back, asking her to explain.

*I am thirty years old. . . . Because I have a physical handicap, it took me five years to complete my AA degree at Pasadena City College. . . . During the season I average 55 hours a week writing five to seven game reports, one or two editorials, researching and listening and/or watching the games.*

Physical handicap. I paused again. I was in no mood to discuss a physical handicap, whatever it was.

I have had these discussions before, discussions often becoming long, teary stories about overcoming obstacles.

Courageous people make me jealous. They make me cry. But at some point, they have also made me numb.

Then I read the part about her working fifty-five hours a week. Goodness. This woman didn't only follow the Dodgers, she covered them like a newspaper reporter.

But for whom? Sarah called her Web site *Dodger Place*. I searched for it, and found nothing. I checked all the Dodger search links, and found nothing.

Then I reread her e-mail and discovered an address buried at the bottom: http://members.tripod.com/spunkydodgers.

I clicked there. It wasn't fancy, rather like a chalkboard, with block letters and big type.

There was a section of "News from a Fan." Another section of "Views by a Fan." But she covered the team with the seriousness of a writer.

The stories, while basic, were complete. Sarah's knowledge was evident.

But still, I wondered, how could anybody find it? Is anybody reading it?

*Nobody ever signs my guestbook.*

Does anybody correspond?

*I get one letter a month.*

I read the Web site closer and realized that she does indeed receive about one letter a month—always from the same person.

So here was a physically handicapped woman, covering the Dodgers as extensively as any reporter in the country, yet writing for an obscure Web site with an impossible address, with a readership of about two.

That "deam" was missing a lot more than an *r,* I thought.

The days passed, winter moved toward spring, and I had more questions.

Sarah Morris always had answers.

*I started my own Web site in hopes of finding a job, but I have had no luck yet. I have gone to the Commission of Rehabilitation seeking help, but they say I'm too handicapped to be employed. I disagree.*

*So what if my maximum typing speed is eight words per minute because I use a head pointer to type? My brain works fine. I have dedication to my work. That is what makes people successful.*

*I don't know how to look for a job.*

A head pointer? I remember seeing one of those on a late night commercial for a hospital for paralyzed people.

It looked frightening. But her stories didn't look frightening. They looked, well, normal.

Now I find out she wrote them with her head?

I asked her how long it took her to compose one of her usual 1,200-word filings.

*3–4 hours.*

While pondering that the average person can bang out a 1,200-word e-mail in about thirty minutes, I did something I've never before done with an Internet stranger.

I asked Sarah Morris to call me.

I wanted to talk about the Dodgers. I wanted to talk about her stories.

But, well, yeah, I mostly wanted to talk about why someone would cover a team off television, typing with her head for an invisible readership.

*I have a speech disability making it impossible to use the phone.*

That proved it. My first impression obviously had been correct. This was an elaborate hoax.

She didn't want to talk to me because, of course, she didn't exist.

I thought, "This is why I never answer all my mail. This is why I will never go near a chatroom."

The Internet has become more about mythology than technology, people inventing outrageous lives to compensate for ordinary realities.

So, I was an unwitting actor in a strange little play. This woman writer was probably a forty-five-year-old male plumber.

I decided to end the correspondence.

Then I received another e-mail.

The first sentence read, "*There are some facts you might want to know. . . .*"

In words with an inflection that leaped off the screen, Sarah Morris spoke.

*My disability is cerebral palsy. . . . It affects motor control. . . . I have excessive movement, meaning when my brain tells my hands to hit a key, I would move my legs, hit the table, and six other keys in the process.*

This was only the beginning.

*When my mom explained my handicap, she told me I could accomplish anything that I wanted to if I worked three times as hard as other people.*

She wrote that she became a Dodger fan while growing up in Pasadena. In her sophomore year at Blair High, a junior varsity baseball coach, Mike Sellers, asked her to be the team statistician.

Her special ed teacher discouraged it, but she did it anyway, sitting next to the bleachers with an electric typewriter and a head pointer.

*We had a game on a rainy day. The rain fell in the typewriter, making it unusable, so Mom wrote the stats when I told her. I earned two letters that I am proud of still.*

She wrote that her involvement in baseball had kept her in school—despite poor grades and hours of neck-straining homework.

*Baseball gave me something to work for. . . . I could do something that other kids couldn't. . . . Baseball saved me from becoming another statistic. That is when I decided I wanted to do something for the sport that has done so much for me.*

And about that speech disability?

*When I went to nursery school, teachers treated me dumb. This made me mad, but I got over it. I hate the meaning of "dumb" in the phrase "deaf and dumb." My speech disability is the most frustrating.*

Okay, so I believed her. Sort of. It still sounded odd.

Who could do something like this? I figured she must be privileged. Who, in her supposed condition, could cover a baseball team without the best equipment and help?

I figured she had an elaborate setup somewhere. I was curious about it. I figured she couldn't live too far from Pasadena. I would drive over one day and we would chat.

*I live in Anderson, Texas. It's about 75 miles from Houston.*

Texas? She didn't explain. I didn't ask. But that seemed like a long flight to see a little rich girl bang on an expensive keyboard.

By now, it was spring training, and she was ranting about Gary Sheffield, and I was hanging out in Vero Beach, and I would have forgotten the whole thing.

Except Sarah Morris began sending me her stories. Every day, another story. Game stories, feature stories, some with missing words, others with typographical errors, but all with obvious effort.

Then, fate. The Lakers were involved in a playoff series in San Antonio, I had one free day, and she lived about three hours away.

I wrote her, asking if I could drive over to see her. She agreed, but much too quickly for my suspicious tastes, writing me with detailed directions involving farm roads and streets with no name.

I read the directions and again thought, this was weird. This could be dangerous. I wanted to back out.

Turns out, I wasn't the only one.

*I'm so nervous about tomorrow. I'm nothing special but a woman with disabilities. I don't know what makes a good journalism story. I don't know if I am it.*

I pulled out of my San Antonio hotel on a warm May morning and drove east across the stark Texas landscape. I followed Sarah's directions off the interstate and onto a desolate two-lane highway.

The road stretched through miles of scraggly fields, interrupted only by occasional feed stores, small white churches, and blinking red lights.

I rolled into the small intersection that is Anderson, then took a right turn, down a narrow crumbling road, high weeds thwacking against the car's window.

After several miles, I turned down another crumbling road, pulling up in front of a rusted gate, which I had been instructed to open.

Now, on a winding dirt road dotted with potholes the size of small animals, I bounced for nearly a mile past grazing cows. Through the dust, I spotted what looked like an old toolshed.

But it wasn't a shed. It was a house, a decaying shanty covered by a tin roof and surrounded by weeds and junk.

I slowed and stared. Could this be right?

Then I saw, amid a clump of weeds near the front door, a rusted wheelchair.

*P.S. We have dogs.*

Do they ever. A couple of creatures with matted hair emerged from some bushes and surrounded the car, scratching and howling.

Finally, an older woman in an old T-shirt and skirt emerged from the front door and shooed the dogs away.

"I'm Sarah's mother," said Lois Morris, grabbing my smooth hand with a worn one. "She's waiting for you inside."

I walked out of the sunlight, opened a torn screen door, and moved into the shadows, where an eighty-seven-pound figure was curled up in a creaky wheelchair.

Her limbs twisted. Her head rolled. We could not hug. We could not even shake hands. She could only stare at me and smile.

But that smile! It cut through the gloom of the cracked wooden floor, the torn couch, the broken, cobwebbed windows.

A clutter of books and boxes filled the small rooms. There was a rabbit living in a cage next to an old refrigerator. From somewhere outside the house, you could hear the squeaking of rats.

Eventually I could bear to look at nothing else, so I stared at that smile, and it was so clear, so certain, it even cut through most of my doubts.

But still, even then, I wondered.

This is Sarah Morris?

She began shaking in her chair, emitting sounds. I thought she was coughing. She was, instead, speaking.

Her mother interpreted. Every sound was a different word or phrase.

"Huh (I) . . . huh-huh (want to show) . . . huh (you) . . . huh (something)."

Her mother rolled her through a path that cut through the piles of junk, up to an old desk on cinder blocks.

On the desk was a computer. Next to it was a TV. Nearby was a Dodger bobble-head doll of uncertain identity.

Her mother fastened a head pointer around her daughter's temples, its chin-strap stained dark brown from spilled Dr Pepper. Sarah then began carefully leaning over the computer and pecking.

On the monitor appeared the *Dodger Place* Web site. Sarah used her pointer to call up a story. Peck by peck, she began adding to that story. It was her trademark typeface, her trademark Dodger fan prose, something involving Paul Lo Duca, about whom she later wrote:

> . . . Offensively, Lo Duca has been remarkable. Entering Friday's game, Lo Duca has batted .382 with five home runs and seventeen RBI. Last Tuesday Jim Tracy moved Lo Duca into the lead-off position. Since then, the Dodgers have won six and lost two, Lo Duca has an on-base percentage of .412. On Memorial Day Lo Duca had six hits, becoming the first Dodger to do so since Willie Davis on May 24, 1973. . . .

She looked up and giggled. I looked down in wonder—and shame.

This was indeed Sarah Morris. The great Sarah Morris.

She began making more sounds, bouncing in her chair. Lois asked me to sit on a dusty chair. There were some things that needed explaining.

*Times* photographer Anacleto Rapping, who had been there earlier in the day, and I had been Sarah's first visitors since she moved here with her mother and younger sister from Pasadena nearly six years ago.

This shack was an inheritance from Sarah's grandmother. When Sarah's parents divorced, her mother, with no other prospects, settled here.

The adjustment from life in Southern California to the middle of scrubby field more than thirty miles from the nearest supermarket was painful. Sarah was uprooted from a town of relative tolerance and accessibility to a place of many stares.

The place was so remote, when her mother had once dropped Sarah, helping her out of bed, and called 911, the emergency crew couldn't find the place.

"But the hardest thing for Sarah was leaving her Dodgers," Lois said.

So, she didn't. She used her disability money, and loans, to buy the computer, the television, and the satellite dish that allows her to watch or listen to every game.

She doesn't have any nearby friends, and it's exhausting to spend the five hours required for shopping trips to the nearest Wal-Mart, so the Dodgers fill the void.

They challenge her on bad days, embrace her on good days, stay awake with her while she covers an extra-inning game at 2:00 A.M.

She covers so much baseball, she maintains the eerie schedule of a player, rarely awaking before 10:00 A.M., often eating dinner at midnight.

Through the cluttered house, the path for not only her wheelchair, but for the entire direction of her life, leads from her bedroom to the kitchen to the Dodgers.

The air-conditioning sometimes breaks, turning the house into a steam bath. Lois totaled their aging van last year when she hit a black cow on a starless night, then missed so much work that they barely had enough money for food.

Yet, Sarah spends nine hours carefully constructing an analysis of Gary Sheffield, or two hours writing about a one-run victory in Colorado.

I asked what her Dodger Web page represented to her.

*Freedom.*

I asked how she feels when working.

*Happy. Useful.*

I had contacted Sarah Morris months earlier, looking for a fight. I realized now, watching her strain into the thick air of this dark room to type words that perhaps no other soul will read, that I had found that fight.

Only, it wasn't with Sarah. It was with myself. It is the same fight the sports world experiences daily in these times of cynicism and conspiracy theories.

The fight to believe. The fight to trust that athletics can still create heroes without rap sheets, virtue without chemicals, nobility with grace.

It is about the battle to return to the days when sports did not detract from life, but added to it, with its awesome power to enlighten and include.

In a place far from such doubt, with a mind filled with wonder, Sarah Morris brought me back.

I had not wanted to walk into those shadows. But two hours later, I did not want to leave.

Yet I did, because there was an airplane waiting, and an NBA playoff series to cover, big things, nonsense things.

Sarah asked her mother to wheel her outside. She was rolled to the edge of the weeds. I grasped one of her trembling hands. She grasped back with her smile.

I climbed into the car and rattled down the dirt road. Through the rearview mirror, through the rising dust, I could see the back of Sarah Morris's bobbing head as she was wheeled back to that cinder-blocked desk.

For she, too, had a game to cover.

*If you see Karros, please tell him to watch his knees in 1999. He used to bend them more than now.*

Sarah sent me that e-mail recently. It was about the same time she'd sent me an e-mail saying she had finally saved enough money to begin attending a college about forty-five minutes down the road in pursuit of her "deam."

I didn't get a chance to pass along her note to the slumping Karros, but it didn't matter.

A day later, he had a game-winning hit. The next game, a home run. The game after that, another homer.

If you watched him closely, you could see that he indeed was bending his knees again.

Eight months ago I wouldn't have believed it, but I could swear each leg formed the shape of an *r*.

# THE PASSIONS
# OF MARIO CUOMO

*Ron Rosenbaum*

Who is that tall, spectral figure haunting the gloomy halls of the state capitol building today? Who is that silver-haired, patrician wraith with the lines of a shattered past engraved on his face?

Could it be—yes—*it's John Lindsay.*

Once the Great White Hope of American liberalism, the shining paladin of urban progressivism—what's he doing here in the lobby of Mario Cuomo's statehouse office?

What Lindsay's doing in the lobby is, in fact, lobbying. The former mayor is here today as a lobbyist for Drexel Burnham Lambert. The high-flying "junk-bond" financiers have hired Lindsay to importune the governor to veto the anti-takeover legislation now on his desk.

Some might relish the ironic appropriateness of this apparition, this Ghost of the Fiscal Crisis Past. After all, here's Lindsay, whom many blame for turning New York City's credit obligations *into* junk bonds, now a paid hireling for the junk-bond kings of the private sector.

Some might relish it, but I don't. Coming upon Lindsay on my way to sit down with Cuomo was like seeing a sad, cautionary specter. Once, in college, from a distance, I'd believed in the shining promise of the Lindsay crusade, believed that he might be the one to translate the ideals of the civil-rights movement into workable realities on the streets of the cities of the North. And then, as a reporter during the dying days of the second Lindsay administration, I'd seen at close hand exactly why Lindsay came to be called the Man Who Gave Good Intentions a Bad Name.

Would it be different with Mario Cuomo? After his electrifying, impassioned keynote speech at the 1984 Democratic National Convention—the one he'd called "A Tale of Two Cities"—Cuomo succeeded to that place in the hearts of the hopeful that Lindsay once had. Only the thought was, the hope was, that Cuomo's different: He's not another Lindsay. He's got the passion for the old ideals, but he knows how to make them work. He's got a kind of passion for perfecting the mechanical details of governing that make the difference between mere good intentions and successful results. Unlike Lindsay, he's got a way with people that turns them on rather than off to his ideals.

And there was something else about Cuomo that encouraged the hope he wouldn't end up like Lindsay: his reputation as a killer debater and a go-for-the-jugular politician. This was the Cuomo who took apart first Ed Koch and then Lew Lehrman in the '82 campaign debates, the Cuomo who's not afraid to trade head shots with Reagan's designated hit man, Pat Buchanan. The guy who took on his own archbishop on theological grounds at Notre Dame.

If Reagan has adopted Rambo as his role model, Cuomo makes you think of the Clint Eastwood character in *Pale Rider:* the mysterious stranger in the clerical collar folk called the Preacher. He speaks in parables of love, but when he runs into resistance from the greedy, land-raping federals, the Preacher's eyes gleam and he takes great pleasure in blowing the feds full of holes.

Has the phrase "linebacker's eyes" ever been applied to Mario Cuomo? It's used to describe the gleam of passionate intensity that certain souls on fire, like Jack Lambert and Jack "Hacksaw" Reynolds, evince in the anticipation of cutting halfbacks in half.

All I knew about Cuomo's brief career as a minor-league baseball prospect was something I read about a fistfight he'd had with a catcher in the Class B league. But I have the feeling he might have chosen the wrong sport: He could have been a linebacker.

This afternoon as he barrels into the conference room in which I've been waiting, he manifests the burly, aggressive physical presence of a crack linebacker. When he sits himself down, he doesn't really sit. He crouches over the table, shoulders hunched forward, elbows advanced, looking like a roverback hanging over the gap at scrimmage, eager to nail an errant ballcarrier behind the line.

And when he senses intellectual error Cuomo shows you those linebacker's eyes. They gleam with pleasure as he blows holes in arguments and demolishes confused lines of thought. I found Cuomo thoughtful, introspective, compassionate, all those things, and he's got a great stern-but-kind-teacher side to him. But when he spots a mistake he's more like Hacksaw Reynolds than Mr. Chips.

In fact the first thing he wanted to do in our conversation was correct a mistake I'd made about him some months ago. Actually it was a mistake Roy Cohn made.

"Cuomo's tough," Roy had told me during my interview with him. "I saw one thing he did that *scared* me."

What was it that scared Roy, a guy who prides himself on not scaring easily? It was a devastating debating move Cuomo pulled on his hapless gubernatorial opponent, Lew Lehrman, in the climactic debate of the '82 campaign—a one-line remark that shocked Lehrman out of his red suspenders and left him for dead in the debate.

But, Cuomo tells me, Roy Cohn's account of that particular Cuomo moment got it wrong.

"Roy is saying 'Cuomo is one guy I'm afraid of because he went charging over to Lehrman, grabbed his wrist—some bellicose gesture like that—and said to Lehrman, "*My, isn't that an expensive watch.*"' Well, that didn't occur at all."

What then did happen?

"What occurred was, we were standing side by side debating and Lew was trying to interrupt my answers. Apparently he had some kind of *strategy* in mind," says Cuomo, barely suppressing his evident contempt for the strategic genius behind this tactic, "and at one point he leaned right over in front of me while I was speaking and jammed his watch in my face. He said, 'Look at the time.' And I never even touched him. I looked at the watch and I said, *'My, that's an expensive watch.'* And the place broke up.

"So it wasn't me going over to Lehrman," says Cuomo, intent on setting the record straight. "It was Lehrman coming over to me. It wasn't me grabbing his wrist. It was Lehrman thrusting his watch in my face."

He pauses and smiles with satisfaction. "It was, however, I who said, *'My, that's an expensive watch.'"*

The distinction seems important to Cuomo: He didn't hit Lehrman with a low blow—it was a counterpunch.

Not that Cuomo takes the whole thing *that* seriously. It was, after all, Mario Cuomo, he reminds me, who sent Roy Cohn a Mickey Mouse watch after reading Cohn's "Cuomo scares me" comments.

"Can you get the note to Roy Cohn about the Mickey Mouse watch?" the governor calls out to his secretary.

The note that Cuomo sent to Cohn along with the Mickey Mouse gift reads: "I would never be unwise enough to debate you as a politician. But when finally the public drives me back to the practice of the law and I find myself head to head against you, wearing this will protect you from the kind of attack I made on Lew."

Setting aside the exact circumstances of the expensive-watch attack, what is it with these tough-guy Republicans like Roy Cohn and Pat Buchanan, the most recent victim of a Cuomo counter-punch? Why, I ask the governor, are these GOP street fighters frightened of Mario Cuomo?

"Because they're making a mistake," he says. "Because they misperceive me. Because they don't know me. I'm the easiest opponent they could have, I'm sure. They just don't know me."

"And what is the misperception they have?"

"They're confused. They think because I stood up and spoke about family and speak about law and order without surrendering to the death penalty, because I can balance a budget and still give more money to people in wheelchairs—they're confused into thinking that because I can do all of these things, which is exactly what they say Republicans are supposed to do, that means I'm going to run for president and then for sure they'd lose."

"And why are they wrong in—"

"Because I'm not running for president," he says. "If they knew the truth, which is, all I'm planning is to run for governor, they could all be relieved. They wouldn't bother with me—they'd go beat up Gary Hart."

"Why have you decided not to run for president?"

"I haven't decided not to run for president," he says, correcting me. "I said I'm planning to run for governor. They think I'm planning to run for president."

And of course an answer like that will not do much to change their minds, if you ask me.

But rather than get into that game, there's someone I'd like to introduce you to now. Someone you'll undoubtedly be hearing more about if Cuomo does run for president. Someone you probably need to know to understand Cuomo as a person and a politician.

Maybe you know about this guy already: the French paleontologist and Jesuit priest whose attempts to speak of spirituality in Darwinian and Einsteinian terms were suppressed by the church until after his death in 1955.

I'm speaking, of course, of Pierre Teilhard de Chardin, Mario Cuomo's spiritual mentor.

I'd been surprised to find that nothing I'd read about Cuomo had focused attention on the importance of Teilhard to him. There had been no mention of Teilhard's inspirational work *The Divine Milieu,* which, Cuomo told me, he'd read "a hundred times."

Cuomo's published *Diaries* hint strongly at the centrality of Teilhard to him. In one typical passage from 1981 he finds himself worrying about money: His wife's unhappy with him for not having gotten bigger bucks out of his law practice, and he's unhappy that the political career he sacrificed the big bucks for isn't really doing much to make the world better.

"I wonder what Teilhard would say about this kind of thinking," Cuomo writes. "Is it a form of weakness? How do I deal with what he would call the diminishments of my own spirit and the diminishments imposed by the world?"

Before going up to Albany to sit down with Cuomo, I brushed up on Teilhard, having been impressed by his speculative evolutionary theory in *The Phenomenon of Man* in college, but being kind of rusty on the details. *The Divine Milieu* is far more explicitly devotional and Catholic: It's an impassioned, inspirational work that takes off from the thesis that the universe of matter and energy revealed by contemporary subatomic physics and astrophysics is not a challenge to faith, but rather further revelation of the glory of Created Being. Yes, we are living in a material world, Teilhard says, anticipating you know who. But the material world (including human nature) is interpenetrated with divine potential—it's a "divine milieu," the way energy is the "milieu" of matter in relativistic physics.

I was curious to find out just how important this vision was to the governor. And surprised at just how passionate he was about it.

Our conversation about Teilhard, which somewhat incongruously followed the one about Roy Cohn and the Mickey Mouse watch, began, nonetheless much like that one, with Cuomo correcting another mistake I made.

This time it was my misreading of a passage in *The Divine Milieu* that I had been certain was a key to Cuomo's character development.

The passage I got wrong comes from Teilhard's introduction, in which he's describing the particular kind of person *The Divine Milieu* will have the most meaning for: "A certain kind of human spirit known to every spiritual director."

What is it about this certain kind of spirit? He's the kind of person who has a taste for the life of this world but a "higher Will" to withdraw from what he sees as the sinful confusion of the fallen world in search for the purity of loving God alone. Someone, in other words, who might be drawn to the priesthood or the monastic life for reasons of self-sanctification but who would be better off, Teilhard wants him to know, embracing rather than rejecting the world.

Is that you? I asked Cuomo.

Right doctrine, wrong guy, he replied—in essence. But before refuting my conjecture about his character he reproved my obvious quick-study job on *The Divine Milieu*.

"If you read it only once, then you are missing all the joy of reading it a hundred times as I have," he told me, "because as you know, it's poetry, a kind of intelligent emoting."

Then he got down to the task of setting me straight on the nature of its importance to his personal development.

"First, let me tell you what I think Teilhard is saying," Cuomo begins. "He devotes the book 'to those who love the world.' What he really says is, God so loved the world that he made man. Now it's very important to remember the context. He was banned. The reason he was banned is that before Vatican II it was common to interpret the Catholic theology in this country as saying this world is an evil place. A series of moral obstacles. The best you can do is repair to the monastery and weave baskets. Monks weave baskets to give their hands something to do in the grim interval between birth and eternity. Teilhard was a reaction to all that. Teilhard was saying that *debases* God. That *demeans* God. God didn't make us to get ready for the next world. He made us to be involved in this world. What he is saying to people like me is: The world is good, involvement is good, pain is good, sorrow is good—Being is good. It's very important to somebody raised in the Jimmy Breslin era, when if girls wore patent-leather shoes the nuns got upset that boys would look under their skirts by the reflection. So what kind of spirit am I?" Cuomo asks, coming back, now that he has defined my terms more precisely, to my original question.

"I'm not a spirit, I'm a struggler, a confused human who knows way down deep that there's something immensely beautiful about this world and who, when he comes across a Teilhard, says, 'Hallelujah! Prayers have been answered,' because Teilhard is one who as a scientist, a paleontologist, was able to say to you with perfect theological probity, 'You're right, Mario. I don't understand it either and I'm smarter than you, but I know that it's beautiful and I know you ought to stay with it and I know the more deeply you get involved in it, the more deeply you become a part of it, the more beautiful it gets and we are building up.' We diminish

physically to build up spiritually, and when it's all over it just begins, so it's—"

"So it wasn't that you were tempted by renunciation," I say,
interrupting Cuomo as the distinction he is making finally dawns
on me. "It's the opposite: You found in him a vindication for a
temperamental preference for this world."

"This world has a significance better than the significance taught
by the old—" He searches for a word for the antiworld Catholic
thinkers. "They weren't theologians because they didn't understand the theology. They were good religious people," he says,
finally coming up with a charitable formulation for the error he
sees in their ways. "Good religious people who concentrated on
sin instead of opportunity."

I hadn't planned to get as deeply into theological questions as
we did, but I think you get a sense of Cuomo's thought process at
its most unmediated—in every sense of the word—when he's talking about such questions as the nature of hell and the continuing
mystery of the origin of evil.

We got into hell and evil when I once again strayed into error—
this time in my interpretation of a particularly cryptic reference to
Teilhard in Cuomo's *Diaries*. Amidst the chaos of his primary campaign against Ed Koch, Cuomo found himself "thinking through
the Apostles' Creed in my mind, the old creed that said, 'He descended into hell.' Matching it up to Teilhard." I had a theory about
what that passage was *really* about, which I tried out on the governor:

"I wondered whether you were comparing your entering New
York State politics to Christ descending into hell?"

"Oh no. No, not really. No," Cuomo says, "because that's
inconsistent with believing as I do that almost all of involvement
is good. So all the pain of politics and all the disappointment of
politics, all the imperfections of politics, that's part of living and
experiencing."

What was it then that he was speculating about in that passage
when he talked about matching up the old Apostles' Creed with
Teilhard?

The theology of hell is "still kind of bothersome" to him,
Cuomo says. "If you look at the old Apostles' Creed and you

compare it to what's said as a creed now—one of the principal differences is that they leave out of the present creed the portion that says Christ descended into hell."

So?

"I concluded from much analysis while jogging that what they're really saying in the new creed is, hell is the *void*. But the old creed suggested there was a *place,* an existence beneath us the way the world is a place. The new creed suggests that the real hell is a nothingness and a vacuum. And that's a colossal step forward. What Teilhard, I guess, would have said is there is a heaven but there is no hell in the sense of punishment."

Questions of hell and punishment lead him to leap to the theological controversy over the nature of evil.

"There is no explanation for evil, obviously, and Teilhard is very clear on that, too, but—"

"No explanation for evil in Teilhard?"

"I don't think anywhere really. There isn't sufficient understanding allowing us to be able to explain evil—I mean not sin, but unexplained pain to children sitting in Vietnamese villages who got their eyes blown out of their heads by explosions they didn't know were coming and that they had nothing to do with. The mother losing four children in a row, the apparently senseless tragedy. My brother's son freezing to death in the backyard at age five out in Copiague. How do you explain that? The apparent injustice. You can't. You read McBrien's two volumes on Catholicism, which is now all the rage theologically for Catholics—he says there's no point in giving a lot of pages to the subject of evil because we don't *have* an explanation."

Returning to Teilhard, I wondered if there might be something more about him that Cuomo identified with. Perhaps the way his heretical tendencies got him in trouble with his religious superiors might have fortified Cuomo in his outspoken disagreement with Archbishop O'Connor over abortion rights.

"Teilhard was a heretic, right?" I began. "He was condemned for—"

"No, no, he was not," Cuomo corrects me heatedly. "No, sir, there was nothing heretical about Teilhard."

"What about pantheism?" I suggest. "Pelagianism?" (The translator's footnotes to my edition of *The Divine Milieu* are replete with cautionary explanations of certain passages of Teilhard that, he says protectively, might *sound* pantheist, or hint at Pelagian tendencies, but are really okay in context. Pelagianism is the early church heresy that suggests that Adam's original sin does not necessarily taint all succeeding generations of mankind—that human endeavor has a potential for good in this world.)

Cuomo is particularly sensitive to my imputation that his spiritual mentor was a Pelagian heretic.

"Oh no, no, no, no," he says, quadruply negative. "He wasn't a Pelagianist either."

If he seems particularly upset about the imputation of Pelagianism, it may be because it's a particularly intriguing heresy to Cuomo. And one he will soon accuse Ed Koch, of all people, of adhering to.

But meanwhile he wants to correct my misuse of the word "heretic" in its application to Teilhard:

"The harshest criticism he got from the church was not that he should stop believing what he believed—he was just told that he was to stop publishing. It was John XXIII, that magnificent contribution to our humanity, who freed him from that and allowed him to publish, but just to seminarians where they could control it with guidance and understanding. And then eventually to the world at large. But he was never declared a heretic. He was to be read with caution."

"I guess what I was getting at is, you've had this public battle with your bishop. Do *you* feel at all like a heretic?"

"If you don't mind, my *cardinal*," he says.

"Your cardinal now. Do you feel at all like a heretic?"

"No. I will be precise on this subject, and it's a great relief to be able to be. I wrote the Notre Dame speech [on his abortion position] only because the archbishop in one of his early appearances was asked on a television show whether I should be excommunicated, and my wife and son were together with me watching the show at the time, and I have never had a more painful moment than the moment of the archbishop's hesitation in answer to that question."

He pauses, a pained expression on his brow. "The archbishop has since many times, not once or twice but many times, made clear that that wasn't his intent, et cetera. But too late. The damage was done and I felt it was time therefore to write my own apologia, which I did with the help of a number of theologians. When I say 'the help,' I wrote it and then distributed it to theologians whom I trusted. I was absolutely certain that I was right theologically, and since then in *America* magazine a couple of the leading theologians, or at least one in the country, have written that my position, whether they agreed with it or not as a matter of prudential judgment, was perfectly sound theologically, so I have no doubt that my position is sound theologically. My difference with my archbishop, now cardinal, is on a political judgment, agreeing that in my own personal life I would instruct those who wished my instruction that abortion was undesirable. What do you do about that politically? Do you try to pass a constitutional amendment which won't pass and which wouldn't do any good if it passed, or do you try to work affirmatively to convince people that there's a better way than abortion? I chose the latter. That's purely a matter of politics and I said so in the speech, and I'm right and I'm sure I'm right."

An admittedly irreverent thought strikes me at this point. How does a guy so concerned with theological correctness react to being named by *Playgirl* as one of its "Ten Sexiest Men"? A bit later I ask him what he thought of the accolade.

"Thank God John Candy made the list too," he says, laughing. "That way I won't take myself too seriously."

"What *is* your attitude toward sexual revolution or whatever you want to call what's gone on for the last twenty years? How traditional are you? Do you disapprove of permissiveness or—?"

"It's not for me to approve or disapprove," he says, criticizing my question before giving a surprisingly impassioned answer. "I don't judge people's conduct that way. I think from society's point of view it would be better if we were less open about sex. I believe we have profaned it. I believe sex is a beautiful gift of God, or whatever—fate, nature. It is a magnificent opportunity to express real feeling. It is God's device for regeneration. It is a lot of beautiful things. It is not improved by the way in which we as a society are dealing with it publicly. I think we fail to teach the reverence for it that we should. I think we have debased it and that's unfortunate. I think we're all losers as a result of that. It means less to this generation than it might have.

"It's a very personal thing. Some people are married and are frequently involved in sexual encounters, some people very infrequently. It's a personal thing. I do think from society's point of view it would have been better if we had not profaned it the way we have. But aside from that, I think as a people it would be better for us if we were more consistent in keeping violence out of our public exhibitions than sex, for all that I've said about the profaning of sex. Even worse is what we've done with violence, and popularizing violence is one of the great social sins of our time. I think those societies, I guess like Scandinavian societies where they allowed people vast freedom when it came to sexual preferences but were assiduous about trying to keep violence out of movies and publications, et cetera, where they can—that was probably a more intelligent judgment than the one we've made as a society."

Moral seriousness of this sort can be a bit of a problem with some. Recently I had dinner with a college friend and his wife who confessed their Cuomo Problem to me. They weren't the first. I'd found a number of Big Chill types who'd opted for the fast lane a bit resentful, hostile to Cuomo for reminding them of ideals—or, they'd say, illusions—they'd left behind.

Whatever was behind it, the way my friend's wife expressed her Cuomo Problem to me was: "I'd be more comfortable with Cuomo if I knew he had some really human faults—you know, even if it was that he binged on cookies at three in the morning—without transforming it into a spiritual lesson."

I ask Cuomo if he would help her out by confessing to me some cookie-binge-type faults. He isn't very forthcoming.

"I have all the faults that everybody has," he insists, "all the appetites that other people have. We control them, each of us, in various ways, but we each sin seven times a day."

Somehow I don't think that was the kind of answer she had in mind, so I try to approach the virtuousness problem from another direction.

"There was something Murray Kempton said—did you read his review of your book?"

"I never understand what he's saying but I love everything he writes," Cuomo avers.

"Well, he was very admiring of you in the review, but he also seemed to suggest that in your diary entries you were putting forward your humility in a somewhat prideful way."

Cuomo laughs. "See. I told you I had faults."

"Would you say it's true, though?"

"If Murray said it, I'll accept it."

I begin to shift the subject when Cuomo interrupts, not content to let Kempton have the last word on his pride/humility quotient.

"I'll say this about Murray: He has a little bit of pridefulness about the way he writes about *my* pridefulness."

Do I seem a bit captious about Cuomo here? Perhaps because we're coming to a subject upon which I find his views genuinely admirable, and I don't want to seem like an uncritical sensibility when discussing them. The subject is racial justice, and I admire Cuomo because I think he's one of the few powerful politicians in America who still takes the unfulfilled goals of the civil-rights movement seriously. Not only takes them seriously but takes seriously the task of making them work in a society that wants to ignore the past by calling itself "postracist," as the fashionable phrase goes.

You can hear how impassioned Cuomo is on the subject of race when I ask him how he would have handled racial relations in New York City differently from Ed Koch.

"There *is* a difference, I think, between the mayor and me," Cuomo says. "I think he uses the notion of *evenhandedness* where

I would use the notion of *equity*. I have heard him say, 'I treat blacks and whites the same way.' That can be misunderstood at a time when disproportionate numbers of blacks are vulnerable. Then people might mishear you and think that what you're really saying is 'I don't care if you're in trouble, I'm going to treat you like the people who are not in trouble.' Now that doesn't make any sense. That's what Marie Antoinette said: Let them all eat cake. So he puts a greater stress on pure equality. I think more about trying to even up the competition. There are some who are left behind through no fault of their own, who need extra help, and I think we should give them the extra help. The analogy I have used is a family with two children, one in a wheelchair, one wins medals for track. That creates a whole series of situations where the one in the wheelchair should get a little more help than the one who can win medals at track. That's not evenhandedness. So there is that difference. And I think when the mayor talks about equality a lot of blacks like it, the ones who are making it, et cetera. But the ones who are at the bottom, who are vulnerable, who are out of work, who are dropouts, think, 'You oppressed us for a couple of hundred years, you enslaved us, you debased us, you tried to dehumanize us, and then you release us and say, "Now you're like everybody else. I'm going to treat you evenhandedly." But that's not right because for two hundred years you created a negative. Now you're going to have to do at least two hundred years of positive to make up for it.' I think that's the attitude that some have that the mayor doesn't successfully respond to."

Did you catch the shift Cuomo makes in the midst of this response? I could hear it in his voice, but you can see it on the printed page, too. He begins with semantic distinctions and argumentative analogies (Marie Antoinette, the family with the kid in the wheelchair) to make his point intellectually.

Then something happens to his voice. He stops speaking in his own first-person voice and begins speaking *in the voice of the victims* of racism ("You oppressed *us* for a couple of hundred years, you enslaved *us,* you debased *us* . . . "), a voice that takes on tones of genuine pain and anger, not just abstract empathy.

In that astonishing 1984 Democratic convention keynote address, Cuomo called on Americans not to cease "to feel one another's pain."* That can be an empty rhetorical formulation. But in Cuomo's case, I get a feeling it's a *description* of a kind of spiritual discipline he practices in his approach to political problems.

There's a fascinating, characteristically Cuomoesque postscript to our discussion of Koch and race, one that provides another revealing glimpse into the governor's thought process. And one that gives me an opportunity—at last—to correct an error Cuomo made, in theological reasoning no less.

I don't know whether or not it was prompted by my mention of Pelagianism in connection with his spiritual mentor, or whether Cuomo just has Pelagianism on his mind these days, but a week after our conversation in Albany a quote from Cuomo appeared in print that accused Ed Koch of "Pelagianism."

When I say "a quote from Cuomo" accused Koch of Pelagianism, I may be on shaky ground, because the quote wasn't directly attributed to the governor. The quote appeared in a Ken Auletta *Daily News* column on Koch and race; Auletta attributes the quote to "a thoughtful public official." Judge for yourself if you think I'm rash in concluding it's Cuomo speaking here:

"The core difference between Koch and, say, Governor Cuomo," the "thoughtful public official" says, "is that Koch is a Pelagian. . . . If a kid from the ghetto can't make it, the Pelagian says it's their responsibility. The fact that God placed that kid in the ghetto, gave him no father, and that he was raised poor, that's of no concern."

While I agree with Cuomo on the merits of the equality argument (if somebody can prove to me it wasn't Cuomo speaking, I promise to enter a Trappist monastery and take a vow of silence), nonetheless I think the "thoughtful public official" has made an error in the logic of his heresiology.

His comparison of Koch to the Pelagians does a disservice to the Pelagians, who were far more generous in their view of human nature than Cuomo's analogy would imply. After all, the

---

*Okay, Bill Clinton ran this into the ground. But Clinton's meretricious use of the phrase shouldn't necessarily discredit the sentiment entirely.

heresy of the Pelagians was their rather optimistic belief that natural man was not inevitably corrupted by original sin and was capable, in fact, of moral good and spiritual improvement. It is the gloomy predestinarian Augustine (who believed natural man, as such, was beyond hope and who in fact was chief scourge of Pelagianism in the church) to whom Koch is more aptly compared.

And, in fact, I'd say that both Cuomo and his mentor, Teilhard, are closer in spirit—on the doctrinal spectrum that runs from Pelagius to Augustine—to the Pelagians, in their love of this world and belief in the possibility of spiritual evolution, than they are to Augustine. Indeed, there's a technical term Protestant theologian Paul Tillich uses that, although Cuomo would probably deny it, fits both Teilhard and Cuomo: "semicrypto-Pelagians." (Here's an issue the newly Catholicized Lew Lehrman could really run with next time he debates Cuomo: Okay, it's an expensive watch, but my opponent is a semicrypto-Pelagian.)

At this point I decided to see what Cuomo's views were on a different kind of heresy. A political heresy. About the lesson of the New York fiscal crisis. The orthodox establishment theology on this point, even among "responsible" New Yorkers, is that New York sinned, that New York and New Yorkers deserve the blame for our plight because our profligate bleeding-heart compassion was blind to hard-headed reality—and the rest of the country shouldn't be taxed to support our profligacy.

The first hint I had that Cuomo didn't buy the self-hating logic of the Blame New York First crowd was that stinging "share the derelicts" wisecrack he had delivered down in Washington a week earlier.

The governor was testifying before a House committee on his opposition to the Reagan tax plan's elimination of state- and local-tax deductibility—a complex, eye-glazing issue no Democrat wanted to touch, but which Cuomo seized on and turned into a moral crusade. One he seems to be winning.

Anyway, an earnest Republican House member from New Hampshire somewhat patronizingly suggested to Cuomo that the committee might deign to offer New York and other high-tax states with large social-service budgets "a portion" of the deductibility they wanted.

Fine, said Cuomo, and we'll send New Hampshire "a portion of our derelicts, our homeless, our illegal aliens, and drug addicts."

I thought that raised an important question the Blame New York First crowd has ignored. "Isn't it true," I ask Cuomo, "that the plight of the northern cities is not due to their immorality but to the costs they incur caring for the victims of southern racism, the vast migration of southern blacks who have sought refuge here?"

"I put it a little differently," Cuomo says, "but I made the same point and that is, we bear burdens that are basically national in their genesis and in present responsibility. Welfare, everybody knows, is a national problem. It's not ours. Not all the welfare cases are indigenous. They can travel here from any part of the country. That's the Constitution."

"Don't you think that in the way the fiscal crisis has been written about, New Yorkers have been unfairly portrayed as immoral and wasteful . . . ?"

"There is a regrettably prevalent view of us," Cuomo says, "as not just wasteful but as loud, even debauched, unpleasant, crude, indifferent to other people. I mean, it's a terribly harsh judgment. And again, it's not everybody of course, but too many people feel that way about New York. There may even be a little jealousy in it because of the spectacular quality of New York City, the bigness of it and the largeness; there may be a resentment about that. There is an intimidation factor as well. People are intimidated by the speed that they see here, the pace that they equate with frenzy. The president was aware of it, and the Republicans were aware of it and played to it by starting their whole campaign for this [tax plan] running against New York. In the president's first speech, he took the opportunity to refer to New York specifically. We're the only state he mentioned."

The talk turns to Forest Hills—and John Lindsay.

Cuomo says he met with Lindsay earlier today about the takeover bill, but sitting across the table from him, he couldn't help but think of Forest Hills.

"We didn't talk about Forest Hills," Cuomo says, "but I can't look at John without thinking of it."

Forest Hills was the beginning of the end for John Lindsay and the beginning of the beginning for Mario Cuomo.

Forest Hills—the revolt of the middle-class Queens community against the Lindsay administration plan to stick high-rise, low-income projects for ghetto dwellers in their midst—was, of course, what brought Cuomo into public life. His ability to "feel the pain" and fears of the angry white residents of Forest Hills enabled him to gain community acquiescence to a scaled-down integrated project that salvaged a workable reality from the blundering, self-destructive good intentions of the Lindsay administration.

"What's the Forest Hills project like now?" I ask Cuomo.

"It's beautiful," he says. "I went back there with Harry Reasoner a little bit ago to do *60 Minutes*. We walked the grounds. Every time I go home to Queens I go past it. I stopped by there the other day with somebody in the car just to show it to them."

"You wrote in your Forest Hills *Diary,*" I say, "that toward the end you thought it might be a turning point away from the attempt to integrate housing or, on the other hand, it might be a turning point for the better where communities are consulted, et cetera. Which do you think it has been?"

"It helped end housing programs," says Cuomo. "The Nixon impoundment was in '72, and we never had another large public-housing program. Forest Hills helped produce a political environment that allowed the federal government to walk away from its obligation for low-income housing, and they have ever since."

"Would you favor a return to some kind of attempt to . . . ?"

"I certainly would, but I'm not going to wait for it. That's why Mayor Koch and I have put together the biggest housing program in the history of the state. It would mean seventy-five thousand units if we could get the legislature to adopt the legislation we need to spend the Battery Park and Port Authority monies."

"You know Democrats have a reputation for being antibusiness. Are you antibusiness?"

"I couldn't be if I cared about those people in wheelchairs and the people out of work, because the place they're going to get a job is in the private sector. You can't make it with the public payroll. You just can't put enough people to work. It costs you too much. So if there's any hope for those eight hundred thousand or so AFDC [Aid to Families with Dependent Children] people, it's in the private sector. That means business. So I'm not only not antibusiness, I am probusiness. Not so that they can all drive Rolls-Royces and wear pinkie rings but so that we can create the base we need to do the things we need for people who aren't given the chance to work because they're too old or too weak or because there simply is no job. So yes, I'm very much pro–private sector strength."

By now time was running out, and so I tried to ask the governor one last question that had been on my mind. But first I had to go through one last corrective struggle:

"Last question," I begin.

"You said that already," Cuomo snaps.

"No, I said *two* more questions."

"No you didn't, you said two more questions *two* questions ago."

"No, no, no."

"Yes you did."

"We'll go back to the tape."

"When you play the tape you'll see what a good lawyer I am."

Okay, it turns out he was right. But I'm still right about his semi-crypto-Pelagianism. And he let me ask my final question anyway.

"I was struck as I arrived today," I begin, "seeing John Lindsay down there with some other lobbyists waiting in line. Here was the guy who was the great hope of American liberalism and now he's a high-paid lobbyist for Drexel Burnham. Do you think you'll ever end up as a high-paid lobbyist for corporations?"

"Hmm. I don't know. I kind of doubt it. The only reason I could possibly do that would be for the money, and I hate to say this, but money has never meant everything to me that it should have. If I were a little more careful about money, I would have had a lot more of it, and I would have had a lot more freedom and probably could have done a lot more things than I have. But now I have a son who I am sure is going to get rich if he keeps his health, and I've told him to go into the law practice. He wants public life. He never said that. He won't say it to me but I know it. He's my blood and he wants public life. But first, I told him, go and make money so they can't commandeer you. You see, if you come to this business needing the job then there is the temptation to do things you otherwise might not if you were secure. So I said, build yourself a secure niche. He'll be rich in no time. Honestly. My daughter, my first, is a doctor. My two girls after Andrea are so beautiful and so bright that they're going to make it.

"Money now means something because it keeps you free to be a public servant. I can settle for one hundred thousand dollars. I don't need two hundred fifty thousand. So I doubt very much that I would wind up that way. I'd like to wind up as a judge, a teacher maybe. Not with a lot of classes. That's too hard. I would like to wind up being free to read, being free to listen to music. So anyway, no, I don't want to be a lobbyist. No. I don't want to finish that way."

He pauses. Suddenly a new notion strikes him: "I want to die sliding into third base." Then his eyes light up: "No, throwing a hook shot. I think ideally I'd like to die with the ball just hitting the net, probably a left-hand hook shot off the back wall."

Cuomo gets up and demonstrates his form for that Final Shot.

"It just hits the net," he says with a smile of triumph. "The bell goes off. That's it."

# LAST TANGO IN TAHITI

### Mike Sager

From the start it sounded ridiculous:
*Find Marlon Brando. Go to Tahiti and find Marlon Brando.*
Yeah? And then what?
*You'll know.*
I'll know?
Hmmm.
What else was I going to do? It was December. It was cold. There was promise of little. Contra-gate, snowplows, New Year's. Suicide season. I needed a mission, a real, choice mission. A quest.

Yeah, that's what I needed, a quest.

I needed to learn something; it was time. Thirty years old, divorce pending. Ready now to turn the page for the big buildup. You have to dare to be bad in this world of ours, you have to try things, you might have to fail. You do what you always do, it's guaranteed to turn out the same. After ten years of stories, I'd learned a lot about other people, and a little about myself, but not nearly so much as I'd have liked. This time, I wanted more than a story. I wanted to bring something back in first person, to write about a difference in my life. . . .

As it was, they suggested Marlon.

I took the job. Wouldn't you?

So now I'm in Papeete, searching for Marlon Brando, walking around in the rain. It is rain like I've never seen before, summer rain, monsoon, a thick, pulsing mist against a white-gray sky, a tin rhythm on a rusty roof, steady, maddening. . . .

I arrived four days ago, flying from just before dusk at Dulles until just after dawn at Faaa. How many hours it took, I cannot say. Across the continent, across the equator, halfway around the world, counterclockwise. Snotty stews, grainy light, a fat man reclining his seat into my lap. Time running backward as I flew forward, yesterday arriving tomorrow, brisket and succotash arriving cold.

Since then, since landing and checking in, setting out for Marlon, everything has taken on the quality of a dream. A weird, suffocating, narcotic dream. My bones feel soft. My underwear is damp. I'm looking for a man who doesn't want to be found. I feel like I'm in a movie.

I haven't located Marlon, not exactly, not yet. But there are traces of him everywhere. Down the street, across the Boulevard Pomare, is a bar called Chaplin's. It's named for Charlie, who directed Marlon in *A Countess from Hong Kong*. There's a picture of Marlon on the wall. He's astride a motorcycle, Johnny in *The Wild One*. Marlon's in the bookstore down the street, too. Pieces of his life, anyway. On one shelf are eight copies of *Mutiny on the Bounty*, six copies of *The Arrangement*, by Elia Kazan. *Mutiny*, you know about: Marlon, then the world, discovers Tahiti. Kazan was Marlon's director. *A Streetcar Named Desire, Viva Zapata!, On the Waterfront*.

Even in my room, there are signs of Marlon. I turned on cable a while ago, found Bogart in *The African Queen*. Bogart won the Oscar for *Queen*, beating out Marlon in *Streetcar*. Later this evening, *Catch-22* is airing. Martin Sheen is in that. He is also in *Apocalypse Now*, playing another guy who goes searching for Marlon, another guy who didn't know what he'd do if he found him.

It's been like this for some time now. Everywhere I look, I see Marlon. His pictures, his movies, his legacy. In a way, I guess, I did this to myself, cooked up the mania and smoked it like a drug, inhaled his spirit into my body, his thoughts into my head.

After I took the job, I set out to study Marlon. I bought a VCR. Night after night, for four solid weeks, I darkened the lights and flipped the remote, and the LCD pulsed and the reels rolled inside their plastic casings. Old moments from Hollywood returned, and Marlon moved in many guises, shadowing first my Sony monitor and, later, the screen inside my brain.

Napoleon, Fletcher Christian, the Godfather, Julius Caesar, Sky Masterson, Jor-El, an eyeball in a cave. Turned-down lips and sleek smooth jaw and high-gloss cheekbones and almond eyes and tousled hair. A brute, a fop, a dandy, a statesman, a queer, a killer, a don, a Nip, a crip, a Kraut . . .

I got kind of obsessed so I stopped going out, and I Xeroxed his pictures and taped them on the walls, and I read every book and every article, during every meal and before bed. I dropped down deep, very deep, into my own kind of Method, and in his wife I saw an old girlfriend, and in his divorce I saw my old wife, and in his art I found a meaning, and in his vision I saw one too. I saw a snail crawl along the edge of a straight razor, crawl along the edge of a straight razor and survive. That was my dream. That was my nightmare. That and the others, gray dreams, half formed, fitful and flickering in the hours before dawn.

And then one day, it hit me. Marlon was James Dean before James Dean, De Niro before De Niro, Newman before Newman, Cruise before Cruise. . . . He was all of it before anyone. Marlon was the template for two generations of actors, and even more, he was the template for two generations of men.

He wore jeans, he did his own thing, he did well. He was tough and sensitive, gifted and crude, he spoke French, and he used words like "ain't." He was talented, he made a lot of money, he gave to the world, he used the world for his own whims.

He was, in a sense, the ultimate man of the '80s, thirty years ahead of his time. So much of what we do today is Marlon. The way he puts on his sunglasses in *The Wild One.* The way he smells his lapel rose in *The Godfather.* The way he cries for Stella.

He led the way, then he disappeared, split from the whole program. The more I began to understand, the more I admired him. A tough mother. An original. He could have been head of the Screen Actors Guild, a politician, the occupant of whatever pedestal this hero-hungry world would have gladly offered. Instead, he went for himself, and we've got Rambo and Rob Lowe.

I started to think that it wouldn't be bad at all to find Marlon Brando, to ask him for some guidance on the world's behalf, to ask him what he thinks, where we should be going, what we should be doing, what is supposed to come next. We need you, Marlon Brando. That's how it formed in my mind. *We need you.* In the '50s, he showed us how to be young. In the '80s, we could use a little advice.

It couldn't hurt.

At the moment, I'm in the terrace bar at the Ibis Hotel, paging through a book called *Brando for Breakfast,* written by Anna Kashfi Brando, one of his two ex-wives. It says here on page 120 that Marlon once knew a duck in Paris.

The rain has stopped, and sun pounds the pavement, raising steam. Ants swarm, mosquitoes buzz; I get this feeling that within the wall of plants skirting the terrace a savage spirit has awakened, and he is causing buds to form and stalks to shoot and flowers to explode. It is hard to breathe. I'm waiting for Angelina.

Beyond the terrace, a South Seas city hunkers beside the concrete docks and the lava rock shoreline. Under a row of palms, traffic swirls, a Third World motor-drone of scooter burps and diesel hums that mixes with the smells of rain and earth and flower and lies close to the asphalt, pinioned between thick clouds and high green mountains.

Minicars line the narrow streets, side wheels parked up on curbs. Sullen French women with hair under their arms sit in sidewalk cafés, drinking pink Campari and writing postcards. American retirees off the cruise ship Liberté deliberate in small groups. Two fat men on a bench share red slices of a freshly caught fish. A Tahitian pimp named Louis, a brown bulldog with thick lips, broad brow, and bowed legs, paces nervously beneath an awning, three packs of cigarettes in hand.

And, forty miles that way, due north from my table in the terrace bar at the Ibis, out the harbor and through the clouds, is Marlon's island, Tetiaroa.

It had come as a bit of a shock, this knowledge, though it wasn't hard to get. I'd been walking down Boulevard Pomare, through the rain and the crowds, trying to figure out how the hell I was going to find Marlon, what I was going to say once I did, what everybody would say if I didn't.

Before I left Washington, I'd had ideas. One involved getting to Marlon's island, sitting cross-legged on his beach in saffron robes, making him curious enough to come to me. Another involved a commando raid on Marlon's island. I'd swim ashore under a canopy of darkness. A hired speedboat, black clothes, with camera and tape recorder and extra tapes and batteries secured in the waterproof scuba bag I'd bought at Hudson Trail Outfitters in Gaithersburg.

When I bought the bag, I'd thought about buying a survival knife, too. Maybe Marlon would be in a cave up a river with an army of stoned Polynesians guarding the landing with blowguns. Who knew? All I knew was what they told Captain Willard before his mission in *Apocalypse Now:*

"You see, Willard," the general had said, "things get confused out there. Power, ideals, morality . . . there's conflict in every human heart between the rational and the irrational, between good and evil. Every man has got a breaking point. You and I do. Walter Kurtz has reached his. Very obviously he has gone insane."

So this is what I'd been thinking as I walked in the rain on the Boulevard Pomare. Part of me was afraid of what I'd find, what I'd do once I got there. I knew the risks, or imagined I knew them. But the thing I felt the most, much stronger than fear, was the desire to confront him.

Then, all of a sudden, I saw the poster. Right there, in the window of a travel agency. Three Tahitians, two girls and a boy, in native dress on a white sand beach, letting go a sea bird.

## TAHITI
### Hotel Tetiaroa
### Marlon Brando's Private Atoll

Hotel Tetiaroa!

I pushed on the door, threw it open, and the woman started spitting French, but I don't speak any French so I started tapping furiously on the window, pointing at the poster. "Can go? Can go? Marlon Brando?" I stuttered again and again, tapping the window, tapping furiously with my fingernail, *tap tap tap!,* and I was sure that at any moment a crack would form and spread and the glass would shatter into puddles on the sidewalk, and my hand would bleed and maybe music would play, just like Willard's in the movie, but I couldn't stop tapping . . . "Can go? Can go? Marlon Brando?" . . . because I couldn't believe this, a travel poster for Marlon Brando's Private Atoll. Marlon running a tourist trap. "Can go? Can go? Marlon Brando?"

"No problem," the woman said. "Cash, check, or Visa?"

Angelina is late. I know she thinks I'm crazy. When I first called her and said I needed help finding Marlon, she was silent a moment. Then she said, "Marlon Brando. He is lost?"

I've decided, however, that I need her. I speak neither French nor Tahitian. And there was that run-in with the local press.

It happened two days ago. I figured I'd find a journalist. The local colleague is always a good bet. He had to know about Marlon. Where he lived, where he ate, things like that.

I played charades with the receptionist at *Le Nouveau Journal,* trying to make my purpose clear. I typed on an imaginary typewriter, did a Godfather imitation. Finally, I said the only thing I know how to say in French: "*Parlez-vous anglais?*"

The receptionist made a phone call. Dany Weus appeared.

Weus is a burnt, thin guy with a pointed face like a mongoose. He led me through a courtyard, up some stairs. A room with three desks. He sat down.

I looked around, crossed the room, dragged a chair over to his desk, smiled, sat. I lit his cigarette and one for myself.

"I've been sent by *The Washington Post* to find Marlon Brando."

'Watergate!" he screamed. "*Washington Post!* Watergate! Bob Woodward! You know him?"

His mouth dropped. He froze. A full minute. Then he snapped to, took out a pad and a pen. "How do you spell your name?" he asked.

I started spelling. M . . . I . . . K . . . "Wait a minute! What are you doing?"

"We make the story of you searching for Marlon Brando. We take picture of you, everything."

Whoa.

Just what I need.

Marlon picking up the newspaper and reading about my search. Marlon hates publicity, hates reporters. The last time he was interviewed was in June 1977, for a *Playboy* Q&A. Marlon granted the interview, he said, to "pay a debt, so to speak" to Hugh Hefner, who several years earlier had posted bond when American Indian Movement leader Russell Means was arrested.

Debt or not, Marlon had kept the *Playboy* reporter on hold for seventeen months. He canceled three times before they finally met, and then he did his best over five sessions in ten days to evade all subjects other than the plight of the American Indian.

Prior to that, on a promotion stump for *Superman,* he fried Dick Cavett on network TV. Ninety minutes on Indians.

On the BBC, the interviewer asked, "Were you able to get into your costume for *Superman?*" Marlon answered, "Well, in 1973, Wounded Knee [the protest] took place."

"I've regretted most interviews," Marlon told *Playboy*. And journalism being what it was, what it is, you can't help but understand. Of course, Marlon being what he was, what he is, well, that hasn't helped either.

In 1946, Marlon dictated the following biography. It appeared in the Playbill for his second Broadway play, *Truckline Café.*

"Born in Bangkok, Siam, the son of an etymologist now affiliated with the Field Museum in Chicago, Mr. Brando passed his early years in Calcutta, Indochina, the Mongolian Desert and Ceylon. His formal education began in Switzerland and ended in Minnesota, where he found the rigid restriction of military school too confining. After a period in which he saw himself as a potential tympanic maestro, he came to New York and studied acting."

It's been that way ever since, Marlon slings crap, the publicists and reporters catch it, gobble, regurgitate. A mythology grows.

Marlon disdains it. Ignores it. Slings more crap. Gets mad. He punches out a photographer, chases a reporter off his island. The press writes about it.

Since 1950, when he appeared as a paraplegic war vet in *The Men,* the first of his thirty-one movies, reporters have called him "The Brilliant Brat," "The Walking Hormone Factory," "The Valentino of the Bop Generation," "World's Highest-Paid Geek." They have pictured him racing around New York on a motorcycle, living like a beatnik in a flat with Wally Cox, living like a recluse, living like a Hollywood star. They have reported he wore blue jeans in public, switched from blue jeans to suits and ties, fathered at least six children by at least four different women, was seen in a restaurant holding a piece of bread and buttering his sleeve.

Reporters have approached him at parties with lines like, "You seem pretty normal," only to have Marlon walk quietly to a corner and stand on his head. They have talked him into doing interviews, only to have Marlon sit catatonic for thirty minutes, then get up and leave.

Reporters have written that he was personally responsible for $6 million of the $21 million cost overrun in the filming of *Mutiny on the Bounty.* They've said he requested that his lines be written on Maria Schneider's rear during the filming of *Last Tango in Paris.* They've said he dogged roles, tyrannized directors, threw temper tantrums.

They have cycled and recycled the story of his youth in Libertyville, Illinois. Young Marlon Brando Jr., Bud to his family, born April 3, 1924. Cherubic only boy, youngest child of a womanizing limestone products salesman and an amateur actress with a fondness for alcohol who was credited for discovering Henry Fonda. There was the time he set his own sweater afire in an elevator in a department store; the time he brought home a bag lady during the Depression; the time he stole the clapper from the bell at military school.

They have quoted his grandma saying that "Bud is always falling for the cross-eyed girls," and an actress calling him a Don

Juan: "If he's Don Juan, he's Don them all." They have uncovered nude paintings of his first fiancée, Josanne Mariani-Berenger, daughter of a French fisherman. They have traveled around the world chasing rumors that his first wife was not really Anna Kashfi, a Hindu from Calcutta, but Joan O'Callaghan, daughter of a Welsh factory worker who was posing as a Hindu from Calcutta. They have hinted that the reason he married Mexican actress Movita was so their son would have a last name; that the reason he stayed with Movita was so their daughter would have a last name.

They have updated the public on every new twist in his fourteen-year court battle over the custody of his son by Kashfi/O'Callaghan; on every new romance; on Rita Moreno's overdose of sleeping pills at his Hollywood home; on a Philippine woman's paternity suit; on France Nuyen's inability to play Suzie Wong on the screen because of her depression after he dumped her.

They have called him a genius and a slob. They have written stories called "Brando: An Explosive Young Man's Fight to Be Himself," "Brando—The Real Story," "My Friend Brando," "Idealism Is a Snare for Citizen Brando," "Brando in Search of Himself."

Said *The New York Times Magazine:* "Brando's riddled with paradoxes. *And* conflicts. *And* inner problems. An extraordinarily complicated Joe trying to understand himself, to come to terms with himself, to uncover his own identity."

In 1977, he told *Playboy,* "I'm not going to lay myself at the feet of the American public and invite them into my soul. My soul is a private place. . . . People believe what they will believe. . . . People will like you who never met you . . . and then people also will hate you, for reasons that have nothing to do with any real experience with you. People don't want to lose their enemies. . . . Why should I talk to anyone?"

No. *Merci,* no. No stories in *Le Nouveau Journal* about my search for Marlon. I told Weus I'd call him Friday. I didn't say what year. If I was going to find Marlon, I would have to be subtle. And if I had to be subtle, I couldn't act like a journalist.

I'd have to come up with something better.

I'd have to go see Benji.

Benji's in exile.

He used to be a captain in the Philippine army. His uncle was a general. The general didn't get along too well with Ferdinand Marcos, so the whole family fled to Tahiti. Now, the general runs a grocery, and Benji works at the Ibis. He arranges cars, recommends restaurants, chats up American women and sends them on the Circle Island tour to see the Blowhole of Arahoho. He looks like someone who can get you what you need.

I set the proposition. I need a translator, I say, someone to help infiltrate the natives who work on Marlon's island, someone to help with a subtle mission. Someone to help find Marlon. Soon.

"And for this someone, you want girl or boy?" Benji asks. His lip curls, then he leers.

"Well, ah, ah, um," I say. "Ah, um. I think girl would be best."

"I see," says Benji.

"If I go with a girl, it would be a good cover for me. Me there with a girl. You know. Oh, of course, separate accommodations. I'm looking for a translator, you understand. Simply a translator."

"I see," says Benji.

"And, you know, now that I think about it, it wouldn't hurt to have a beautiful girl, either. You know, Marlon loves beautiful, exotic women, and, like, well . . ."

Angelina arrives at the terrace bar an hour late. She shakes my hand tentatively, sits at the table with her knees together and her purse balanced in her lap. She wears a flower behind her ear, and a pareu, a native length of cloth. She has tied it in such a way that it looks like a gown, and she wears it with an easy elegance, a languor, a . . . well, Benji has done all right.

It is hard to know what she is thinking as I tell her of my plan. The true language of Tahiti is a silent one, conveyed with a downcast glance, a lift of the chin, a raising of the eyebrows. She smiles now and then in the velvet shadows of the sunset; she pouts, giggles, breaks my heart with the bright whites of her eyes. She seems willing enough to go on a trip and make some money. She seems to trust me. But she just can't understand. Why am I searching for Marlon Brando?

I try to explain. I can't. It started out as an assignment, but it's becoming more and more like life. Anyway, it doesn't matter. I've got reservations for two on Tetiaroa. Tomorrow, we fly.

I wake to a clattering breeze beneath a coconut palm, a melody of fronds like wind chimes. The sand is soft ivory, warm to the touch, with a crust of coral like fresh ice on deep snow. Red ants skitter across a footprint, hermit crabs in painted shells motor sideways, probing with tiny claws. The vegetation is lush, a blend of vines and flowers and leaves and fruits and coconut palms that bend the water's edge, curved and vain, ripe with green nuts. The lagoon teems with fish, feeding in bands and swirls of aquamarine and amethyst and emerald. A half-mile distant, a coral reef breaks the waves, but here on the beach, only a dim echo of the roar is heard, and all is calm.

This is my second day on Marlon's island, mid-morning. I must have fallen asleep. I was up until 4 last night reading *Marlon Brando: The Only Contender,* by the author of *Doug and Mary, Lenny, Janis and Jimi: All the Stars in Heaven.* I'm still a little woozy. I rub my eyes, blink them back into focus.

Hmmm.

On the beach, ten feet south, a most beautiful pair of breasts. Smooth, brown, tapered in repose, they rise and fall gently with breath. I lean back on one elbow, admire. Scraps of lust and poetry float across my memory, and I have an urge to reach, to touch, to feel the softness against my palms and fingertips, but I cannot.

I am searching for Marlon Brando, and the breasts are those of my translator, Angelina, a softly sculpted girl of twenty on an ivory beach in string bikini bottom who speaks English, French, and Tahitian.

Angelina stirs.

I snap gaze, search blue.

Marlon discovered Tahiti in 1960, when he came here to shoot *Mutiny on the Bounty.* His *Bounty* was a remake of Clark Gable's of 1935. (Gable's leading lady, Movita, became Marlon's second wife.) When he got here, Marlon stayed in an expensive bungalow, attended by beautiful wahines. He played his conga drums with the natives, met Tarita, made a movie, discovered a good thing. By then, Marlon was thirty-seven. He'd been making movies for ten years. He was arguably the biggest star in Hollywood.

After *I Remember Mama* and *A Streetcar Named Desire* on Broadway, Marlon had gone to the coast in 1949 to film *The Men*. Next came the movie version of *Streetcar*, *Viva Zapata!*, *Julius Caesar*, *The Wild One*, *On the Waterfront*, *Désirée*, *Guys and Dolls*, *The Teahouse of the August Moon*, *Sayonara*, *The Young Lions*, *The Fugitive Kind*, and *One-Eyed Jacks*.

By the time he got to Tahiti, he had been nominated for an Oscar four times, had won once and on the way had inspired what became a whole new generation of Method actors—leading men like James Dean, Paul Newman, Jack Nicholson, and Robert De Niro, who drew from the tentative mannerisms, the untrained voice, the raw emotions, and the brutal reality that Marlon had brought to the screen.

It is said by some that Marlon's acting helped redefine the concepts of masculine sexuality in our culture. He played men who acted one way, felt another. He reversed the old, simple, John Wayne kind of concept that a man can be judged by his actions, that he can be held responsible.

"Because the typical Brando hero of the early Fifties was ambivalent and emotionally confused," wrote a contributing editor to *Harper's* magazine, "he could not summon the courage and maturity that had formerly been elements of a film hero's virility. Instead, he projected a kind of teenaged eroticism, intense and unfocused, which derived emotional power from an impossible passive yearning. Frustration was the bottom line of his sexuality, the frustration of a man who cannot control his fate."

And so it was that Marlon and his sexuality became the subject of intense debate and scrutiny and replication, and so it was that people began expecting him to throw raccoons. Marlon never had much liking for denizens of Hollywood, the "funnies in satin Cadillacs" who lived in "the cultural boneyard." He once told

James Dean that Dean was mentally unbalanced and ought to see a shrink. Of Frank Sinatra, Marlon said, "Frank is the kind of guy, when he dies, he's going to Heaven and give God a bad time for making him bald." The two biggest Hollywood gossip columnists of the day were Louella Parsons and Hedda Hopper. Marlon called them "The Fat One" and "The One with the Hat."

Marlon, obviously, was not impressed. He did things the way he wanted to do them. From the first, he bucked the system of studios and contract players. He was among the first modern actors to receive a percentage of gross earnings, to have script and casting approval, to start his own production company, to produce and direct his own film, *One-Eyed Jacks*. And he was one of the first to discover what nobody else, to this day, seems able to accept: Great actors should stay actors; they only lose by trying to be more.

And lose Marlon did. As was inevitable, when his films started lagging at the box office, Hollywood began swiping back. Times were bad. He was estranged from Movita, his pregnant second wife of several months. He was named in a paternity suit by a Philippine dancer. And his first wife was still dragging him through court. Associated Press reported, on November 19, 1959, that Anna Kashfi "threatened Mr. Brando with a butcher knife and threw a tricycle at him. She says he beat her, threw her to the floor, and terrorized her. Each says their violent battles, which included hair pulling and spanking, were the other's faults."

At work, Marlon became more and more of an attitude problem. He brought the raccoon to the set. And rubber spiders. He tyrannized directors with script changes, arrived late, wore earplugs during takes, gained so much weight during the course of production that obtuse camera angles had to be employed by the end of filming.

Marlon began talking about hanging it up for good. He diversified—this too, before his time—studying Eastern religions and meditation, traveling to Southeast Asia, playing his conga drums, lending his image to political causes.

In fact, when MGM came to him in 1960 with the idea for a remake of *Mutiny on the Bounty,* Marlon was more interested in promoting a film biography of Caryl Chessman, a rapist who had recently been executed in California. On the night Chessman had been put to death, Marlon stood outside the walls at San Quentin prison and mourned.

At a meeting at his Hollywood home with producer Aaron Rosenberg and director Carol Reed, Marlon pitched Chessman's life for two hours. The men listened, they shook their heads no. Then Rosenberg proposed an alternate idea. If Marlon would agree to do *Bounty,* he could leave right away for Tahiti. Marlon could cast his Polynesian leading lady himself.

And so it was that Marlon came to Tahiti, and so it was that he bought his own atoll, thirteen islands in a lagoon four miles across, protected by a coral reef. Half a world away from Hollywood, his wives, his problems, it was called Tetiaroa.

Tetia means "man standing alone." Roa means "far away."

It was perfect.

"Sleep well?"

"Yes, thank you," says Angelina, stirring from her mid-morning nap on the beach on our second day. "Did you find Marlon Brando yet?"

"Cute. Very cute," I say. "How come you like making fun of me?"

"I not make fun. I ask question."

"Oh. Okay. How about I ask you question? What ever happened to you last night? You disappeared right after dinner."

"I not disappear," says Angelina.

"I didn't see you."

"I tired, that all," she says, and she giggles.

"Tired is right, *tired out,*" I think, but I don't say it. No sense getting mad. I hired her to infiltrate Marlon's people. I just didn't think she'd get so far so fast.

The twin-engine, twelve-seater plane had broken cloud cover five minutes out of Tahiti, and thereafter the sky was clear, the ocean a vast cloth of wrinkled blue, curved at the horizon. After twenty minutes in the air, the plane made its approach, a full circuit of Marlon's sunny atoll, then landed on the airstrip, a patch of packed sand and concrete scissored like an off-center part through five square miles of jungle.

A dozen smiling Tahitians dressed in pareus and Hawaiian surfer shorts met the plane. The only other passengers were four members of a French film crew. They'd just finished shooting a miniseries sequel to *Mutiny on the Bounty*. An older woman, Simone, led us to our bungalows, rustic dwellings of ancient design spaced randomly among coconut and pandanus and breadfruit and ironwood trees.

Angelina and I followed at the rear. Marlon's island. Here at last. As I walked, I figured we'd take it easy, check things out, be subtle. . . .

Then all of a sudden, Angelina was marching toward Simone. The line stopped. Angelina and Simone talked. They giggled. Angelina pointed to me. Simone looked back. Everyone in line looked back. Then Angelina and Simone giggled again. Simone shook her head.

Angelina returned. She smiled and averted her eyes.

"Listen," I began, "from now on—"

"She say Marlon Brando not here."

That was yesterday. Now, this morning, I'm on the beach with my thoughts, the palms, the lagoon, the hermit crabs in painted shells, Angelina's breasts. Of course, I don't believe Simone. I've come, what, ten thousand miles? Of course she was going to say he wasn't here. You spend ten years writing stories about people who don't want stories written about them, and you learn a few things. Marlon pays all these people to keep people like me away.

But that's to be expected. No one said it would be easy. I'll find him.

I already know a lot more than I did yesterday. Between Angelina and myself, we have found out that there are seventeen employees here, and about ten of their children visiting for the Christmas holidays. The Hotel Tetiaroa itself consists of fifteen guest bungalows, which are rarely full all at once. There's a reception area, a dining room, a gift shop (T-shirts that say "Marlon Brando's Private Atoll"), a thatched lobby with a TV and a VCR, a bar on the beach called Dirty Old Bob's Bar. (Dirty Old Bob, I had heard in Papeete, is a ham radio operator in Honolulu. Marlon and he used to ratchet-jaw often.)

All the buildings are built on concrete slabs with native materials. The beds in the bungalows have mosquito nets, and the bed frames and furniture are fashioned of coco wood, cloth, and twine. The walls are made of woven pandanus fronds, decorated with pieces of driftwood. Instead of bathroom sinks, there are giant clam shells with metal faucets. There is electricity, but only at certain times of the day, and only until 10 at night. Without the hum of the generator, there is just the loud soothing sound track of the tropics: the sea birds, the palms, the mosquitoes, the waves.

Bringing Angelina along was a good idea. She fit right in. She seemed to like prying into other people's lives. After the incident with Simone, I had a little talk with Angelina, and later, she'd drifted over to the picnic table near the bar where Marlon's people sat. She sat herself down, started in giggling. I left her alone with them for a while, then ambled over. She invited me to join.

The conversation was lively, and, occasionally, Angelina would translate something. Or she would say so-and-so spoke English, and I would try, but so-and-so wouldn't speak. Most of the time, I drank, offered menthol cigarettes all around, tried to smile at the appropriate time as they jabbered in French and Tahitian.

The old lady with the frizzy afro is Grandmere. She comes from Bora Bora. Her job is taking care of Marlon. She's been with him for twenty years. She remembers once she had to take Cheyenne, Marlon's daughter by Tarita, to Aspen for a reunion of some of Marlon's kids. It was so cold she thought she would die.

Popi is white-haired and grizzled, black, a native of New Guinea. He wears five shark teeth around his neck. His real name is John. He was given the name Popi by Christian Devi Brando, Marlon's son by Anna Kashfi. Popi says that he and Devi were working to clear the airstrip one day when Devi suddenly hugged him and said, "From now on, you're my Popi."

Charles and Suzanna are from Vanuatu. They are first cousins, and they live together. Suzanna used to be a radio announcer on Vanuatu, but Charles got tired of fishing and making copra, the work of his father and his father before that. They came here five years ago. They work a few hours a day—Suzanna running the bar, Charles doing odd jobs with the other men. They make about $500 a month each. Their rent is free. A small amount is taken for food. They will stay forever.

Matahi is from Morea. He is round-bellied and half toothless and is married to an American woman who is at home in Papeete. He speaks English, but not so well considering he lived in the San Fernando Valley for twenty years. When *Bounty* was being filmed, he was hired as a carpenter and built sets. After the movie, he moved to California, got married, toured the country for a French airline with a Tahitian song and dance troupe. He remembers going to a party once at Marlon's house in Hollywood. There was no address given on the invitation. The instructions were to drive to a certain place and then follow the pareus that had been hung from bamboo poles.

There are several here from Bora Bora, Tarita's home island. Tarita is the mother of two of Marlon's six kids. She spends half her time on Tetiaroa, half in a house Marlon built in Papeete. Marlon also has three houses in Bora Bora. Tarita and her daughters, Cheyenne (by Marlon) Miamiti (named by Marlon for Tarita's character in *Bounty*), and Reatua, will be flying in this afternoon to celebrate Christmas.

And then there is Teri'i. He's twenty-three, has been here two years. He got the job on Tetiaroa after meeting Marlon and Tarita's son Tehotu in the bars in Papeete.

Tehotu runs the hotel, but he is presently in California. At twenty-six, he is roughly the same age as three of Marlon's four other sons. He loves to party, Teri'i says. He's a good surfer; he's good with girls. He prefers to be known by his mother's family name, Teriipaia, rather than by his father's.

Angelina and Teri'i took to one another instantly. I have to admit that he is something, a Polynesian Renaissance man with sculpted muscles, crafted cheekbones, a parrot tattooed on his shoulder.

Yesterday afternoon, after the giggles and the beers and the menthol cigarettes around the picnic table, Teri'i had invited

Angelina for a walk along the beach. I went along, though I was pretty sure I wasn't invited.

Teri'i carried a fishing spear, six feet long, three rusty iron prongs, as he sure-footed along the sand. A few hundred yards down the beach, he stopped, waded out into the lagoon. He was still a moment, then he frowned, then he jabbed. He came back to the beach with something on the end of the spear about the size of a flattened basketball, brown and covered with spines like a porcupine. He threw it on the sand. He grunted, spoke.

Angelina translated. "Teri'i say if you step on this thing, is very bad. Baddest thing in world. It can kill."

Teri'i turned the thing over with his spear. Tiny transparent appendages wriggled like worms underneath.

"If you step," Angelina translated, "you turn over like this, stick foot on wiggly things. They suck all poison gone."

Teri'i grunted, jabbed the thing again, strode on. I shivered, hurried after him.

Next was a marijuana field. Waist-high plants here and there among the scrub. Teri'i picked a bud off one plant. Fat and green, sticky. Then he spoke in English. "Is very good! Party! Get big stoned!"

Then Teri'i jumped a coco tree and climbed twenty-five feet to the top. He knocked down some green drinking nuts. Teri'i presented Angelina with the tender meat from the inside of the young coconut, and I got a taste, too.

Angelina says she learned English in New Caledonia, where her family had moved when her father was stricken with gout. Later, her father's visa ran out, and they were forced to return to Tahiti. Angelina had to drop out of school and go to work in a hotel to help support the family.

One day, Angelina says, an Italian checked into the hotel, and he fell in love with her. A deep, unrequited love. He left Tahiti, returned, stayed for several months. Each night, he'd play solitaire in the lobby while she worked behind the desk. Sometimes they talked. Once she played cards with him. He kept asking her to dinner. She kept saying no.

Finally, on the eve of his departure, she accepted his invitation.

He cried.

She fell in love.

Her Italian friend, as she calls him, has been here again recently. He flew in when he heard about Angelina's gynecological surgery. She's recovering now, and her friend's back in London. Soon, he'll send for her. She'll finish her education. They'll get married.

Or something like that.

Anyway, after the coconuts, on the walk back to the bungalow, Angelina stopped translating, and she and Teri'i switched languages; the rolled r's and throaty tones of French were replaced with the guttural singsong of Tahitian. They walked together, elbows almost touching. I walked six paces behind. They acted like I wasn't there.

Damn. Even if this was a story, not life, I couldn't help feeling that Teri'i had snaked me. Not that I had any claim, but hell, we'd just gotten there, I hadn't even had my chance. I could tell I had lost, and there was no comfort in the fact that I had lost to the better man. Or at least to a man better suited to Paradise.

I walked, sulked. Presently, I felt myself shrug. Who cared? I wanted Marlon. That's what I'd come for. Work first, R&R later. Let Teri'i have her. Maybe it would help.

Then I remembered. I smiled.

Gynecological problems. Did they have those in Paradise?

"Come on Marlon. Come on, man. Show yourself. I know you're here, Marlon. Come on, Marlon. . . ."

Hacking through the jungle on Marlon's island, beating back brush with a driftwood machete. I have a pack on my back, I'm wrapped tight, walking a step at a time on the balls of my feet, chanting under my breath to Marlon. He's close, real close. I can feel him sucking me in, repelling me even as I move closer. Something rustles the brush. I freeze. Behind me, no, left.

A clearing. A cat. Old tom, half an ear.

He sits, stares, weirds me out. A sign, maybe, or a sentinel.

I was too young for Vietnam, but this is what it was like, I know it now, just like *Apocalypse Now,* a mission through a jungle, a quarry I cannot see, a reason that has become too confused to understand. Like war, like love, the desire within me is strong, burns in my head like the midday sun. Odds? There are no odds anymore. I'm on point, I'm close, walking a path that snakes through the days and weeks of my mission like a main circuit cable plugged straight into Marlon. I want him. I need him. I have to see him and I will, I will find him.

The jungle is all weirdness and sounds, a thick, primitive, evil thing, lewdly fertile and engorged. Plants with eight-foot leaves, vines like arms, roots like legs; a coconut falls twenty feet away and my heart stops. I think of heads.

I had set out two hours ago. Past the tourist bungalows, past the beachfront huts where Marlon's people live, across the flaming airstrip in the heat of day and into the breathless jungle.

At random I followed tractor treads, gauged their age by the hardness and the wetness of the print. I found the landfill, an empty pit dug in the sand, the cement foundation of a grand-looking house that was never finished. I found a wire on a tree and followed it half a mile into the brush, tree to tree, until it stopped, ran down to the ground, and connected to a transformer in the middle of a clearing. The ground was soft, but it didn't seem like anything was buried underneath. I made a note to come back later with a shovel. Underground complex?

I'd discovered the tools earlier, before entering the jungle, in a large work shed near the bungalows, along with the generator, some old bicycles, an old trail bike, a huge land mover. There were some doors in a corridor behind the concrete work area. I got a thick screwdriver and found a bathroom behind one door, some books in a shelf behind another.

They were Marlon's books, all right. *The Encylopedia Americana. How to Be Rich,* by J. Paul Getty. *A Sioux Chronicle,* by George B. Hyde. *Tao, The Three Treasures,* by Bhagwan Shree Rajneesh. *Ham Antenna Construction Projects.* His cassettes, too. "Stress Management Training Program," "Biofeedback Relaxation Training."

Manuals on everything. Hydroponics, solar energy, refrigeration, birds. In the beginning, Marlon had a lot of plans for his island. He said he wanted to bring new-age technology to Tahiti, to find ways of helping modern men blend with the environment, of helping primitive man coexist with it. Little got done. It cost too much, most likely.

There is evidence of the burden in his choice of roles during the '60s—dogs like *The Ugly American, Bedtime Story, Morituri, The Chase, The Appaloosa, A Countess from Hong Kong, The Night of the Following Day, Candy*. Today, you can't even get them on video.

"I need money, I make a film," Marlon said during that period. It was obvious.

At the end of another trail through the jungle, I found old stones arranged in a rectangle, ten feet long, three feet wide. The ruins of a *marae,* a Polynesian place of worship, an outdoor temple for offerings, dances, rituals.

In antiquity, Tetiaroa was owned by the royal family, the Pomares. It was a summer residence, a site of religious festivals, a fashionable watering place for chiefs from the north end of Tahiti. They came by sailing canoe, repaired to shady groves, ate lightly of fish and coconut, recovered from war and from the ravages of fermented *ava.* Some say virgins were sacrificed in maraes like this one, some say it was people who broke taboo; some say there was cannibalism, some say the cannibalism was limited to the eating of an enemy's eye. Whatever. There is a weird feeling about the place, a palpable force, a vibration. Forget it. Push on. . . .

Two more hours, the jungle breaks on the far side of the island. My skin burns, my whole body throbs with welts and bites. To the left is a clearing. A house.

It is vaguely Japanese—square pavilions, with a crude boardwalk connecting the pavilions into a large rectangular compound. A cool breeze blows through ironwood trees, and the fine long needles whisper and sway. There is no one around.

The pavilions are mostly wood, the walls are large sheets of Plexiglas in frames that can be raised. Everything is nailed shut. There is a pavilion with a stove and a sink, one with a low table for eating, one with empty shelves. Seven pavilions in all, they stretch perhaps two hundred feet on the long side of the rectangle. The last room, beachfront, has a bed, a mosquito net, four chairs, a desk.

The frames around the windows in this pavilion are screwed, nailed, padlocked, secured with 2-by-4s. All the windows but one are opaque. I wipe a circle with my hand. A large can of bug spray, a jar of Nescafé instant coffee, a wooden salad bowl, a refrigerator, toothpicks in a shot glass. Some tools piled on the floor, a bird cage covered with a towel. Driftwood, an African fright mask, strings of worry beads, the bleached skull of an animal, two fly swatters hanging from wooden beams and struts that support the roof. Near the bed, two scarred conga drums.

Congas.

Hmmm.

Congas!

Marlon plays congas!

This is it. This is it!

Marlon's room. Marlon's things. I have found Marlon's things!

I pull out a pad, take notes. Marble desktop . . . flowered blue tablecloth . . . shell necklaces . . hoovering each detail like a line of drug, buzzed beyond belief. So long. So far. Now I am here. Only a half-inch of Plexiglas, some wood, some nails, some screws separate me from Marlon Brando's possessions. Things he has touched, things he has used. God, imagine what could be in those two small metal file cabinets! What could be in that desk! . . . Petal brand facial tissue (white) . . . three forks . . . a coffee cup . . . magazines . . . *Popular Science,* May 1985: Good-bye records and tape! Here comes the laser disc revolution! . . . *Scientific American,* March 1985! . . .

And then . . .

I didn't even notice.

On the magazines.

Little labels.

MARLON BRANDO

-----MULHOLLAND DR.

BEVERLY HILLS, CA 90210

I am overcome with something and I jump off the porch, tear back through the jungle on a dead run in the direction of the work shed. His address, his address, I've got his address, and now I want more, I want more, I want a crowbar.

I pull up hard at the edge of the jungle. Go to the shed across the clearing. Search the benches, the floor, the shelves. A big closet. There, at the bottom. Rusty, three feet long. A crowbar.

Feel the weight. Shift it hand to hand . . .

Wait.

Wait.

What am I doing?

No, no. Whoa.

I ain't gonna do it.

I ain't gonna do it.

Calm down.

Marlon isn't here.

Marlon is not here!

Those magazines. They're a year and a half old. His place is shut tight. There is nowhere else on the island for him to be. I've looked everywhere. I've searched in grids. On the way in, the plane had buzzed low over the entire atoll before landing. We were not more than fifty feet above the thirteen islands in the atoll. I would have seen something if there was anything to see. A clearing, a roof, something irregular in the unrelenting tangle.

Simone was telling the truth. Marlon's not here. Tehotu is in California for Christmas, Teri'i had told Angelina. They're probably at Marlon's house in Beverly Hills. At Marlon's house.

Okay. I know where he is. I am with Marlon's people. He will hear of it. He will know I am searching for him. Break into his place, he'll know that, too, probably before the sun falls. No. I must play a different game. Subtle. Smart. Human.

I replace the crowbar, head back toward the bungalows. I'd told Angelina before I left to meet Tarita's plane. I'll see what she found out. I'll talk to her and decide what's next. I'll formulate. I'll make a plan. I'll get to him, no problem. Now I know where he is.

At the bungalow, there's a note on the door, stuck between the fronds.

Mr. Sager (Mike):

I have taken the 3:00 plane back to Papeete.

Good luck finding Marlon!

FAAEVA, Angelina.

PS. You can give my salary to Benji. He will see that I get it.

"You ever see his movies, Teri'i? Movies. You know, *Apocalypse Now, Superman, Godfather . . .*"

"*Godfather!*"

"*Godfather?*"

"Oui, *Le Père.*"

"Is good for you? *Godfather?*" I ask.

"Okay. I no like movie," Teri'i says. "Is too much bad. No good for the eyes. I like look sunset."

"It is beautiful here, isn't it?"

"Yes. And sea. All day color change. Is not only one sea, is many seas. Here is very good for me," he says, pressing his fist to his heart, sweeping it outward.

I never spoke again of Angelina, and neither did Teri'i. It didn't seem important. It was as if she had never been here, a footprint on the beach that the wind had blown away. She was forgotten, at least in speech. But it still nagged. Why did she leave?

The music was good in Teri'i's bungalow, 95-Rock from Papeete on a boom box that took six D batteries to run. In the days that followed, I came often to his bungalow, and we became friends. Maybe he felt bad about Angelina, but I doubt it. Probably, it was more simple than that. I liked him, I was nice to him. He liked me, he was nice to me. That is the way Tahitians are. They are not people of theory, they are people of heart. What needn't make a difference doesn't have to. What seems right is what is.

Teri'i's place was on the beach, plywood and thatch with a millionaire's view. I'd show up, and we'd sit on crates and stare at the horizon, or we'd giggle and try to talk trash. Most times, we ran out of vocabulary. And sometimes, when that happened, it hurt, for there were things I wanted to say.

Being there with Teri'i in his bungalow, and with Charles and Popi and Serge and the others who came to hang out, I learned to do as they did: to empty my mind completely, to forget about yesterday or tomorrow. I learned why Tahitians don't have need of a word of apology; and I learned the deep peace of dreamless sleep, the richness of the glow of the dawn.

And, in time, I found myself doing as Teri'i did, as all the rest of them did. I found myself saying, "Here is very good," and then nodding my head yes, pressing my fist to heart, sweeping it outward.

Thanks to Angelina, I knew the names of all Marlon's people. I played soccer in bare feet on the beach with the other guys, and lolled in the warm, salty lagoon afterward, floating as they did, like a hippo, arms out and feet just touching the soft sand on the bottom, water just below my nose. I learned how to spot a fish by the ripple of the water, how to navigate an outrigger canoe through the shallows by the depth chart of the different hues.

I got very brown, and with my shaved, tanned head and earring, new guests thought I was an employee of some sort, a weird one of Marlon's people. They came over, smiled tentatively as tourists do, asked, "Where's the good fishing?"

I said what Teri'i had said to me. "Good fish everywhere, just throw in line."

At night, when the generator was off and the guests were asleep, there were a million stars, and Marlon's people would sit around the picnic table singing. I hummed along, and after a few days, Matahi taught me how to play the songs on guitar. Once in a while, they'd let me sit in, and as I strummed I felt part of something warm, something old, something very right.

I met Tarita, but I didn't come on like a journalist. I told her my first name, greeted her not as Marlon's wife, not as a movie star, but as any other of Marlon's people. I did watch her closely, from afar, admiring her still-beautiful face, her still-lithe figure, seeing now and then in my mind the scene in *Bounty* when she dances so sensuously for Marlon.

Tarita had been a waitress when she was picked from a group of sixteen native girls for the movie part of Maimiti, daughter of the chief, wife of Mr. Christian. After arriving in Tahiti to choose his leading lady for *Bounty,* Marlon had set up shop in a hotel in Papeete, brought each of the girls into his second-story room and threatened to jump out the window. Tarita got the part because she giggled the least when he threatened.

Her career ended with *Bounty,* and she resumed the simple life of her youth. On Tetiaroa, she spends much of her time gardening. She fishes a lot, too, usually with Grandmère, sometimes with all three of her daughters. They were a sight out there in the lagoon, the five of them, all topless except Grandmère, throwing hooks baited with squid over the side, pulling up huge fish. I got in the habit, when she went out fishing, of watching the lagoon for the return of her boat. When she dropped anchor, I'd be there, coincidentally, to help drag the catch ashore.

The second time I helped, she smiled. She said I was nice. "Not like any other guest."

I thought a lot about meeting Marlon, about how the two of us would get along once we met. If this was his place, then I knew I'd like him. Perhaps he'd like me, too. Maybe, I mused, I would write his biography. He'd set me up on my own island. That one, there, across the lagoon.

I hadn't found Marlon, not yet, but I had found something of him, an important something. A man who would do this—buy an island, people it, shelter them with goodness and nature, create a small peaceful nation in the midst of the widest of oceans—this was a man worth finding.

It was time to go to L.A.


"Mr. Sager, isn't it?" says Cynthia. "What can we do for you?"

I had flown back to Papeete after a week on Tetiaroa, leaving to hugs and even songs from Marlon's people, feeling that it was time to go, knowing I'd be back.

The next day, I went to see Cynthia at the Bureau de Tetiaroa, at Faaa Airport. Cynthia is a former airline stewardess, originally from Maui, Hawaii. She runs all of Marlon's Tahitian interests. She speaks with Marlon often, it is said. In fact, according to Teri'i, she had just returned from Los Angeles.

"Well," I say, pulling up a chair, reaching into my pocket. "Let's start with this." I give her my card.

"You're a journalist?" The tone in her voice. She might have said, "You're a child molester?"

"Listen. I'm not going to ask you any questions. . . ."

"Good, because I can't answer any."

"I just want to tell you something. Okay? Please?"

And so it is that I deliver the most impassioned speech in a life of impassioned speeches, starting with, "Cynthia, I'm not a scoop slob running around looking for a quote. I don't give a damn about actors or movies. . . ."

I tell Cynthia about my assignment, my preparation, my obsession. I tell her about watching all the movies, reading all the books and the magazines, feeling how Marlon felt, hiring Angelina, going to Tetiaroa, helping Tarita with her fish and her plants.

Then I tell her all about the mess America is in. Urine testing, the banning of *Alice* in *Wonderland,* Rambo, College Republicans, Tom Cruise, demographics, no-smoking sections in restaurants. Loss of freedoms, right-wing fascists, Contra-gate, all the rest.

And then I say:

"Cynthia, let me tell you what I think. Going to Marlon's island, reading about him, learning about his life, I have come to think of Marlon as a visionary. A visionary, Cynthia. He was one of the first actors to produce and direct. He was one of the first to get percentage of gross. He was one of the first to study Eastern religion, and he went to Southeast Asia before anybody even knew about the war. He gave up one of the starring roles in *Butch Cassidy and the Sundance Kid* because Martin Luther King Jr. had just died. Did you know that, Cynthia? He cared so much about civil rights, and when King died he was too broken up to work.

"Marlon has bought an island and established his own country, a paradise. The United Islands of Brando. He has sat alone for years and taken the time to read and learn and think. He's got ideas. He's got foresight. He's got . . . Let me put it this way, Cynthia: America needs Marlon. We need to ask him what comes next.

"I want to talk to him about this. I don't want to talk acting. I think acting is stupid, I think Hollywood is a cultural boneyard. All those idiots running around in satin Cadillacs. Forget all that.

Forget it! I want to talk about how to make the world a better place. I want Marlon's opinion. *The Washington Post* wants Marlon's opinion.

"Cynthia, I'm here. I know Marlon is in Los Angeles. I want to see him. I'll fly tomorrow. I'll see him for five minutes, or I'll listen for as long as he wants to talk. Tell him that, Cynthia, tell him that for me. Tell him—"

The phone rings.

Damn.

I had her going. Her eyes were wide, and she was nodding her head like a puppet. Of course she thinks Marlon is a visionary. She's been working for him for fifteen years. And, truth be told, I believe it, too.

Cynthia jabbers in French. My name is mentioned. What's going on? Is that him on the phone? I know he has a network, but . . .

Cynthia hangs up.

She smiles.

She beams.

"That was Tarita. She was calling about something else, but I told her you were here and what you said. She said you were a really nice person. She couldn't believe you were a journalist! Isn't that funny?

"She said I should call Marlon for you. When are you leaving for L.A.?"

"Yes?" says the voice in the metal box. "What do you want?"

"Package for Mr. Brando," I say, looking nonchalant, waving at the three different cameras set to my right and to my left and over there, near a tree behind the ten-foot iron fence guarding Marlon's canyon compound.

I am in L.A., and if my mission is starting to feel at all like the movie, at all like *Apocalypse Now,* then this is the Kno Long bridge, the last outpost that Captain Willard passes on his way up the river to find Kurtz. All the flares and lights, the psychedelic music, the stoned-out soldiers. Too much going on, no one in charge. That's L.A. Obscenely expensive cars, palm trees with no coconuts. It is cold, 50 degrees, and raining. The sky is brown at the edges. At night from the hot tub I can count all five stars in the sky.

First thing upon arrival, I did as Cynthia instructed. I called Marlon's assistant, Pat Quinn.

Pat was in *Alice's Restaurant.* She's been with Marlon for twenty years. I did my speech again, and she ate it up. She gushed. She was so glad I liked Marlon's island. She'd heard all about me. Cynthia had called. She'd talk to Marlon today, she said.

He'd call, she said.

For three days, each ring of the phone was another needle in my brain, and I was back to the straight, hard reality of seventy-eight different cable channels and not a show I wanted to see.

Each day I drove up into the hills and coasted past Marlon's house, perched atop Mulholland, atop Benedict Canyon, a rich view of the valley and the mountains to the north. I stared up at the sharp concertina wire that is wrapped around his fence. Come on, Marlon. Come on. Call, Marlon. Call.

Then I hurried back. I didn't want to miss the call.

For another day and a half I left messages for Pat. Then, late one night, she answered the phone herself.

"How you doing, Pat?" I was friendly, nonchalant.

"I can't converse with you!" she shrieked.

"What about Marlon. What about—"

"I can't converse with you!"

She slammed the phone. I slammed it back.

In the ensuing days, I tried other things. I called Marlon's other assistant, Aiko. I called a woman in L.A. that I'd met on Tetiaroa. She'd been there resting. She used to work for Quincy Jones. Quincy had been to Tetiaroa. He is friends with Marlon. No go. A friend's father knew someone who knew someone who once had Marlon to dinner. He worked that angle. I called Marlon's bookkeepers, Brown and Kraft.

And I called Cynthia. She was glad to hear from me. I told her what had happened with Pat. She said she didn't know what to think.

Then she paused a moment, as if deliberating. Then she said, "Well, you know, Marlon's got a lot of problems right now. All the new tax laws, that stuff, he's been meeting with accountants, day and night, trying to solve his problems. That's why Tehotu is there. He's helping Marlon get some other things done that have been bothering him."

I thanked Cynthia. She wished me luck.

I wasn't giving up, not yet. I was offering Marlon a good product: an opportunity to speak his mind. If accounting had him down, politics would get him going. It would be good therapy. We could work together, write a good story about something important, something that mattered to Marlon. Okay, okay, the biography and the island would have to wait. Obviously, he wasn't in the mood for that. But that didn't matter. Right now, all that mattered was meeting Marlon. I wanted to look him in the eye, to hear his voice, to see him walk across a room. I wanted to smile and raise eyebrows, play a few Tahitian tunes, anything.

And so it was that I went to Radio Shack and bought a tape recorder, then drove up to Mulholland, parked overlooking a canyon. I lit a cigarette, started the tape. I felt out of breath. My voice quavered.

"Marlon Brando," I began.

"Please forgive this further intrusion, but I just hung up from Pat Quinn. She said she could not converse with me. I don't understand.

"Sir, in the two months I have spent learning about you, visiting Tetiaroa, meeting your extended family, experiencing my own solitude, I have become involved, fascinated, and respectful. I flatter only the facts in concluding that you are a man with vision.

"What I am offering is this: a ten-thousand-word article in *The Washington Post Sunday Magazine*. One million copies of the magazine are distributed each week. You can direct the subject matter. Any cause or concern. The choice is yours.

"You have, I guess, gotten reports from your people concerning my handling of this assignment. As you know, I took no pictures of your family. I did not intrude. I conducted myself as a decent human being.

"I know you want to be left alone. But I also know that you care about many things, and that you care about doing good.

Together, I think, we can do a little good for the world. The choice is up to you. If you say no, I will respect that. I will give up, eventually.

"Will you please answer?"

When I finished, I put the tape recorder, along with some of my clips—the Great Peace March for Global Nuclear Disarmament, columns I had written against urine testing, demographics, use of wealth for things instead of for ideas—into a large Ziploc baggie. I chose the baggie because I could seal it, and because Marlon could see that there wasn't a bomb inside. I hoped it would make him curious, this little dog-and-pony show in a Ziploc bag. Maybe he would listen.

So now I am at Marlon's gate. I've told the voice in the box that I have a package for Marlon.

After an interval, the voice says, "Drive slow and stay to the left."

The gate creaks open. There's a red sign advertising security inside. "Armed Response," it says.

Marlon's compound is dense with foliage. There's a fenced-in area a hundred feet up the driveway, and as I drive slowly past in my red Suzuki jeep, two giant dogs throw themselves at the gate and howl.

The road forks, I stay left. A line of shrubs is blocking the driveway. Suddenly, the shrubs swing open. An asphalt parking area. I pull in. There's a Jeep Wagoneer and a gold Mercedes 380, and three little houses, low-slung, cement, nothing fancy, painted light orangey brown, and a common in between.

A sign in the driveway says, "Stay in Car. Attack Dogs on Premises."

After a few seconds, someone comes walking toward me. He's got a Doberman on a leash. He's wearing a white T-shirt. He looks exactly like Stanley Kowalski, exactly like Terry Malloy, exactly like Marlon's picture on the cover of *Marlon Brando: The Only Contender*. I can't believe it. The resemblance.

"Tehotu! What's happening!"

The kid is stunned.

I introduce myself to Marlon's son.

"Oh, yeah," he says, and shakes my hand. "Cynthia said you'd be coming,"

"Teri'i told me to say hello," I say. "He wants to know when you're coming back. Christ, I can't believe you missed New Year's Eve down there, I hear it's a real party. Oh, and I'm supposed to tell you that Charles . . ."

I am yammering away like a fool, but I can't help it. Jesus Christ, this kid looks like Marlon. Turned-down lip and sleek smooth jaw and high-gloss cheekbones and almond eyes and tousled hair. Christ, he is Marlon with a tan, a young Marlon in his prime, Marlon when he was turning Hollywood upside down, long before the wives and the press and the crap that drove him away from the world. Standing before me, he is a vision of the Marlon that I've lived with in my mind, asleep and awake for six long weeks. Here, right here, right before me.

I regain my composure, shut my mouth. I hand Tehotu the baggie with the recorder and the clips.

"Listen," I say. "Tell your dad [your dad!] that if he thinks I'm a jerk and he doesn't want to talk to me, I'll go away. But ask him please to answer. Have him say something. Just something. You know . . . well, ask him to please call."

Tehotu smiles.

I think of the beach and the stars and the lagoon. I smile, raise an eyebrow, giggle.

"He's out right now, but he'll be back soon," Tehotu says, and then he smiles again. "I'm sure he won't think you're a jerk."

Three more days.

Rain, cable TV. Sherman Oaks, California.

No call.

I *am* a jerk!

The hell with Marlon Brando. The hell with searching for Marlon Brando. He doesn't deserve a story. He doesn't deserve to be alive. I don't care if he talks to me or not. What do I have to ask him anyway? What could he possibly have to say of any relevance at all? He's an actor! Who cares? Why the hell should I waste my time searching for . . .

Okay.

One more try.

One more try.

One more try and that's it.

I buy some bagels, some coffee, two newspapers, and a pair of binoculars. I drive up to Mulholland. I park at a curve. I stake out Marlon.

I didn't want to have to do this. This is exactly what I've tried not to be. A scoop slob looking for a quote, a tidbit to take home and put in the first paragraph of a regurgitated story about Marlon Brando's life. A doggie bag to warm in the microwave.

But I accepted the job. *Go find Marlon Brando.* I've traveled eighteen thousand miles. I've spent a lot of money. Everyone thought I was going to fail, and when I get home, I'm going to have to look them in their faces. Marlon said in *Last Tango* that in order to live your life, you have to look first into the maw of death. In order to be a journalist, maybe sometimes you have to look first into yourself. You have to get a quote.

Birds soar the canyons, Mercedes-Benzes and Jaguars and BMWs screech around the curves on Mulholland Drive. People stare into the window of my red Suzuki jeep. They see a guy with a black Nikon cap and sunglasses and binoculars on a stakeout. I know what they are thinking. Something like what I'm thinking about myself.

Four hours pass.

Then, movement.

Up there, a break in the trees. Three hundred yards away, a porch in Marlon's compound.

I raise the binoculars,

Tehotu. He's carrying a saw and a board.

Then, Marlon.

Marlon Brando.

Him.

Focus.

Marlon is fat. He looks tired and worried. He is bald on top with a fringe of white hair around the sides. He is wearing a blue bathrobe. He points here, points there, appears distracted.

It has been been thirteen years now since he made *Godfather* and earned his second Oscar, which he refused to accept, and about $21 million in salary and percentages, which he did accept. After that came *Last Tango in Paris, The Missouri Breaks, Superman, Apocalypse Now,* and *The Formula.* For the last three, he made more than $10 million for less than thirty minutes on-screen.

Since 1977, Marlon has said nothing to the press. "I'm not going to lay myself at the feet of the American public and invite them into my soul. My soul is a private place," he told *Playboy.*

Through the binoculars, I see Marlon, but I see nothing of the Brat, the Slob, the Valentino of the Bop Generation, the Walking Hormone Factory, the man standing alone far away, the visionary. I see nothing of Terry Malloy, of Stanley Kowalski, of Fletcher Christian. . . . Christ, he was beautiful then. Christ, he was good. Good enough to change Hollywood forever. Go to the movies now, you see him. Newman, Redford, Nicholson, Pacino, Hoffman, Cruise, Penn . . . before all of them, there was Brando.

Now, here is Marlon.

An old guy. Fat, bald, blue bathrobe.

It begins to rain.

I key the Suzuki, it putters to life. I drive toward Marlon's gate.

For six weeks now I've been searching. I Xeroxed his pictures and taped them to my walls. I read every book and every article, during every meal and before bedtime. I dropped down deep, very deep, into my own kind of Method, and in his wife I saw an old girlfriend, and in his divorce I saw an old wife, and in his art I found a meaning, and in his vision I saw one, too. I walked his ivory beaches and floated in his blue lagoon. I picked out a place for my own bungalow on a lonely atoll in the middle of the South Pacific, and I knew that someday I'd return.

And over the weeks I realized that Marlon was the template for two generations of men, the ultimate man of the '80s, thirty years before his time. He'd shown us how to be young, then he'd split the whole program. And I started thinking that maybe it wouldn't be bad at all to find Marlon, on the world's behalf, to ask him what he thinks, where we should be going, what we should be doing, what it is that is supposed to come next. We need you,

Marlon Brando. That's how it formed in my mind. We need you. In the '50s, he showed us how to be young. In the '80s, we could use a little advice. It couldn't hurt.

Now, I am pulling into Marlon's driveway. I edge up even with the little metal box. There's a button to ring. One button to Marlon. Quote city. Pay dirt.

Behind the iron gate, a car rounds the bend, descending the hill from Marlon's compound. It's heading straight for me, an old import, a Toyota or something. It stops. A hand reaches out of the window. The gate opens. The car rolls forward, stops. The door opens. A woman. She's fortyish, Japanese. It's Aiko, Marlon's other personal assistant. After Pat had told me she "couldn't converse," I'd called Aiko maybe thirteen times. She never returned my calls.

Aiko walks through the gate, toward the mailbox. She doesn't even look at me, sitting behind the wheel of the Suzuki. It's like I don't exist. She just walks to the mailbox, opens it, starts taking out some mail.

"Aiko?"

She turns.

"I'm Mike Sager."

"Oh, yes, Mr. Sager. How are you today?"

How are you today? "Fine," I say. Listen, I wonder—"

She cuts me off. "We got your package," she says sweetly, and then she smiles. "We forwarded it to Marlon, to his next stop, wherever it is he's going. I'm sure he'll get back to you on the matter soon."

Forwarded it? She's lying to my face! I've just seen Marlon, fat and bald in a blue bathrobe. He's up there on the porch. "Wherever it is he's going." Give me a break. I look at Aiko, then I look over toward the iron gate. It's open. My Suzuki is idling. I could run to the jeep, floor it, spew gravel. I could be in Marlon's compound in a few seconds. I could get to Marlon. It would probably take the police fifteen minutes to get there. By then I could get a quote, at least. Then I could get arrested. I'd have an ending for my story. I'd have an ending with Marlon. Or maybe I'd have a beginning. Maybe Marlon would be impressed with such a ballsy move. Maybe we'd become friends before the cops got there. After all, I'd carried Tarita's fish. I hadn't taken pictures of his daughter. I'd shown myself to be a good human being. "That's okay, Officer. Mr. Sager will be staying. . . ."

On the other hand, maybe he'd shoot me.

I think of *Apocalypse Now*. Before Captain Willard goes up the river, the general tries to prepare him. "You see, Willard," the general says, "things get confused out there. Power, ideals, morality . . . there's a conflict in every human heart between the rational and the irrational, between good and evil."

Captain Willard, of course, was a soldier. A hired gun, an assassin. He had a job to do. He did it.

Me, I'm a journalist. It's a strange profession, not unlike Willard's, though I don't kill anyone. What I do is scrape people's insides, pull out their guts, display them on a page. I tell them it's the people's right to know, and I stick my foot in the door. I dog them, I posture, I say what they want to hear. I get my story, just like Willard gets his man.

This time, I'd wanted it to be different. I'd junked the journalist technique, gone for good human being. I'd figured I could show myself to Marlon as a man worthy of meeting, and somewhere along the line, things got confused, and I came to believe that I was.

Marlon knew better, of course. All the dog-and-pony shows in all the Ziploc baggies in the world would not have changed his mind. I thought I was being a person. But Marlon knows I'm just another reporter looking for a story. Six weeks ago, I didn't care one iota about Marlon. Then I got the assignment, then I decided I wanted to meet him, then I decided on the approach. Good Human Being. Aiko knows this. That's why she's lying to my face, and that's why she seems to be enjoying herself so greatly. Because my face isn't my face. It is the face of all journalists, of all the scoop slobs who have stalked and staked out Marlon for thirty years. I am searching for Marlon, trying to get my story. That is the reason I have come. There is no other.

From the start it sounded ridiculous. *Find Marlon Brando. Go to Tahiti and find Marlon Brando.*

Yeah? And then what?

*You'll know.*

I'll know?

Hmmm.

I look at my Suzuki, at Aiko's Toyota, at the open iron gate, at the rows of sharp concertina ringing the compound. I want a quote, but Marlon wants to be left alone. If I really was a good human being, I'd leave him alone.

"Ah, listen, Aiko. I have to be leaving town. I have another story to do. Here's my card. When Marlon gets to wherever he's going, he can reach me at this number."

I walk back to the Suzuki, put it in reverse, back out, drive away. I take the next plane home.

# ACKNOWLEDGMENTS

I must thank the usual suspects in my career, especially for an anthology that is really an outgrowth of a lifetime of work and learning. In my youth, Ed Lambeth, to whom this book is dedicated, opened my eyes to the boundless possibilities that fine journalism allowed. My old friend Steve Weinberg has always been an inspiration, as have my colleagues and friends Mike Sager, Pete Earley, and Joyce Hoffmann. I was blessed with fine and tolerant editors in my years at *The Washington Post Magazine*. At the time, I thought I was finding my own way. Looking back, Stephen Petranek, Jay Lovinger, Bob Thompson, and John Cotter were actually directing my journey. I owe them big time. My former editor Terry Karten also taught me much about doing a personal book.

For this project, many colleagues offered invaluable advice. Thanks to Madeleine Blais, Carl Stepp, Jon Franklin, Anne Fadiman, Stephen Lyons, Norman Sims, Kevin Kerrane, Chip Scanlon, Roy Peter Clark, Patsy Sims, Dick Weiss, Joe Mackall, Dan Lehman, Philip Gerard, David Remnick, Chip Brown, and Mark Kramer. Thanks to the University of Illinois Department of Journalism for providing research assistance. Thanks to Amber Jenne, Amanda Grish, and Luiza Ilie for doing that work and to the university's College of Communications library director Lisa Romero for many years of help. Thanks also to Carey Checca for research she did as an independent studies student on the topic of personal journalism. Thanks to the reference librarians at The Urbana Free Library for frequent fast-lane fact checking.

At Grove/Atlantic, thanks to my editor, Morgan Entrekin, for advice on this book and on a previous book of personal journalism. Thanks also to his editorial assistant, Daniel Maurer, and the book's excellent copy editor, Don Kennison. And thanks to my agent, Sloan Harris, at ICM.

Finally, as ever, thank you to my wonderful wife, Keran.